BLUE GRASS AIRPORT
AN AMERICAN AVIATION STORY

Editor: Fran Taylor
Project Manager: Amy Caudill, Blue Grass Airport
Designer: Suzanne Dorman, Dorman Design
Contributing Designer: Kristine McCombs, KEM Creative, LLC

Library of Congress Control Number: 2013957986

ISBN 978-0-9881911-2-9

Printed in The United States of America
First Edition: 2014

West High LLC
www.westhighpublishing.com

www.bluegrassairport.com

BLUE GRASS AIRPORT

AN AMERICAN AVIATION STORY

Presented by Blue Grass Airport in collaboration with Fran Taylor

Introduction by Story Musgrave

CONTENTS

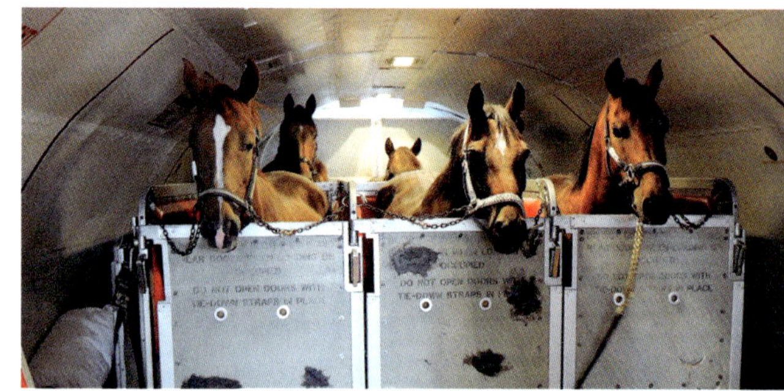

FOREWORD

From the Lexington-Fayette Urban County Airport Board

Many central Kentuckians hold fond memories of our airport. However, most do not realize the place of honor Lexington has earned in America's rich aviation history.

From Charles Lindbergh's landing at Halley Field in 1928, to the subsequent growth of Lexington Municipal Airport at Glengarry Field/ Cool Meadow, it was a humble, yet meaningful start. Add to that the war years and birth of Blue Grass Field, and we learn a great deal about commercial aviation and our community. Yet, these fascinating stories have not been available from a comprehensive source until now.

Creating *Blue Grass Airport: An American Aviation Story* has been an enriching experience for everyone involved. As soon as the airport board authorized staff to proceed with the project, the detailed task of researching, collecting and cataloging the stories, facts and photographs began. Countless residents joined in the process, sharing first-hand knowledge and personal memorabilia. Oral histories now preserve these recollections for future generations.

Some of the area's most accomplished writers were enlisted to combine reference materials with their own research to culminate in the book you are about to read. You will be delighted to learn, among countless other lost or forgotten facts, that Charles Lindbergh and Eddie Rickenbacker are two of the nationally known aviators who played a part in Lexington's history.

We appreciate the generous contributions the following airport partners made to help produce this book: ATS Construction; Gresham, Smith and Partners; HDR, Inc.; Keeneland Association; Messer Construction; Powell-Walton-Milward; Republic Parking System; Stites & Harbison, PLLC and TAC Air. Their commitment to this project affirms their lasting role in Lexington's aviation history.

This book would not have been possible without the remarkable stories and photos from the *Lexington Herald-Leader's* archives.

Join us in celebrating our culture, our life and the joy of aviation as told here. For, as Socrates so aptly put it, "Man must rise above the Earth – to the top of the atmosphere and beyond – for only thus will he fully understand the world in which he lives."

Lexington-Fayette Urban County Airport Board (2013):
Nancy Wiser, Chair
Larry C. Deener, Vice Chair and Treasurer
Doris Benson, Secretary
Roszalyn Akins, Member
W.V. Alford, Jr., Member
James Coles, Member
Chuck Ellinger, Member
Richard Hopgood, Member
J. Robert Owens, Member
Kelley Sloane, Member

Blue
Grass
Airport
Terminal Lobby

By Story Musgrave

INTRODUCTION

My first experience of the Bluegrass was when touring the USA as a teenager. I came in from Louisville on Versailles Road, stopped in at some unknown (to me) but spectacular jewel of a race track and discovered Keeneland; went across the road and explored an equally unknown but gorgeous little airport that turned out to be Blue Grass Field; and kept going down the road past a beautiful farm called Calumet.

As I continued on to downtown Lexington, it came upon me that at this point in my travels I had entered into another land. After cruising around in the warm welcoming atmosphere of downtown, I followed a trail of horse symbols on a map. I didn't know what they meant, but being a farm kid I had to find out.

Traveling west on Main Street, I came upon a place in full and beautiful bloom, the Lexington Cemetery. I continued on over Price and Georgetown Roads and turned right on Berea Road – all the time guided by horse symbols on the map. Heading East on Ironworks Pike, I finally found those horses, the lush blue grasses and the entrance to Spindletop Hall. Further down the road the spirit of the place became mesmerizing, even hypnotic. By the time I turned back toward town on Paris Pike, I can only say that I was possessed by it. It was addictive to the extreme, and there and then I made the decision that I would return to this country at the first opportunity – and I did.

That is what this book captures. It is about spirit: the spirit of the Bluegrass and the way that Blue Grass Field embodies that spirit in its history, its beauty, its operation and its ambiance.

The book begins with an existential history that is at once the birth of the airport but also the birth of aviation and an exposition of an era of America. It illustrates its rich history in poignant dramatic scenarios of particular people and events. It knits together the ethereal nature of flight and the magic of Bluegrass horse country. It creates an understanding of the present while reading about the past. It shows how the airfield ultimately reflects the character of the land and the culture and is enriched by those attributes.

I have flown out of Blue Grass Airport for half a century. It is here that aviation became my calling; here that I pursued all the ratings and flew as a private pilot and charter pilot and flight instructor for Bohmer Flying Service and Lexington Air Taxi.

You are cleared for takeoff – not by just any air traffic controller, but by a LEX controller. Their words are the same, but their tone, courtesy and compassion are clearly their own – reflecting the spirit of the place. This charm is infectious and pervasive. In whichever direction you depart, you sail along over undulating waves of grass.

This country is known for its grass – literally and figuratively, Bluegrass. The airport is located on a gentle slope of grass and is surrounded by grass – mile upon mile of Bluegrass pastures.

You visit the small, neighboring airports and you land on grass. You are immersed in that amazing blue-green color, caressed and calmed by it. And it is the horses; the fields of horses that you remember. You depart on Runway 27 and look down right into the heart of Keeneland. And, like any truly aesthetic experience, you know its depth by how your body reacts to it. As you fly over the track you begin to relax and your body sinks deeply into the seat.

After visiting more beautiful farms than you can count, you turn back to the airport and approach from the northeast. The path to touchdown on Runway 22 takes you directly over Calumet where the spirit of this place again and forever possesses you. As you finally pass over Man o' War Boulevard and touch down at what will always be Blue Grass Field to me, you know that you are home.

Story Musgrave was a NASA astronaut for more than 30 years and flew on six space-flights. He gained his pilot's license while in Lexington during the mid 1960s pursuing post doctoral degrees at the University of Kentucky. He is perhaps best known for his role in repairing the Hubble Space Telescope.

In 1907, Roy Knabenshue flew his California Arrow airship in Lexington at the Blue Grass Fair. He is pictured with the airship at the St. Louis World's Fair in 1904.

Lexington Catches
FLYING FEVER

BY SCOTT MAY

Lexington was no different from any other city in the early 1900s. Aviation was in its infancy and the nation was fascinated. Articles about the latest technological development, the flying machine, began appearing in newspapers regularly. In 1902, a play called "The Aeroplane" opened at the Lexington Opera House. The "pretty little play," as described in the *Lexington Leader*, made a profit of $100 during its brief run, a small fortune in those days. People were mad for the idea of flying!

Stories of Orville and Wilbur Wright were abundant, and as time went by fascinating new "aviators" emerged. Their accomplishments were hailed heartily and their tragedies seemed almost inevitable. Both sold newspapers and spurred interest. Countless "daredevils" fueled the public's growing appetite for the thrilling spectacle of flying.

Lexington's first taste of aviation came when the Blue Grass Fair brought Toledo, Ohio's Roy Knabenshue and his airship to Lexington in 1907. Although the airship was only a manned balloon, the seed was planted, but it lay dormant; for the next few years, the citizens of central Kentucky could only read and dream about the wonders of manned flight.

The introduction of a real "flying machine" did not occur until 1910 when a young Canadian aviator, J.A.D. McCurdy, flew his Curtiss biplane at the Blue Grass Fair on August 6 and 7, 1910. The crowds cheered and applauded as McCurdy took flight. McCurdy reached a dizzying altitude of more than 75 feet during the initial two flights. After his ace mechanics made some adjustments, McCurdy took off for a third flight. A staggering 150 feet in altitude was achieved during the final flight of the day and the crowd went wild. Move over jockey great, Isaac Murphy! A new hero was delivered to Lexington in the form of J.A.D. McCurdy.

McCurdy came to Lexington again on August 9, 1911. He was scheduled to fly as

The Wright Brothers, from Dayton, Ohio, became heroes with their aviation feats. This 1909 photo shows them with their Model A aeroplane in France.

J.A.D. McCurdy brought his flying machine to Lexington in 1910 and 1911. It was powered by a French-made Gnome motor.

the Chesapeake & Ohio railroad to Winchester.

A year later, on June 2, 1912, the *Lexington Herald* was full of news about another exciting aviation event: the Aviation Meet and Automobile Races, featuring Berger's aviators, a group of daredevil pilots. Prominent businesses added aviation themes to their advertising, and articles covering the occasion were plentiful.

The event was held at the Kentucky Association racetrack in Blue Grass Park, where the flying show quickly transformed the infield of the track into an aerodrome. Temporary hangars were erected facing the grandstands so the spectators could watch the preparation of the flying machines. The aircraft then used the remaining space for taking off and landing.

The aviators arrived in the days before the event with their "mechanical birds" and included some of the top pilots in the nation. Each pilot was known for a different aviation record. One pilot showed up unannounced, creating a stir in the already excited crowd. Pilot Héctor Worden joined fellow aviators Paul Peck, Oscar Brindley, Eugene Heth, Leonard W. Bonney, Louis Mitchell and Alfred Bolognesi, all sponsored by Berger Aviation Company.

Monday, June 3, 1912, was an historic day for

part of the Blue Grass Fair festivities. He arrived by train and his flying machine arrived later in the day. Part of his demonstration was to fly from the fairgrounds in east Lexington, most likely leaving from the Kentucky Association racetrack on the eastern edge of downtown at East Fifth and Race Streets and following

1912

A gallon of gas is 7 cents.

The *Titanic* sinks on April 15.

Harriet Quimby is the first female pilot to fly across the English Channel.

Italian airships are used to bomb Turkish troops.

Edgar Rice Burroughs publishes *Tarzan of the Apes.*

The first *Keystone Kops* film premieres.

Explorer Robert Scott perishes in Antarctica.

Woodrow Wilson defeats Teddy Roosevelt.

A branch office of the U.S. Postal Service was established at the Kentucky Association racetrack in 1912 for Lexington's first "aerial mail" delivery. Bad weather canceled the flight, which was to be made by Paul Peck.

Berger Aviation Company turned the Kentucky Association racetrack in downtown Lexington into an aerodrome during the Aviation Meet and Automobile Races in 1912. The track, which is shown during a typical race meet, closed in spring 1933; its facilities were torn down in 1935.

Lexington. Four aeroplanes graced the skies above the racetrack at the same time, the first such spectacle in Kentucky. A monoplane performed a solo flight after the opening sequence. The crowds were treated to multiple flights and aerials lasting upward of 15 minutes. Flights continued throughout the day with the aviators giving rides to newspaper reporters and to daring members of the crowd. The first day of the Aviation Meet was declared a roaring success.

Tuesday, June 4, promised even more excitement. The crowd's interest was growing as the aviators promised more entertainment and delivered it as Oscar Brindley set an altitude record that afternoon by soaring to more than 5,000 feet. But, the real heart-pounding moment came when the flying machine flown by Leonard Bonney fell 50 feet from the sky as his engine failed. The Wright biplane struck a wire fence stopping just a few feet short of a railroad car. Miraculously, Bonney emerged from the crumpled airplane with a few bruises and scratches – but lucky to be alive. He had wrestled the out-of-control airplane to prevent it from crashing into the gathered spectators in the infield of the racetrack.

The remainder of the meet was successful despite uncooperative weather, which extended it through Sunday. Crowds grew larger each day as tales of those "magnificent men and their flying machines" spread.

History was to be made when aviator Paul Peck flew mail collected at the event to Winchester, Kentucky. Local Postmaster Wilbur R. Smith had gained prior approval from the Postmaster General in Washington, D.C., to establish a branch office of the Lexington post office at the racetrack during the event. A clerk from the post office stamped each letter with a special aerial postal stamp. Winchester was chosen as the destination over the state capitol due to Frankfort's lack of a suitable landing area.

Unfortunately, foul weather forced Peck to cancel

Aviator Paul Peck

the attempt. It hardly seemed to matter – the air show had already made history. The estimated attendance for the three-day show was 50,000 people!

AVIATION COMES OF AGE

World War I had a mixed effect on aviation in the United States. Civil aviation slowed during the war, but interest in the military's use of aircraft increased. The military brought great developments to the in-dustry, along with the creation of exciting aviator superstars. These pilots were deemed "aces" following successful air-to-air combat victories (usually five or more), and the daring maneuvers they employed became the foundation for future barnstorming and air shows. One of the most famous of these flying aces, Eddie Rickenbacker, would ultimately play a role in Lexington's aviation history.

Barnstorming was the next big step for aviation. Former military pilots returned to the States and began crisscrossing the nation with their aerial shows. These events gave people the opportunity to meet the aviators and see the flying skills that had been the subject of so many enthralling wartime news articles.

Lexington did not host any air shows immediately after the war, but several World War I pilots returned to Lexington and brought their love of aviation home with them. Lieutenant Jesse O. Creech was one of the most prominent. While in the Army Air Service, Creech had earned the Distinguished Service Cross and the Distinguished Flying Cross. He earned the title "ace" by shooting down seven enemy aircraft and was a true hero. After the war, Creech settled in Lexington. Ted Kincannon, another World War I ace, relocated from Texas a few years later.

As early as 1921, several Lexington businessmen had expressed interest in promoting an airfield but were unsuccessful. To increase awareness, former Lieutenant Creech flew from Chicago on June 18, 1921, as part of a publicity stunt. He landed in the field of Dr. Samuel H. Halley's farm on Leestown Pike.

The purpose of the flight was to launch Creech's new aviation venture and the "hook" to attract media interest was the idea of bringing a live pig along on the flight (a gift from a meat packing company in Chicago) to be presented to Lexington Mayor T.C. Bradley. Despite conflicting media reports, the pig was not handed off in Chicago as planned and was not on the flight. The flight took four hours while Creech flew at an average speed of 75 miles per hour with only one stop at the Indianapolis Motor Speedway.

More importantly, Creech's flight on June 18, 1921, marked the first "commercial" flight to Lexington. His flight in a new Avro three-seater aircraft launched

WHAT IS A FLYING ACE?

Enemy pilots at first simply exchanged waves or shook their fists at each other. Due to weight restrictions, only small weapons could be carried on board. Intrepid pilots decided to interfere

The Red Baron

with enemy reconnaissance by improvised means, including throwing bricks, grenades and sometimes rope, which they hoped would entangle the enemy plane's propeller.

In October 1914, a handgun from another plane was used to shoot down an airplane for the first time over Rheims, France. Once machine guns were mounted to airplanes, either on a flexible mounting or higher on the wings of early biplanes, the era of air combat began.

A flying ace or fighter ace is a military aviator credited with shooting down several enemy aircraft during aerial combat. The actual number of aerial victories required to officially qualify a pilot as an "ace" has varied, but it is usually consid-ered to be five or more. The few aces among combat pilots have historically accounted for the majority of air-to-air victories in military history.

The most storied ace in history is Manfred Albrecht Freiherr von Richthofen – better known as "The Red Baron" – who is credited with 80 air combat victories in World War I while flying for the Imperial German Army Air Service (Luft-streitkräfte). By comparison, American hero and World War I ace Edward "Eddie" Ricken-backer had 26 documented aerial victories.

WWI flying ace, Eddie Rickenbacker

The gracious veranda at Dr. Samuel Halley's Meadowthorpe Farm. Dr. Halley allowed part of his farmland to be used as the first airstrip in Lexington.

the beginning of the Lexington Aviation Company. Creech acted as the general manager and chief pilot for the flying service.

It was not until 1926 that a formal attempt was made to establish an airfield in Lexington. A committee formed by the Lexington Automobile Club and Board of Commerce heard presentations by Creech. Recent legislative acts made it possible for any community to acquire and maintain an airfield. The *Lexington Herald* reported in November 1926 that Lexington was the first city in Kentucky to promote plans for the development

of an airport. The plans also involved an effort to have Lexington included in one of the new airmail routes.

THE FIRST AIRFIELD

The committee did not give up on its dreams, and in May 1927 its persistence paid off. The committee and Dr. Samuel H. Halley came to an agreement, and Lexington's first official airfield came into existence. The airfield was located on Dr. Halley's estate, named Meadowthorpe, on Leestown Pike, approximately two miles from downtown. The hangar was

Dedication of Halley Field on June 11, 1927

at one end of the large field where 200 and 204 Boiling Springs Drive are now located in Lexington's Meadowthorpe subdivision. The airstrip became known as Halley Field.

World War I ace Ted Kincannon was the first manager of the Lexington Municipal Airport at Halley Field. Kincannon, with the assistance of fellow pilot Jap Lee, brought two aircraft to Lexington on May 27 and announced that he would commence services including flight instruction. Kincannon's flight school offered courses in motor mechanics, repair, aircraft set-up and the mechanics of flight. The cost of the school was $200.

His classes began the next day with eight students.

The airport was not dedicated until June 11, 1927, just three weeks after Charles Lindbergh's famous transatlantic crossing. Three U.S. Army airplanes and the Lexington Airways Company provided flight demonstrations. Army pilots flew the Curtiss pursuit planes from McCook Field near Dayton, Ohio. Lexington Airways Company, managed by Kincannon, flew passengers in five of its commercial airplanes.

Perhaps the biggest story in Lexington's aviation history occurred on March 28, 1928. Seventeen-year-old Melvin Rhorer had been assigned an important task that

"This is not Lindbergh's 'dilapidated old plane'... but is a replica of the famous 'Spirit of St. Louis' snapped at Halley Air Port," reads the caption on this photo from *Kentucky Progress*. Seventeen-year-old Melvin Rhorer (at left) guards Lindbergh's airplane overnight.

– Lexington Leader, 1928

Lindbergh and Jap Lee at Halley Field in 1928

Colonel Charles A. Lindbergh

morning. He was recruited by Lee and Kincannon to lay out a 100-foot circle using limestone to mark the field's location for a special visitor.

Later that Wednesday afternoon an exact duplicate of the *Spirit of St. Louis* touched down at Halley Field. Lee and a *Lexington Herald* reporter had taken off moments earlier to greet the airplane and guide it to the field. After touching down at 2:33 p.m., four persons emerged from the aircraft: Colonel Henry Breckinridge of Lexington (legal advisor), Major Thomas Lanphier, Captain E.S. Land and Orin Root, Jr. The pilot remained in the aircraft until shortly after the passengers had deplaned. After securing the aircraft, the pilot, Charles A. Lindbergh, emerged.

Lindbergh's trip to Lexington was supposed to be a secret. Only his host, Dr. Scott Breckinridge – brother of Henry Breckinridge – and Kincannon were aware of the details of the visit. Lindbergh had requested in advance that crowds not be allowed to gather at the airport and also let it be known to his hosts that he would not be available for interviews with the media.

Word of his arrival, however, got out almost immediately, and crowds of people came to the airfield to view the replica of the world-famous *Spirit of St. Louis* airplane (varying only by the size of its fuel tanks) that Lindbergh had flown from New York to Paris. Of course, they also hoped to see "Lucky Lindy" himself. While people streamed to the airfield, Lindbergh rested and visited with Dr. Breckinridge at his residence on Russell Cave Road.

The next morning, when Lindbergh and his passengers were ready to depart, they found that word of his visit had spread. Nearly 3,000 people gathered at Halley Field to catch a glimpse of Lindbergh, known internationally as the "Lone Eagle." Lexington Police

THE LEXINGTON LEADER

THE WEATHER
THUNDERSHOWERS TONIGHT AND FRIDAY,
MUCH COLDER. PROBABLY FREEZING.

FINAL EDITION
CIRCULATION LARGEST WHERE BUSINESS
IS GREATEST

TWENTY-TWO PAGES TODAY   LEXINGTON, KY., THURSDAY AFTERNOON, MARCH 29, 1928   PRICE FIVE CENTS

LINDY PLANE BARELY MISSES TREES AT HOP OFF

NO VETO FOR FLOOD CONTROL MEASURE, VIEW

Vote on Such Legislation Is Expected to Be Overwhelming.

TAXES TO BE AFFECTED

Coolidge and Mellon Trying to Hold Down Expenditures by Congress.

Plane Lindy Flies Today

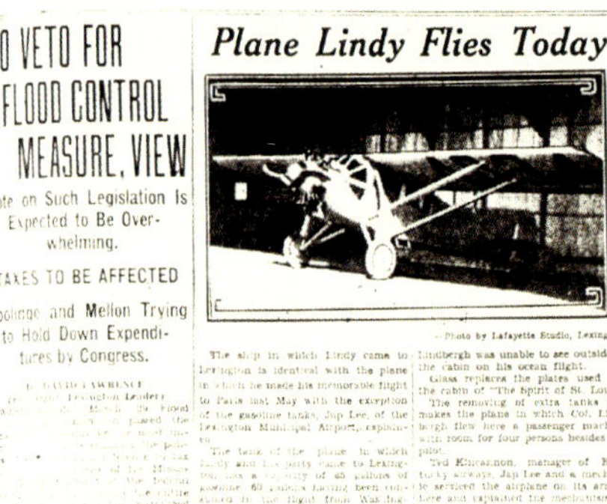

Lindy Says Lexington's Airport Too Small For Present Aviation Needs

U. S. ASKED TO GUARD POLLS DURING PRIMARY ELECTION ON APRIL 10

CHICAGO, March 29 (AP)—The United States government today was asked to guard Chicago polls April 10 when voters mark their answer to a turbulent, bomb-studded primary election campaign.

Palmer Anderson, U. S. Marshal, has forwarded to Washington a recommendation that he be authorized to use 500 deputy marshals in Chicago that day.

LINDY AVOIDS THE CROWD, GREETS YOUNG ADMIRERS

Favored Few Shake Hands With Flyer at Home of Dr. Scott Breckinridge.

VISITS SHOOTING GALLERY

Reporters Who Waited at Gate Are Rewarded With Glimpse of World Hero

EAGLE'S FLIGHT HERE SURPRISED ENTIRE NATION

Lexington First Stop Since Announcement of Public Retirement.

Just After Lindy Arrived

The photograph shows Col. Charles A. Lindbergh just after he arrived at Lexington's airport Wednesday afternoon. Lindy is the tall man and he is talking with Jap Lee, noted airplane pilot and mechanic at Halley Field.

Personal Charm And High Type Of Manhood Strike Those Who Met Lindbergh

CROWD OF 2,000 WATCHES AS SHIP SPEEDS TO NORTH

Party Takes Off for Cincinnati, Then Eagle Will Return to St. Louis.

PILOT'S SKILL IS SEEN

He Accelerates Motor Quickly to Clear Second Group of Trees Ahead.

Captain Austin Price and 15 of his officers were summoned to the field to control the crowd. Lindbergh ignored the onlookers with the exception of a busload of children from the Shriner's Hospital, whom he acknowledged with a friendly wave as he prepared for takeoff. At approximately 10:22 a.m., the aircraft piloted by Lindbergh lifted off from Halley Field heading west for St. Louis.

Great debate has taken place about what happened next. During Lindbergh's takeoff, his plane barely cleared a line of trees and wires near the end of the field. Some felt that it was due to his plane being heavily loaded with passengers and fuel and that the field was too short, but rebuttal was offered in letters to the editor in the *Lexington Herald* the following day. One of the writers was Kincannon. In his letter he described Lindbergh's near miss as a result of a shift in wind causing the aircraft to drop slightly. Other aviators such as Lee and Creech agreed with Kincannon's assessment.

A *Lexington Leader* headline screamed, "LINDY PLANE BARELY MISSES TREES AT HOP OFF," but comments he later made about the airfield were conflicting. Part of the confusion resulted from the statement offered by Creech. He had spoken with Lindbergh at Dr. Breckinridge's home the morning he was preparing to leave. Creech indicated that in an aviator-to-aviator chat, Lindbergh said he liked Halley Field and that it was excellent for a city the size of Lexington but was thought to be too small for commercial operations.

Lindbergh's visit to Lexington was considered by many to be the best advertisement for Lexington and its future in aviation. He was the ultimate icon of his time and considered the greatest aviator in the world. C. Frank Dunn was quoted in the *Lexington Herald's* "Aviation Notes" as saying, "Lexingtonians who aided in the establishment of the airport should now feel more than repaid for their efforts."

Lexington, the first city to have an airport in central Kentucky, was soon joined by other cities. By August 1928, the cities of Berea, Danville and Harrodsburg had established their airfields. Berea's field was developed in the spring of 1928, but it saw little traffic. Harrodsburg's Eastland Field was dedicated on June 16, 1928, as part of the city's 154th anniversary celebration.

Airports in Frankfort, Winchester and Paris were still in the planning stages.

A SECOND AIRFIELD IS CONSIDERED

The first mention of replacing Halley Field was an announcement made on October 29, 1929. The founders and incorporators of Lexington Airways, Inc. planned to significantly enlarge their operation and expand their services. Harkness Edwards, one of the investors, announced that the fleet of aircraft would soon be increased with 10 new Aeronca monoplanes and that two tracts of land were being considered for its base of operations. The opening of a new field was expected to happen within several weeks, but the location was not announced since negotiations were still in progress.

As they made their optimistic announcement (ironically on a day that would later be known as Black Tuesday – the day the stock market crashed in 1929), little did Harkness Edwards and his colleagues at Lexington Airways know the rocky times that lay ahead. The nation would soon face its most devastating and economically challenging period in history – the Great Depression.

Since the city's lease of Halley Field was to expire on April 15, 1930, Fayette County appropriated $1,500 in February 1930 for the lease of a new airfield; the city's share of funding was practically assured. Fred Bryant was named site committee chairman, and he worked with University of Kentucky engineers who began surveying three sites under consideration.

The lease on a new 250-acre airfield was finally announced in the local papers on February 28, 1930. Glengarry Farm, owned by J. Blythe Anderson on Newtown Pike, five miles from the city, had been leased for $20 per acre annually for a period of 10 years. An option was included for the purchase of the tract for $500 per acre at the end of the lease. Lexington Airways was given exclusive use of the field and planned to build a hangar, operate a flying school and help finance capital improvements in exchange for the privilege. The lease was ratified on March 3, 1930, but it would be some time before any more would be done to bring the proposed airport to life.

The impending creation of a new field did not mean the end of flying at Halley Field. Lexington's airport

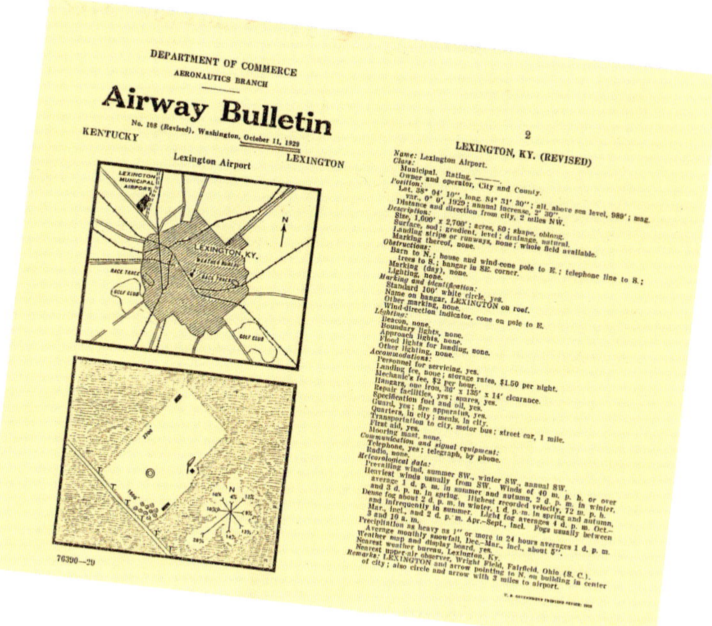

Department of Commerce 1929 Airway Bulletin on the Lexington airport, which became known officially as Halley Field in 1930.

was one of only two airports in Kentucky – the other in Louisville – listed in a magazine titled *Airports*. The magazine listed only those airports that were accepted as models for the size of community they served.

On April 15, 1930, the lease on Halley Field expired. Though the lease on the new field on Newtown Pike had been negotiated and ratified, it had yet to be signed. The new lease was dependent on Lexington Airways getting cooperation from the Curtiss Flying Service to form the proposed flight school and commercial flight services. Dr. Halley graciously granted the continued use of Halley Field until the deal on the new field was closed. The Board

Halley Field facilities were rudimentary but served as a base of operation for Kentucky Airways.

of Commerce airport committee then met to consider a month-to-month lease of Halley Field.

On May 1, 1930, it was announced that a one-year lease on Halley Field was signed by a group of fliers. Bruce King, Monroe Bradley and Swope Loughridge planned for work to begin immediately to improve the airport. They intended to provide services such as passenger service, sightseeing flights, flight training and sales and servicing of aircraft. The three also planned to add a cabin-style aircraft to their fleet consisting of a Waco, Arrow Pursuit and Arrow Sport. Their lease resulted in the airfield's official name being changed from Lexington Municipal Airport to Halley Field.

Plans for another airport materialized in February 1931 when two men, George Wurtz and William B. Loughridge, took an option for a 55-acre tract of land on Nicholasville Pike owned by James Lowry, presumably near the area where Lowry Lane is now located. It was their intention to open an airport in the following months. Although the article appeared in the *Lexington Herald* on February 5, 1931, no other mention could be found as to the proposed airport.

When Wurtz spoke of Lexington's need for an airport to the Fayette County Farmers Union on March 7, 1931, he declared that aviation in Lexington was behind the times and more support was needed in order to estab-

"Fearless" Freddie Lund lost his life during a 1931 air show at Halley Field.

lish a first-class airport for Lexington. In January 1932, Wurtz presented the airport committee of the Board of Commerce with a second proposal to acquire a 300-acre tract of land located on Bryan Station Pike near Easton Road. George Wurtz was also known for being the head of the U.S. Weather Bureau in Lexington.

HALLEY FIELD CARRIES ON

Business at Halley Field continued to flourish in 1931. In March, the Lexington Cab Company expanded its operations to include aviation. The airplane taxi service was thought to be the first in Kentucky and offered: "air service to any place at anytime," a flying school and aerial photography. A special "night flight" service was also an option. Sightseeing trips over the city cost $1.50 per person while a trip for two to Louisville or Cincinnati was $18.50 and $22.50, respectively. Lexingtonians and visitors from nearby cities enjoyed the night sightseeing trips over Lexington for months following the launch of the new sightseeing service.

Announcements of an air show and races to be held at Halley Field filled the Lexington newspapers the last week of September 1931. The aerial meet (as it was called then) and races were scheduled for Friday, Saturday and Sunday, October 2-4. Arrangements were made for more than 12,000 visitors and 5,000 cars. Attendees were amazed as airplanes raced around the triangular course at speeds of more than 180 miles per hour.

Tragically, during the last day of the show, the good-natured excitement turned to horror as the spec-

While the airstrip at Halley Field could easily accommodate small aircraft, as aircraft became larger the length of the field became an issue.

The name Meadowthorpe preceded the Lexington subdivision by 100 years. It was the name of a well-known stock farm owned by Jacob Hostetter. A two-story Greek revival house was

Dr. Samuel H. Halley

built on the property around 1849. After his death in 1886, the farm was sold to William H. Cheppu, a well-known Lexington bookmaker.

On April 28, 1892, in order to pay off an overdraft of $32,000, Cheppu sold it to Colonel James E. Pepper, owner of the Pepper Distillery, a massive distillery complex located in downtown Lexington on Manchester Street. At the time, Meadowthorpe Farm consisted of 222 acres on the north side of Leestown Pike. The price of $275 per acre was the highest that had ever been paid for a Bluegrass farm. If Pepper had followed through on his original intentions, a magnificent castle would have been built on the property and he certainly had the means to do it. Instead, he decided to remodel and enlarge the existing house and added a new front gable inscribed with the name and date: Meadowthorpe 1892.

Although the estate was officially deeded to Pepper's wife in 1898, after Colonel Pepper's accidental death in 1906, heirs sold it to Dr. Samuel H. Halley, president/general manager of Fayette Tobacco Warehouse. He and his family lived there at least through the

Meadowthorpe subdivision in the 1950s

Residence on Meadowthorpe Stock Farm in Kentucky.

1920s and allowed part of the farm to be converted to an airstrip, which later became Lexington Municipal Airport – Halley Field. Their home was the scene of many gala parties and having one of Kentucky's only two airfields at the time on the property must have made life at Meadowthorpe interesting.

The storied farm ultimately fell victim to "progress." On October 13, 1949, the Planning and Zoning Commission approved Meadowthorpe Subdivision, Section 1, consisting of 158 lots and owned by H.R. Taylor. The new subdivision contained three streets running perpendicular to Leestown Road: Glendale and Hillsboro Avenues and Boiling Springs Drive, where the original Halley Field hangar was located.

Source: Meadowthorpe Neighborhood Assoc.

> 66 *Grandfather [Dr. Samuel Halley, owner of Halley Field] was not a pilot or an airplane owner. As I have been told, he was fascinated by machines, modernization and gadgetry — and I think he enjoyed the publicity. I believe he simply got caught up in the craze of the day and offered the relatively flat land for the field … He was an extravagant man. One who rented private trains to take friends to a play or concert in New York — a man who paid caddies from Lexington Country Club to attend Kentucky football games to cheer for Washington and Lee, wearing W&L apparel he had purchased for them. So I believe he was thrilled to have airplanes in his front yard and especially thrilled to have Lindbergh land there.* 99
>
> — Sam Halley, grandson of Dr. Samuel Halley

Air Climbers of America at Halley Field - 1930

Glengarry Farm in 1904

tators witnessed a mid-air collision between two racers. Freddie Lund, one of the nation's more famous stunt fliers, was killed in the collision witnessed by his wife and the crowds below.

Lund was given a funeral with full military honors in Lexington the following day and Lund's body was placed in the receiving vault of the Lexington Cemetery until it was determined whether his body, accompanied by his widow, would be returned to California or to his childhood home in Minnesota.

In 1932, Halley Field became the focal point of several disheartening events. The first came when the operators received notice from the state air board and county fiscal court in early March stating that there had been complaints of improper flight operations. Complainants indicated that airplanes had disregarded proper warming-up procedures and often flew too low over the city. Two crashes in the following months coupled with the earlier complaints resulted in the Board of Commerce withdrawing its support of the operations at Halley Field in June 1932. The lease with Dr. Halley was later canceled in August 1932, but before the end of the month the airport received a reprieve and flights in and out of Halley Field resumed.

GLENGARRY FIELD/COOL MEADOW GETS ITS START

In February 1934, the city again took an option on a portion of the 165-acre Glengarry Farm owned by J. Blythe Anderson on Newtown Pike. The stately Italianate home where Anderson resided overlooked the proposed airfield. The fields and wooded hills of Glengarry had been used by Union troops as an encampment during the Civil War following a battle with Confederate troops at nearby Taylor's crossroads in mid-July 1862. The Union soldiers under the command of Colonel Metcalf, Captain John B. Castleman and Lieutenant Lawrence Jones were forced to retreat toward Lexington and stopped at Glengarry. In the years to come, the farm would be used to train and race Thoroughbreds.

Glengarry Field became the scene of numerous air circuses and festive events during the 1930s. Fasig-Tipton Thoroughbred auction sales company is now located on the site of the former airfield.

The 100-acre site was chosen after inspectors with the Federal Bureau of Aeronautics determined it met federal government specifications. The approval came at a crucial time. In order to begin construction, applications had to be submitted to the state Civil Works Administration (CWA) in order to procure needed funding. The CWA funding would pay for the labor while the city would pay for the equipment and materials needed to construct the airfield. CWA was a division of the Federal Emergency Relief Administration, which provided work relief for a large number of men during the winter of 1933-1934. The application needed to be submitted as soon as possible in order to be eligible for existing funds. Funding for CWA projects was slated to end in May 1934.

Financial problems began to plague the construction of the airport almost immediately. These problems continued throughout the construction, frequently delaying work. Federal funds were cut and local funding budgets were questionable. However, due to some creative financing arrangements and reinstatement of federal funds, work began in May 1934. On May 14, 1934, city commissioners passed Ordinance 264 authorizing the lease of approximately 100 acres on Newtown Pike from Blythe Anderson and other members of his family for the new airport.

By January 1935 the majority of the work had been completed, but the airport still lacked hangars, office buildings and lighting. Some aircraft had used the new airport despite its work being incomplete, but the majority of aircraft were still using Halley Field.

In the meantime, efforts to procure a hangar and lighting for the airport continued. In June 1935, city and airport officials began visiting various cities to inspect hangars at their airports. The inspections resulted in the opportunity to purchase a hangar from the Robertson Airplane Service in St. Louis, Missouri, for $1,500.

A surprise response to a request for funding assistance was received in late July. The response was from Brigadier General Oscar M. Westover, the acting chief of the Army Air Corps. Ed Wilder, executive secretary of the Lexington Board of Commerce, had written General Westover regarding the construction of the airport and also suggested its designation as a possible military base. Lexington's airport, according to General Westover, could be considered at a later time to be an intermediate station providing for the transcontinental movement of military aircraft. Airports, such as the one in Lexington, were provided for in a federal bill, which approved construction and designation of airports as air defense facilities. Wilder's letter was placed in line for

An airshow at Glengarry Field draws a crowd.

consideration. Although the airport was not selected, this letter could have very well been the foundation for Lexington's next airport, Blue Grass Field.

The American Legion announced in July that an air circus would visit Lexington's new airport for two days, opening July 20, 1935. The circus would be part of the American Legion's state convention festivities. A crowd of more than 1,500 people attended the opening ceremonies. The following day, July 21, City Commissioner Sam McCormick christened Lexington's new municipal airport on Newtown Pike as "Glengarry Field."

Despite the airport's lack of amenities, business was flourishing. Lexington Air Taxi Service was incorporated on August 9, 1935, and began operations on September 1, 1935, with a new $10,000 Bellanca six-passenger cabin airplane with chief pilot and manager Paul "Dixie" Hosier in command. By the end of the month, 108 passengers had flown on a 25-mile sightseeing excursion with the company and an additional 19 passengers were taken to Cincinnati. A

sightseeing trip to Dix Dam in central Kentucky was later added to the list of flight offerings.

The all-metal 55-by-120-foot hangar purchased in early September 1935 was shipped by rail from St. Louis and arrived on the 28th of the month. The 100,000-pound metal structure was reassembled on the north side of the Newtown Pike landing field at the end of a macadam (crushed stone) road already constructed into the airport.

Improvements to come included the placement of additional markers throughout the county. These markers would be painted on major roads leading to Lexington. Since pilots frequently used roads as part of their navigation, these new markers would help pilots, who had not yet reached the city, find the airport. Markers had already been painted on the rooftops of several tobacco warehouses and large industrial buildings in town, pointing the way to the new airfield.

The airport was given a more official name by Resolution 165 passed by the Board of Commissioners on December 9, 1935. It provided that the airport oper-

Waiting for customers, but the price is right! Since people didn't have a lot of discretionary dollars to spend after the Great Depression, prices such as $1 (and up) for sightseeing and $4.50 for a lesson made flying affordable.

ated by the city be designated and known as "Lexington Municipal Airport, Glengarry Field."

NEXT STEPS AND CONTROVERSY

Cumberland Air Lines announced tentative plans for creating a "feeder" air service to Lexington in January 1936. The air service would use Lexington to connect flights between Cincinnati, Middlesboro, Knoxville and Chattanooga. Lexington's location was strategic and the feeder service would bring much desired commerce to the city. The service would include a combination of rail and air travel connecting Lexington with a nationwide system.

It was in March 1936 that the airport became the focal point of controversy. An ordinance was introduced on March 26 that would allow the airport to be leased to, and operated by, Lexington Air Taxi Service, Inc. (Lexington Air Taxi). Under the lease agreement, the city would still be responsible for the annual rental of the property from Blythe Anderson for $1,500. Lexington Air Taxi would then lease the airport from the city for $1 per year. The company would be responsible for all maintenance and operating costs. Lexington Air Taxi would also be required to observe all rules and regulations of the city and federal department of commerce. The field at this time was managed by Shirley Lyons, who was employed by the city as airport manager at an annual salary of $1,200. This arrangement would reduce city expenditures by more than $3,600 and the city would also be relieved from liability for injuries arising out of accidents at the airport.

Opposition arose from more than 1,400 citizens and aviators who signed a petition protesting the proposal. John Sutherland, opposed to the lease, argued that major cities serviced by national airlines, had not "surrendered" control of their airports. By surrendering control of the

Lexington's first air taxi, a new $10,000 Bellanca six-passenger cabin aircraft, was brought in from Dayton, Ohio. Paul "Dixie" Hosier, chief pilot and manager of Lexington Air Taxi (fourth from the left in front of the plane) is standing next to his wife.

Miss Jeanette Martin, holder of two world records and star of the 1936 Flying Aces Circus, prepares to do her famous "death ride" in which she stands on the top wing of the airplane while the pilot does a series of loops, spins and barrel rolls.

airport to a single company, all other businesses, competitive and otherwise, could be excluded from doing business at the airport, creating a monopoly. If the city was to maintain control, other businesses and airlines could rent hangars and other buildings from the city and offer competitive business. The airport board studied the proposal presented by Lexington Air Taxi and recommended that the airport remain under the city's control.

Another issue in opposition to Lexington Air Taxi's lease arose when a second bid to lease and operate the airport came from Herbert Boggs and Company with a bid of $100 annually. A third bid came in from Paul L. Brown, the president of the Lexington Aero Club, Inc. The Aero Club's bid was high at $120 per year. However, Lexington Air Taxi was the only bidder to submit a report of financial responsibility.

The board of city commissioners met on April 2, 1936, and consisted of Mayor E. Reed Wilson, Florence S. Cantrill, James P. Kelly, R. Mack Oldham and Dan Regan. Despite the protests, the board suspended the rules and voted in favor of adopting a revised ordinance to replace the original. The revised ordinance would allow anyone with an airworthy aircraft to use the air-

port for passenger carrying purposes. The rest of the conditions remained unchanged. Under the suspension of rules, the ordinance went into effect immediately. The proposed ordinance passed with a vote of four to one. Commissioner Regan was the sole dissenting vote. Just before the end of the session, the board approved city manager James O'Brien's appointment of Paul Hosier as a special patrolman at the airport.

On April 12, 1936, shortly after Lexington Air Taxi assumed control of the airport, new air service consisting of daily flights between Lexington and Louisville was announced. The air service to Louisville would begin on April 20, departing Lexington at 12:30 p.m. daily and returning between 5:30 and 6:00 p.m. each evening. Lexington Air Taxi had purchased a "three-place" Curtiss-Wright cabin monoplane earlier in the month in preparation for the announced route.

The new airport had been open since July 1935, but there had yet to be any official dedication ceremony. The airport committee brought this issue to Mayor Wilson in a letter sent on May 13, 1936. In the letter, W.C. Smith, chairman of the committee, requested the matter be brought before the city commissioners and a date be set for the dedication. The committee emphasized that such a ceremony would help attract attention from across the nation, thus encouraging air travel through Lexington.

A dedication ceremony would also draw attention from airmail cover collectors throughout the nation seeking a special cancellation mark commemorating the occasion. The envelopes would then be sent via airmail to Louisville and Cincinnati and put on national airlines. The airport committee seeking the special cancellation had already received more than 100 envelopes. A number of the letters, some from as far away as Canada, had been sent more than two years earlier in anticipation of such an event.

Although the formal dedication would not come for some time, the airfield was becoming known for its aviation activities – including air circuses. The Flying Aces Circus arrived in Lexington on May 16, 1936. The show, slated to last a little over two hours, was scheduled for the next day with a demonstration of aerial combat and a parachute jump from 10,000 feet. Additional acts would include wing walking, precision flying and other aerobatic flights.

More than 10,000 spectators lined the airfield, with shuttle buses bringing them from the city hall garage. Those deciding to drive themselves were charged 40 cents per person or $1.50 per carload, and they were

1936

Gas is 19 cents per gallon.

Margaret Mitchell's epic *Gone with the Wind* is published.

The Bureau of Air Commerce begins to set up a nationwide air traffic control system.

The Spanish Civil War begins.

Track and field athlete Jesse Owens wins four gold medals in the 1936 Berlin Olympic Games.

The Brooklyn Dodgers fire manager Casey Stengel.

FDR is re-elected to a second term as president.

Edward VIII abdicates the throne for Wallis Simpson.

Glengarry Field became known as Cool Meadow (or Coolmeadow) Airport around 1940.

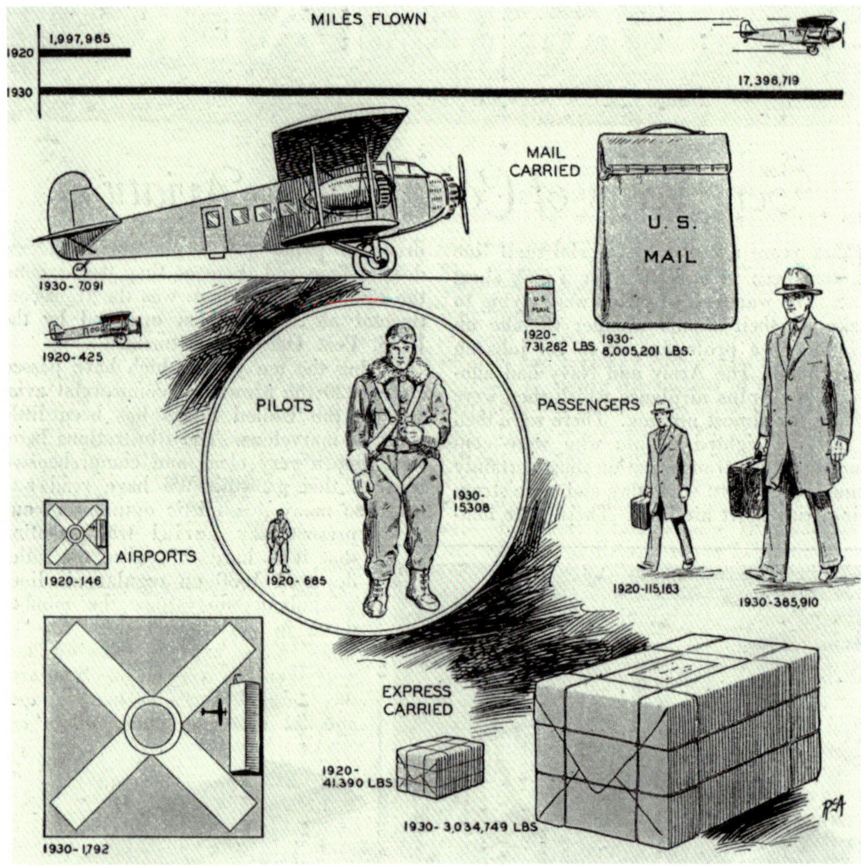

An illustration from *Modern Mechanics* shows the dramatic growth in commercial aviation in the decade between 1920 and 1930.

An aerial view of Cool Meadow (formerly known as Glengarry Field) taken around 1950. Although Blue Grass Field was in operation by then, Cool Meadow continued to be used until 1953.

not disappointed. The performances were well received and the air circus left town without incident.

During the same month, A.M. Papania, the vice-commander of the local American Legion post, announced that funding from the Works Progress Administration (WPA) had been obtained to aid in the marking of the city for air travelers. The program called for 214 towns in Kentucky to be marked to aid aviators in navigation. The WPA allotted $134 to be used to mark buildings in Lexington. Several buildings had already been marked. Those buildings were to be re-marked, and a survey of buildings suitable for new markings began immediately.

The directional markers, which were in disrepair at Lexington's airfield, were part of an extensive system of airline markers throughout the country. These markers were similar to road signs for motorists. Since 1927, the Bureau of Air Commerce and WPA crews had marked more than 13,384 towns and had more to do. Markings were to be placed every 15 miles. The WPA crews were also responsible for improving more than 1,300 of the nation's 2,000 airports, which ranged from simple graded fields to large commercial airfields.

Within two weeks, two buildings had been located for marking – the hangar at the airport and the G.F. Vaughn Tobacco Company re-drying plant on Angliana Avenue. The airport hangar was an obvious choice since it had no formal markings to distinguish it from any other barn when observed from the air.

LEXINGTON'S AIRPORT MISSES THE MARK

A scathing report on the airport's condition was released during the first week of August 1936. On August 6, an article appeared on the front page of the *Lexington Herald*. The article, along with photographs, listed the deficiencies and lack of upkeep at the airport. Lexington Air Taxi Service had spent several thousand dollars on the airfield, yet it was described as not much more than a landing field and dangerous to those not familiar with it. The field still lacked lights for locating and landing at night; the directional markers on the roofs of buildings had faded; there were no restrooms; it had a dirt floor in the hangar; and the markers on the ground were hidden by grass and weeds, which were allowed to grow waist-high. Hangar doors did not exist until just a few weeks prior, and when the doors were installed they lacked locks. The absence of locks left stored aircraft with no security.

Also missing were electricity and telephone service. The lack of electrical power meant no lighting for the field or its beacon. Airports used for night flights were to have beacons, which could be seen from 40 miles. The beacons were to be placed 50 feet or more above the ground to be visible from that distance. The windsock at each airport was required to be lit at night, and lights were to be placed along the boundary marking the airfield. The landing areas were required to be illuminated by high intensity floodlights located at each end. Those landing at the airport "after hours" would have to make their way to a home across the road to use a telephone.

Refueling aircraft was problematic since the gasoline was stored several hundred yards from the hangar in a fairly decrepit wooden shack, and there was no pumping station. Fuel had to be carried in five-gallon cans making for strenuous and lengthy refueling. The conditions at the field had deteriorated so badly that pilots threatened to take their planes and operate from another field. The airport operator, Lexington Air Taxi Service headed by Ernest Welsh, strongly urged the city to take over the operation of the airport by purchasing the field.

Despite the city taking more active oversight in the next couple of years, it seemed that Lexington was always chasing the funds needed to bring the airfield up to date.

In October 1938, the members of the Bluegrass Aviation Club took the initiative to have a beacon installed at the Lexington airport. In an announcement on October 20, the club indicated that the purchase of the beacon would be the first step in procuring the equipment needed to modernize the airport.

In retrospect, it was too little, too late. It would take more than a beacon to become a modern airport worthy of attracting commercial airlines. Despite some high points with air circuses and airmail promotions, it became all too obvious in the months and years to come that Lexington needed a "real" airport.

Halley Field and Glengarry Field (later renamed Cool Meadow) had both been outpaced by the rapid growth of aviation and America's increasing appetite for flying as a preferred means of transportation. Although the grass landing field of Cool Meadow would remain in service for 15 years longer, many would soon be clamoring for an airport that would help Lexington keep pace with progress. ✈

Lexington Herald front page story on August 6, 1936

The Birth of BLUE GRASS FIELD

BY RENA BAER

It is fairly safe to say that when cities woo passenger airlines these days, they have the basics covered before they go courting – paved runways, night lighting, a terminal building. It is almost inconceivable that they wouldn't. However, this was not the case in 1940, when Lexington officials met with Delta Air Lines and Eastern Air Lines representatives to try to convince them to bring air service to the Bluegrass.

Delta had been eyeing the city as a stop between Cincinnati and Atlanta, and Eastern wanted to make Lexington one of several hops from Washington, D.C., to St. Louis, Missouri. But the decision was not theirs to make. The Civil Aeronautics Administration (CAA) decreed all commercial routes, sending inspectors to make recommendations.

Quite obviously, the first thing they noticed was that Lexington did not have a "real" airport. It had some airfields with fairly level pastures that served as runways and a grow-

ing aviation community, but it certainly wasn't on par with the more established regional or national airports.

Lexington Mayor T. Ward Havely was ready to put the city on the country's flight map. The 45-year-old Central Rock president, who had just been elected in 1939 and taken office in 1940, saw the time as right. Two years earlier, the Civil Aeronautics Act had repealed the federal ban on aid to airports, and the Works Progress Administration (WPA) was awarding funds for cities to build or improve existing airports. The country was being put back to work.

Additionally, the ominous prospect of the United States being drawn into a second World War grew ever more likely as Britain and France declared war on Germany following the invasion of Poland in September 1939. The inevitability of war, and Germany's unprecedented and unrelenting strategic bombing of the United Kingdom beginning in 1940 (kill-

> **THE ACCOMPLISHMENT OF [AN] AIRPORT IS THE BIG STORY OF 1940 FOR LEXINGTON. IF THE SPIRIT OF 'ALL HANDS ON DECK' AND 'NOW, ALTOGETHER' CAN CONTINUE TO PREVAIL THERE IS NO TELLING WHAT MAY BE ACHIEVED IN THE YEAR THAT IS JUST AHEAD.**
>
> – *LEXINGTON LEADER*, 1940

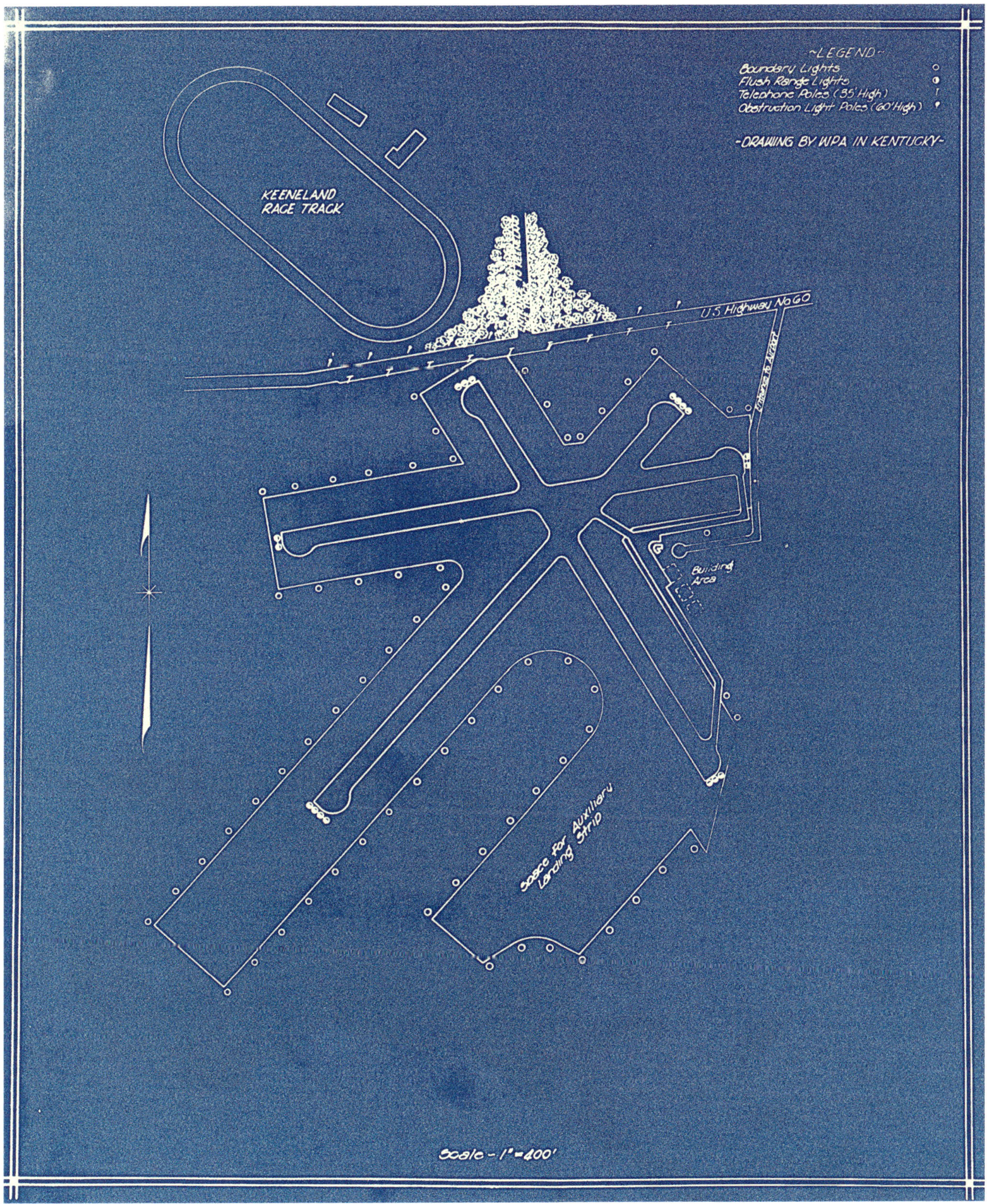

This site plan drawn by the Works Progress Administration shows the proposed airport on Versailles Pike across from the Keeneland Race Course.

ing 40,000 people in an eight-month period), fueled America's growing awareness that a national air defense system would be critical in the event of war.

With the tide in his favor, Havely gathered community support for the project. The city pledged a possible $100,000 bond issue while the county mulled a $50,000 bond issue to purchase land for the airport. With the local pledge to buy the land, Kentucky's U.S. Senators A.B. Chandler and Alben W. Barkley

This Herb Block editorial cartoon from 1940 shows military commanders reaching the conclusion that airplanes had a role in battle.

pitched Lexington's bid for a new airport to the War Department and CAA in early June 1940.

In August, the *Lexington Leader* supported the project in no uncertain terms when it published an editorial entitled "The Time for an Airport."

"There is no possible investment that the city could make that would more certainly guarantee the future than … providing land for an airport. If the unfortunate war in Europe has demonstrated anything it has proved that the future must look to

the air, both for defense and for travel and perhaps large commercial transportation." Such was Havely's state of mind when he attended a mayoral conference on national defense and airport development in New York City. Though most of the cities represented had populations of more than 100,000, Havely explained that the War Department and CAA were considering Lexington, with a population of less than 80,000, as a site for a large airport because of its central location.

Meanwhile, Delta and Eastern were having a difficult time getting the CAA to approve their proposed routes through Lexington. Two examiners recommended not only against the inclusion of Lexington, noting it did not have a suitable airport at present, but also against both of the entire routes, saying they could not find justification for them.

Lexington's official representative in airport dealings, J.E. Marks, traffic manager of Lexington's commerce board, was all for getting the routes approved, even if they did not include Lexington for the time being.

"If we can get the transports to fly over Lexington, we will find some way to bring them down [here] for business," he said.

Delta representatives were not giving up and came to Lexington in late September to gain support for the route. They declared that, in anticipation of the new route, Delta had already purchased a fleet of new 21-seat Douglas DC-3 planes that would arrive in January.

FUNDING IS IDENTIFIED

Lexington's federal bid for an airport began looking up in December 1940. In an effort to beef up national defense, $40 million had been earmarked earlier in the fall for airport construction and improvement nationwide. In a list of projects, the CAA had allotted $57,000 toward Lexington's airport. A few days later a WPA grant catapulted the amount to $200,000 with the possibility of $627,500 if all went as planned.

The funding, however, hinged on securing public money for the airport site.

"In no case will we permit our funds to be used in lieu of local contributions pledged by the sponsors of WPA projects," said Colonel Donald H. Connolly, administrator of CAA, when the appropriations were an-

Delta purchased a fleet of Douglas DC-3s in the early 1940s. The DC-3, with its speed and range, helped revolutionize air travel when it was introduced in 1936.

nounced. He further stipulated that the money would only go to projects being built on government land with a free-and-clear title.

So far, Lexington had neither a site nor the money to purchase one. And without both, Connolly had made it abundantly clear that federal funding would disappear.

Members of the Fayette County Fiscal Court quickly convened with representatives of the city and the county. Havely estimated the land would cost $160,000 and immediately announced that the city, which was approaching the end of its fiscal year, would put up $80,000 in cash – if the county would do the same.

County officials said they heartily favored the project but were unsure whether they could get the money. Their fiscal year had six months remaining and their budget could not be legally altered to accommodate the request. The amount also represented one-fourth of the county's income. Their answer would have to wait a few days.

The meeting also raised a question about whether the 600 acres off Versailles Pike opposite Keeneland Race Course had been chosen as the location of the new airport. The Lexington mayor answered that 10 sites had been submitted but no decision had been made.

As the county struggled to come up with its share, the CAA awaited confirmation on its offer, ticking off the hours before the money would go to another airport project in Kentucky.

1940

Gas is 18 cents per gallon.

Cartoon characters Elmer Fudd, Woody Woodpecker and Bugs Bunny make their debuts.

The Battle of Britain, the first major campaign to be fought entirely by air, commences with Germany attacking British convoys in the English Channel.

Adolf Hitler orders German bombing attacks on London.

FM radio is demonstrated to the FCC for the first time.

Winston Churchill is appointed Prime Minister of the United Kingdom.

The Chicago Bears defeat the Washington Redskins 73–0 in the 1940 NFL Championship Game.

Minimum wage is 30 cents an hour.

As the deadline approached, the *Lexington Leader* again put the pressure on with a headline begging the question, "Airport Ever?" Mayor Havely announced that if Lexington and Fayette County are unable to provide a site for the new airport by January 15, the federal government will consider allocating the funds earmarked for the local field to another community in this area.

Shenandoah Farm, with its large expanse of relatively flat land, became the site of choice for the new airport.

Aware that nearly $700,000 to fund community infrastructure was slipping away, several Lexington businessmen and bankers stepped forward with a plan: They would front the money and be paid back in installments.

Though the federal government required a clear public title on the land upon which the airport would physically be built, no such title was needed on the buffering acreage. Under the plan, a local bond business would form a non-profit holding company, place a mortgage on the outlying 200 acres needed, and then five-year bonds would be issued and paid off by the county at $16,000 annually.

A SITE IS CHOSEN

With funding secured, Havely announced on December 29 that the results of the search had, in fact, landed on Shenandoah Farm, across from Keeneland. The CAA had approved the Versailles Pike site as the only possibility among the choices, and the county and city had obtained a 60-day option to purchase the farm from its owner, Frances McChesney Van Meter.

Lane W. Wilcox of Chicago, CAA district airport engineer, had inspected the site and nine others earlier that week. He found the tract across from Keeneland ideal, writing to Havely that it would give Lexington

"a splendid airport."

"The aeronautical features involved are, at the outset, a distinct advantage; the natural terrain lends itself very well to the establishment of runways aligned in the necessary directions," he wrote. "The site is located on relatively high land, which provides natural, clear approaches that are essential to safe operation of all types of aircraft and aircraft service."

The cooperation among the city, county and community was dually noted in the *Lexington Herald* editorial that appeared on Christmas Eve. "The accomplishment of the airport is the big story of 1940 for Lexington. If the spirit of 'all hands on deck' and 'now, altogether' can continue to prevail there is no telling what may be achieved in the year that is just ahead."

Word of the new airport put the wind under Delta's wings, and by the end of January 1941, the airlines had secured authority not only to fly from Cincinnati

Senator A.B. "Happy" Chandler was instrumental in procuring federal funding for Lexington's new airport. Chandler served Kentucky in many capacities – as senator, lieutenant governor and governor. He then went on to become commissioner of baseball, and under his leadership Major League Baseball became racially integrated.

In this adaptation of a 1938 illustration. a pink airplane with blue wings denotes the Lexington Municipal Airport at Glengarry Field, which was located on Newtown Pike.

Warren Wright, Sr., owner of Calumet Farm, which is adjacent to the proposed airport site, leads Whirlaway off the track at Keeneland. Whirlaway won the Triple Crown in 1941.

in a public office. There isn't a city in the United States with a better mayor."

A month after the Versailles Pike site had been identified publicly, Wilcox talked to the newspaper about the site's many advantages and pointed out that the runways could be configured so as to not draw objections from neighbors. The engineer also talked about specific plans for the airport.

Most of the air traffic, he told the *Lexington Herald* in early February 1941, would land from a north or northeast direction and take off in a south or southwest direction, due to prevailing winds, though three landing strips would be built. These strips would later be paved and upgraded as soon as the appropriations were available, Wilcox said.

A 5,000-foot strip would extend from the southwest to the northeast; an east-west strip would be 2,500 feet; and another 2,500-foot strip would run "approximately" north-south. The hard-surfaced runways would be 150 feet wide and laid out immediately after the tract was grubbed and graded.

The airport, Wilcox said, would eventually rank with those in Cincinnati, Louisville and Indianapolis – other Class 3 fields. This meant that Lexington would be only one grade below the largest airports in the country such as New York's LaGuardia and Chicago's airport, which were Class 4. Meanwhile, it would serve private planes and itinerant fliers.

Wilcox further noted: "The airport should materially increase the commercial interests of horsemen in the Bluegrass area." It was a point well taken by the Bluegrass community.

AND THE PROTESTS BEGIN

In retrospect, Wilcox's comment about the horsemen was most likely in response to a yet-unpublicized protest against the airport launched a couple of months earlier by Warren Wright, Sr., the wealthy horseman

to Atlanta, but also to make stops at Lexington's new airport and Knoxville, Tennessee. Representatives from Transcontinental Air Transport and Western Airlines also were visiting Lexington to collect information to establish service between Washington, D.C., and St. Louis by way of Lexington, in competition with Eastern for the route.

To oversee the airport construction project, Havely and the county judge announced in late January that an airport advisory board would be created to attend city and county meetings on the airport. The board would make recommendations pertaining to construction and later serve as an advisory group on its operation.

Havely's forward thinking and hard work had not gone unnoticed. Earlier in January, the *Lexington Herald* offered the following annual performance review of his first year as mayor: "Mayor Ward Havely, elected to the office of mayor, has done as intelligent, as quiet, as thoughtful and painstaking a job of real business work, without upsetting or running contrary to the city manager act and without grandstanding, as we have seen done

who owned famous Calumet Farm, located across the road from the proposed site. Wright had been sending telegrams to officials from his residence in Miami Beach, Florida, asking that the Shenandoah Farm site be withdrawn from consideration. He claimed the airport would be "an annoyance" and "decrease the value of nearby property."

At Wright's insistence, the CAA sent Wilcox back to Lexington in January to look over all the sites again – and eight additional ones. The CAA airport engineer was even more effusive in his praise for the Versailles Pike acreage after his repeat inspection, insisting the property was the only one that justified a large expenditure of federal money.

City, county and federal officials all politely refused to back down as Wright took his protest public. He created a petition, to be presented to the city council, that listed a mere 14 signatures, albeit the signatures of some very well-known horsemen, including Leslie Combs, whose farms also were in the vicinity.

In response to the forthcoming petition, Havely left no doubt how the issue would resolve. "I have just re-turned from Washington, where I have had conferences with high-ranking government officials. They assured me that federal funds would be furnished for the construction of the airport regardless of protests."

Havely stressed the project had been certified as "important to national defense."

Even as several petitioners withdrew their names (in light of having learned all the facts, they said), Wright appealed for a construction delay, going to the highest authority on the matter, Major Lucius D. Clay, executive head of the Army and Navy Board of National Defense. Clay sent back a message by way of not responding to the request. Wright expressed his disappointment through a spokesperson but acknowledged Lexington needed an airport for both military and commercial use (though his backyard was not his preferred location) and said he would protest no further than the petition that was to go before the city council.

On the evening of March 6, 1941, a crowd of business and civic leaders, dressed in their Sunday best, filled the city commission chambers, worried that further delays would cause Lexington to lose the promised federal dollars.

Wright's petition was read, summarily, politely discussed and dismissed after it was once again stated that only the Versailles Pike site was suitable for the airport. The city commission voted unanimously on its final action to purchase the Versailles Pike property, drawing applause from the audience.

Construction would begin by March 15, 1941, Havely said, with the clearing and marking of the site, and the new airport would be finished and ready for commercial aircraft by June 1942. Havely added that the property around the new airport would be properly zoned to ensure "the avoidance of objectionable establishments," which further clarified at the time consisted of

On March 6, 1941, the city council approved purchase of the airport site despite objections from some prominent Lexington horsemen.

T. Ward Havely
Mayor of Lexington, 1940-1943

"small stands and gathering places that do not fit into the atmosphere at all."

Four days ahead of schedule, the first shovelful of earth was removed to place a small concrete marker on the northern boundary of the property. Over the next few weeks, nearly 175 WPA workers were expected to arrive for the first phase of construction, funded by the original $200,000 that the CAA and WPA had yet to release.

A MAJOR SETBACK

On April Fools' Day 1941, everything came to a halt. A small army of attorneys, on behalf of tenant farmer Alex Fugette, obtained a temporary restraining order demanding that work on the property stop immediately. Fugette claimed he had entered into a yearlong oral contract with Van Meter back in September. He charged that the city and county were ignoring that agreement, and unless restrained by the court, the construction would destroy crops he had already planted for harvest. The 46-year-old farmer said he would suffer a loss of $4,024.25 if he was deprived of the land.

City and county officials were shocked not only by the claim but also by the fact a judge had granted the restraining order. Fugette, they said, had approached Havely back in December with his concerns. In turn, Havely had told him the county and city were willing to reimburse him for money and labor expended preparing for his 1941 crops. (In his suit, Fugette had not asked for money but for a permanent injunction until the case could go to trial.)

Quickly recovering from their astonishment, city officials asked Fayette Circuit Judge Chester D. Adams, who had issued the temporary restraining order, to dissolve it. City counsel requested an immediate hearing on the injunction, stating that any delay would be risky. Final federal approval on the project was expected within less than a month.

Also under speculation was whether Fugette and Wright were in cahoots. Putting that speculation to rest,

Crops on tenant farmer Alex Fugette's land were at the center of a controversy and legal action that put the new airport in jeopardy in 1941.

the three law firms representing the tenant farmer said Fugette was the lone client in the suit, which they had filed against the city, county, Van Meter and the airport holding company.

At a hearing on the temporary restraining order held April 9, Fugette said he remembered going to see Havely in December, right before the mayor left town on the train to go talk with Van Meter about the property. But, contrary to Havely's recollection of events, Fugette maintained that he did not tell the mayor he would be satisfied if the city and county paid him for the crops he had already planted for harvest.

During the hearing, city officials said that Fugette came back to them in March, after the city had decided to purchase the property, saying that he had a verbal agreement with Van Meter to rent the farm from March 1, 1941, to March 1, 1942. Fugette, in his own answers, said that the verbal contract was made in September 1940 and valid through September 1941.

Judge Adams rejected the temporary injunction, stating that farm leases customarily ran from March to March, and a September-to-September lease, if there had even been one, made no sense.

"It does not seem reasonable that a man of Mr. Fugette's experience in farming would have leased a farm from September 21, 1940, to September 20, 1941,

because he would have known the tobacco might not
be ripe by September 20 and that the corn could not be
shucked and cribbed by that time … No man would
want to take a chance on losing a part or all of a tobacco
crop, after putting in the toil, the sweat and the backache
necessary to raise it."

Adams said he made his decision to deny the injunction based upon the lack of proof of an oral agreement
with Van Meter, though he did raise the point that
upon further appeal, Fugette could ask for damages
even if he could not determine an exact amount.

Rather than appeal to a higher court, Fugette's lawyers
amended their petition on the grounds that the farmer
had no other choice than to seek a
permanent injunction because none of
the parties being sued had any money
to pay damages if he offered sufficient
proof that he did have a valid lease.

Under pressure to have all the airport construction contracts let by June
or lose federal funding, the city began
proceedings in May to obtain a writ
to have Fugette evicted from the property. Fugette and his attorneys, at the
same time, launched a new tack, saying that since 90 days had passed since
his lease had ended and he still had
possession of the property, his lease, by
law, had been automatically extended
for another year.

As the legal wrangling continued,
residents had to be content to watch
commercial planes fly past Lexington.
Delta's Cincinnati-to-Atlanta route had
been inaugurated on April 14, with
two roundtrips being made daily. A
Lexington Herald correspondent made
the trip, noticing how quickly Lexington
was below them. "You don't even have
an opportunity to get acquainted with
the stewardess, in this case a young lady
named Miss Birdie Perkins."

"From Lexington on south, things
are a little better. The crew has time to
circulate about and make the customers feel at home.
And if you don't think you could feel at home 8,000
feet in the air moving at 160 miles an hour, you don't
know Miss Perkins."

In an effort to secure a route from Washington,
D.C., to St. Louis, with eventual stops in Lexington
and other points between, a Kentucky contingent of
well-regarded politicians, businessmen and educators
headed to Washington on May 20 to testify before the
CAA. Transcontinental & Western Air and Eastern
Air Lines were both vying for the route. The local supporters said train service was insufficient and airline
service needed to be established. George "Brownie"

Governor Keen Johnson (on left) meets with a representative of the War
Production Board in Washington.

Photographs show progress on grading, filling, laying out runways, creating spillways and pouring concrete. In some of the photos, Keeneland and Versailles Pike can be seen in the background. The Works Progress Administration brought in the men for the site work, which took place from 1941-1943.

Mayor T. Ward Havely offers a hand to Carolyn Cassidy of Louisville, the reigning Miss American Aviation of 1941, at the groundbreaking ceremony on July 31.

Leach, former sports writer for the *Lexington Leader* and publicity director for Keeneland Race Course, told the CAA board that Kentucky had a $30 million racing industry with constant travel by owners, breeders, jockeys and managers, as well as fans, who needed the air service.

Meanwhile, Havely was also in Washington for the testimony and to meet with the CAA and WPA about the Lexington airport project that same day. Havely telephoned the *Lexington Herald* long distance that night to let them know the $200,000 finally had been released and actual work would begin the next morning. Havely said federal authorities wanted the first phase to be completed quickly since the airport had been certified as necessary under the national defense program. So pressing was the need to act quickly that 50 workers from the Fayette County WPA rolls were to begin work at the site the next morning.

The CAA had also approved some changes to the original plan, including the addition of an auxiliary landing field for training purposes and to relieve possible congestion on the main field. The width of the landing areas was also expanded from 500 feet to 700 feet.

As workers grubbed and cleared the extensive property over the next few weeks, an unlikely volunteer was named to the airport advisory board – Warren Wright, Sr. Assured zoning would prevent objectionable and unsightly buildings from marring the bucolic landscape, Wright accepted an appointment by Havely to the Lexington and Fayette County Aviation Board.

Meanwhile, Fugette and his band of attorneys had not abandoned their fight, even as all the property around his farmhouse and crop fields was cleared and graded while he continued to live there. In July, though, Judge Adams ruled that the county and city were entitled to immediate possession of the farmhouse, outbuildings and fields. Adams did include a provision allowing Fugette to harvest his final crops provided he did not interfere with work on the airport.

Fugette was not going to make it easy, though. Only after the city and county agreed to pay him $1,000 and his litigation and attorney fees of $815 did the tenant farmer agree to leave the property, and his crops, by the end of August and take no further action.

TIME FOR A GROUNDBREAKING

Work on the first phase was well under way, with the site cleared and leveled enough to host a groundbreaking ceremony on July 31, 1941. In honor of the occasion, Kentucky Governor Keen Johnson and Senator Chandler spoke to the crowd about the potential of the new airport.

"I share with you the hope that this airport may have to serve only peaceful purposes," Johnson told a small, but stalwart, crowd which had been soaked by a cloudburst an hour earlier and then dried by a blazing sun.

"But if it ever becomes necessary for our defense, it will be highly important that we have it."

"If we were to need an airport here to defend this section of Kentucky, we'd need it mighty bad."

Havely talked about how the airport had come to fruition through the efforts of many and how he hoped there would never come a time "when this airport will have to be used to launch bombers on their way to destruction."

For all of the mayor's hard work bringing the yet-unnamed airport to Lexington, he was honored at the groundbreaking by being the first passenger to deplane from the airfield's inaugural flight, piloted by Harry Bullock, president of the Blue Grass Aviation Club.

In the weeks following the groundbreaking ceremony, the city commission further tried to recognize his contribution by passing a resolution to name the new airport Havely Field.

The mayor, not one to self-aggrandize, respectfully requested the resolution be withdrawn, leaving the question of a name open for the next few years, during which time the U.S. would be drawn into war.

The airport project would progress slowly until peace was declared in 1945.

THE WAR YEARS

As 1941 drew to a close, so did the first phase of the airport's construction, with more than one million cubic yards of dirt moved and the runways graded. If all went as planned with the $600,000 second phase — which included paving the main runways and installing a system of lights and markers, and later an administration building (the predecessor of what would now be referred to as a terminal) — commercial planes would be touching down in Lexington by spring 1942. Finally, Lexington would get its airport and service to points north and south, and perhaps, east and west.

But it was not to be. On December 7, 1941, the Japanese bombed Pearl Harbor, irrevocably changing history's path and American lives as those first bombs and torpedoes exploded.

In Fayette County, security had already been fortified at the Lexington Signal Depot in Avon. Like the

airport, the Signal Depot was still under construction. Both projects had begun around the same time and were most likely tied to one another behind closed doors in Washington. At the time Pearl Harbor was bombed, the sprawling U.S. defense base several miles east of Lexington was stockpiling logistical and com-

In 1942, the Stop Over Station on Esplanade Alley in downtown Lexington became a popular gathering place for men in the Armed Forces.

munications equipment for the Signal Corps, the division responsible for military transmissions.

"Our precautions are as tight as you can get them," Colonel Laurence Watts, commanding officer of the depot, told the *Lexington Leader* the day after the massive strike, "Every precaution has been taken, and we have been increasing our guard there steadily."

Watts told the *Lexington Leader* he had not yet

Blue Grass Field in September 1945 (Versailles Road is to the left of the runways.)

mid–May 1942, paving was well under way. The project involved the pouring of 218,000 square yards of concrete, or 44½ acres. All of the men on the job were WPA laborers who were new to the work they were performing and had to be trained, with the exception of one crane operator and a mixer operator who had previous experience. Older personnel continually had to train younger workers due to the constant turnover caused by the war.

By July, all non-defense WPA projects were halted in seven central Kentucky counties, and the workers were reassigned to Lexington's airport. At the peak of operations, 500 men were employed and transported daily from Fayette and surrounding counties. The paving was completed by October 24, and in December 1942 the U.S. Army took over the airport.

Without lights, an administration building or money from the government forthcoming with which to purchase them, the airport could not be used as a full-fledged military facility. Instead, it became an auxiliary training field for Bowman Field in Louisville, one of the nation's busiest airfields during the war.

received official orders from Washington, but he anticipated supplies to and from the base would increase.

Two months later, in February 1942, the depot was receiving and shipping out more than supplies. Thousands of men, and later women, from across the country were sent to the Signal Depot to train in radio communications and "to become the voice and ears of Uncle Sam's fighting forces throughout the world."

Entry into the war had mobilized all of central Kentucky. Young men were lining up to serve their country, giving the state the highest percentage of enlisted men in the nation. War bond sales were exceeding quota, and thousands of tons of scrap metal were being collected to keep the country's steel mills going, a wartime necessity to forge the guns, tanks and planes needed to fight the enemy. Civil Defense groups were formed in Lexington to mobilize and train community members in the event of an air raid.

Throughout this time, the airport project languished somewhat because of wet and snowy weather, but by

Crew of the first plane to land at Blue Grass Field included (left to right) Technical Sgt. J.F. Gruber, Sgt. H.L. Pospical, Co-pilot Lt. H.J. Schofield and Capt. W.W. Wilson. Capt. Wilson was formerly a student at the University of Kentucky.

The yet-unfinished airport also became a vital means of cargo transport in and out of the Lexington Signal Depot.

It also served as headquarters for the Lexington squadron of the Civil Air Patrol (CAP), an organization of volunteer citizens with prior aviation experience who underwent further training in military operations and defense to become members. Formed nationally in 1941, just prior to the attack on Pearl Harbor, part of CAP's main duties were to prevent

A crowd gathered on July 11, 1942, to watch the first airplane land on the paved runway at Blue Grass Field. This U.S. Army B-25 bomber was being flown from Meridian, Mississippi, to Wright Field in Dayton, Ohio.

anyone unauthorized from flying and to make sure wartime air restrictions were being heeded. In Lexington, CAP also engaged in recruiting missions and took a very active role in flying personnel and light freight for the Lexington Signal Depot. To this day, the CAP still exists in Lexington.

As an auxiliary airport for Bowman Field, Lexington often provided a leg for glider-pilot training runs. Because of the lack of CG-4A gliders for tactical training, glider pilots at Bowman Field had to train in light aircraft. Dead-stick spot landings were practiced regularly, frequently over two sets of 50-foot barriers placed close together to teach glider pilots the technique of short-field landings.

On the morning of September 10, 1943, a line of 30 light aircraft headed on a round-robin to Lexington, flying at 700 feet. The trip to the Bluegrass was uneventful, but on the return, during a left turn directly into the sunlight, two aircraft in the middle of the formation violently collided. The aircraft flown by Flight Officer Robert Sutherlin went into a flat spin and crashed into the field below, killing the pilot on impact. The other pilot, Harold Roth, was fatally injured when he jumped from his aircraft too close to

the ground for his main parachute to deploy.

Flight Officer Charles Edward Skidmore, Jr. did not see the crash but sensed something had happened when his friend Flight Officer Leon Spencer's aircraft left the formation and dived toward a field below. Skidmore could see that two planes had crashed and were burning. Suddenly, he saw Spencer's aircraft, which was buzzing the field, pitch down sharply and crash.

Skidmore (whose son documented this account with the help of Spencer) pulled back on the stick to gain some altitude and instantly saw a field ahead in which he could land. So shaken that he could not find the brakes, Skidmore rolled to a stop in the field before colliding with anything. He jumped out and ran to the adjacent field, where two men were trying to extricate the unconscious but moaning Spencer from the fuel-leaking aircraft.

With the help of two other glider pilots who had just landed, Skidmore took over the rescue, with the three men trying to hoist the engine off of Spencer's legs and right foot without injuring him further. As they worked, two men stood just inches behind them with lit cigarettes dangling from their lips. Skidmore asked the men to back up and put them out. When they wouldn't, he drew

TUSKEGEE AIRMEN:
A Stirring Success Story with Kentucky Connections

In 1941, when Congress mandated that the Army Air Corps develop an African-American combat unit, the contract was awarded to the Tuskegee Institute. The historically black university had already invested in the development of an airfield, had a proven civilian pilot training program and its graduates performed highest on flight aptitude exams.

At the time, there was no precedent for black military pilots. And, in a time of "separate but equal," many Americans were skeptical that any black man could pass the rigorous tests and training required to become a top-notch pilot.

But soon, young black men who possessed the physical and mental qualifications for aviation cadet training came to Tuskegee, Alabama, from every corner of the country, with large numbers from New York, Washington, Los Angeles, Chicago, Philadelphia and Detroit. They trained in P-40s, P-39s, P-47s and P-51s, initially to be pilots, and later to be navigators and bombardiers.

Above and Right: **Members of the 332nd Fighter Group attend a briefing in Italy.**
Below: **Major James A. Ellison reviews the first class of Tuskegee Airmen. The airplane is a BT-13.**

The Tuskegee program officially began with formation of the 99th Fighter Squadron – an entire service arm that included ground crew as well as pilots.

First deployed to the North African campaign, the 99th distinguished itself for outstanding tactical air support and aerial combat in the 12th Air Force in Italy.

To identify themselves, they painted the tails of their aircraft red, thus becoming known as the "Red Tails." The Red Tails soon became recognized for their tenacious bomber escort cover.

After being awarded with two Presidential Unit Citations, the 99th joined the all-black 332nd Fighter Group, which received yet another Presidential Unit Citation for its longest bomber escort mission, which was to Berlin. The 332nd destroyed three German ME-262 jet fighters and damaged five

Willa Brown Chappell

additional German jet fighters without losing any of the American bombers or any of its own fighter aircraft to enemy fighters.

Before long, white bomber pilots requested the "Red Tail Angels" as their fighter

escorts, while the distinctive aircrafts doubtlessly discouraged enemy fighter pilots from attacking bombers escorted by the 332nd.

By the end of World War II, 450 graduates of the Tuskegee program had been deployed to the war in Europe. They shot down 111 enemy aircraft and destroyed another 150 on the ground. They flew in more than 15,000 sorties and more than 1,500 missions. The Airmen's success during World War II – not losing a single bomber to enemy fire in more than 200 combat missions – is a record unmatched by any other fighter group. The combination of pre-war experience and the personal drive of those accepted for training resulted in some of the best pilots in the U.S. Army Air Corps. Sixty-five of these great pilots gave their lives in combat and 32 were captured as prisoners of war.

From 1940-1946, Tuskegee graduated close to 1,000 airmen, with women entering the program in several support fields in later years.

After the war in Europe ended, large numbers of black airmen decided to remain in the service, but because of segregation their assignments were limited. Many white units were undermanned post-war and needed qualified people but were unable to get the experienced black personnel because of the military's segregation policy. Additionally, while their success in combat was undeniable to those directly involved with the Tuskegee Airmen, the Red Tails faced racism and harassment from other military units.

The newly formed U.S. Air Force initiated plans to integrate its units as early as 1947. Then in 1948, President Harry Truman issued an Executive Order that directed equality of treatment and opportunity in all of the United States Armed Forces. This order, in time, led to the end of racial segregation in the U.S. military.

This was also the first step toward racial integration throughout the country. The outstanding record of accomplishment and the superb valor of black airmen, during and after World War II, were pivotal early factors in the historic social movement to achieve racial equality in America.

Today, African-Americans are well represented in the United States Armed Forces, from new recruits to four-star generals.

The Commonwealth of Kentucky was first to name a portion of a highway system in honor of the Tuskegee pilots. In August 2007, the section of highway I-75 in Fayette County was designated the "Tuskegee Airmen Memorial Trail." The trail was extended to the entire length of I-75 in Kentucky in July 2010.

Ground crew awaits return of the squadron.

The late Brigadier General Noel F. Parrish, from Versailles, Kentucky, was the white commanding officer of Tuskegee Army Air Field during World War II. His unique legacy is his role in the training of almost 1,000 African-American aviators and command of more than 14,000 ground support personnel at Tuskegee.

Glasgow, Kentucky, native Willa Brown Chappell trained many of the men who became Tuskegee pilots. She eventually became the coordinator of war-training service for the Civil Aeronautics Authority, the first black female officer in the Civil Air Patrol and the first black woman to hold a commercial pilot's license in the United States. She was posthumously inducted into the Kentucky Aviation Hall of Fame in 2003.

Source: Aviation Museum of Kentucky - Kentucky Aviation Hall of Fame

his Colt .45 and convinced them it would be a good idea.

Spencer survived the crash, and after a long rehabilitation was placed back on flying status in August 1944.

WOMEN WILLING TO FIGHT

Such was the risk many pilots took during the war, including women, who in 1942 and 1943 were completing Civilian Pilot Training and War Training Service programs in the hopes of filling positions as test and training pilots so that men would be free for combat duty overseas. Both Transylvania University and the University of Kentucky offered such programs to men and women. Other college-educated women who were willing to get their private pilot's license were also considered. In Lexington, several women took up the mantle.

One such woman was Barbara Huger, who wrote a

letter for Blue Grass Airport's 50th anniversary, describing her days training to get her pilot's license at Cool Meadow, most likely in 1942, before the Lexington airport had been finished.

"I was approved for the program, provided I undertake to get a private pilot's license, at my own expense, before going into Air Force Training … I took and passed the necessary tests. It turned out there was a field near Lexington where one could have lessons, and when my kind aunt and uncle agreed to take me in for the duration, I was on my way.

I had no car; very few people did. Gasoline was rationed and there was no public transportation to Newtown Pike. Irvine [Scrivner Jr., Huger's cousin] remembers that I arranged to be picked up by a small van from the field. It had solid walls, was entered through doors at the back and had benches against each wall.

The field was just a good-sized pasture with sod run-

A new class of WAVES (Women Accepted for Volunteer Emergency Services) are sworn in on November 11, 1943, in front of Lexington's courthouse.

ways. *There was a small structure with a desk and a
telephone and an ice chest with Cokes. I can't remember a
hangar. The planes were tethered. There were two instructors. They were patient and skillful, and they had to have
been very brave. It embarrasses me terribly that I cannot
remember a name. There were very few people about as
a rule; I was never there on weekends. I can't remember
any sort of instruments. I only experienced contact flight
… and a windsock directed one's comings and goings …
I have two indelible recollections of lessons. I finally made
an unaided landing, of which the instructor said, mildly,
'That wouldn't have cracked an eggshell.' What a triumph!
And then came the stall and spin bit … When I came
through one on my own, I could only wonder what miracle
had kept my body from being pulled through that bucket
seat, and my moccasins had departed my feet."*

Huger, though, never continued her training as
the country's need for the program had been quickly

A largely female workforce made thousands of parachutes for the war effort at
the Irving Air Chute factory in Lexington in 1943.

filled. Among those who filled it was Transylvania
University graduate Elizabeth Moody Wagner, who
after training was chosen for a highly selective program to see whether 10 hand-picked women could
make capable instructors for male Army and Navy air

Transylvania University's campus becomes a training center for Army Air Force recruits in 1944.

cadets. Wagner proved an able pilot with a knack for teaching and was assigned to train air cadets at Centre College in Danville.

Despite the war opening up new flight paths for women, it still came with a huge toll in the loss of life and limb. Though women accounted for a small percentage of casualties, deaths of sons, brothers and fathers constantly hit the newspapers and their families with heart-wrenching blows.

Sadly, Mayor Havely would not live to see the opening of the airport he had so tirelessly supported. In early February 1943, the Lexington Optimist Club had recognized him as the outstanding citizen of 1942 for his perseverance, indefatigable energy and unswerving optimism in bringing the airport to fruition. Havely expressed his surprise and appreciation at the honor and gave credit for the airport to all those who had cooperated with him. He then left for Florida to try and regain his health, which had been in decline

Other improvements in July 1944 include the installation of Weather Bureau equipment.

for several months. Upon his immediate return to Kentucky, he went to St. Joseph Hospital where he died March 22, 1943.

In 1944, Havely Field was once again put forth as a name for the airport by the city commissioners, while county commissioners pushed for Chandler Field, in honor of Senator Chandler. A petition signed by 1,203 asked that it be called Umstead Field, in honor of Lieutenant Colonel Stanley M. Umstead, a Lexington native and test pilot for the Army, who at that time was considered "the dean" of all Army pilots, flying 350 types of experimental planes. Another suggested name was Lexington Airport.

The quest for a name intensified in mid-August as the end of World War II approached and an airport manager was being named to take the helm. On August 21, 1944, city and county officials made a decision: Blue Grass Field.

"For more than two years each side stood by its

choice," said Mayor Mack Oldham, who had been appointed after Havely's death, "but finally we realized the airport had to be named, so we got down to business tonight and named it."

A month earlier the city and county had each voted to provide $20,000 to construct a building that would house administration, a weather station, and radio and lighting equipment. Lights had also finally been put on the runways after the War Production Board, the federal agency allocating materials and labor during the war, had refused to make provision for them a year earlier.

At the meeting announcing the naming of Blue Grass Field, Lexington native and owner of Imperial Oil Company Peter Powell was unanimously endorsed as airport manager. A graduate of Annapolis, he had also been an aviator, as well as an aviation instructor, and had retired from the Navy in 1933 to enter the oil business. Later, he would be elected one of nine national directors of the American Association of Airport Executives during its 20th annual convention. This was considered an honor for any airport representative – much less one representing a fledgling airport like Blue Grass Field. An architect for the airport building, John F. Wilson, was also named. All seemed well on its way.

But, true to form, it wouldn't happen without additional delays and further controversy.

In November, plans for construction of the terminal building were approved,

A 55-foot beacon was installed at Blue Grass Field in July 1944. At night, the light from the beacon can be seen for almost 30 miles.

but due to priorities on material and labor, the War Production Board's Louisville branch delayed construction. In the meantime, the city decided the hangar from Cool Meadow should be relocated to Blue Grass Field and bid it out to an operator for lease, an idea that did not sit well with Blythe Anderson, who owned the land at Cool Meadow. He sued, saying the city had abandoned the hangar when its lease ran out. A judge, though, felt differently and ruled in favor of the city.

In June 1945, the War Production Board eased up, allowing the construction of a terminal building so long as not more than 25 men at a time were used for construction. A month later, the Robert D. Short and Company was awarded the contract for $64,959 and would build only the lobby area and add the wings later.

When the Army handed the airport back over to the city and county on August 15, 1945, Charles Bohmer was selected as the base operator, but Anderson's lawsuit had slowed down construction to a crawl. It wasn't until October, after ground had been broken for the new administration building, that the hangar was dismantled, moved to Blue Grass Field and reassembled. Now, all that was missing was commercial air service, but it wouldn't be long in coming – at least not in comparison to the previous five years of waiting. ✈

Peter Powell, first manager of Blue Grass Field - 1946

Flowers are presented to the crew of the first official passenger flight to land at Blue Grass Field. Delta Air Lines and Eastern Air Lines compete to see which carrier is first to serve Lexington. Delta wins by a mere two hours.

IT'S OFFICIAL
We Are a Commercial Airport!

BY ROBERT BOLSON

When World War II ended in late 1945, the United States embarked upon an unprecedented period of economic prosperity, driven by the increase in industrial production markets brought about by the war.

Airplane manufacturers revamped their bomber design to produce planes that carried up to 80 passengers. Filling those planes with commercial passengers, however, was a challenge for the nation's airlines as people still customarily rode trains and drove automobiles in preference to commercial aviation. But as larger and more comfortable planes were designed and built, the airlines began to attract more and more passengers as the overall flying experience continued to improve while becoming more affordable.

During the 1940s, United Airlines, American Airlines, Eastern Air Lines and Trans World Airlines (TWA) dominated the major transcontinental routes. But by mid decade, fewer than 10 million people had ever flown on a commercial flight, and international routes still barely existed. That was all about to change.

With thousands of experienced aviators available after the war, a large number of new airlines soon sprang up to serve specific regions of the country. The pre-war airline companies took trunk routes connecting major cities, but there were many feeder routes to smaller or more remote destinations, soon to be granted. The first feeder airlines established included such names as Allegheny, Bonanza, Frontier, Ozark, Pacific and Piedmont.

The year 1945 heralded a boom in commercial air travel options, and passenger counts surged to new levels. Air traffic grew steadily as improvements in travel time and decreases in fares made flying an appealing alternative for an increasing number of people. Airfields grew larger, grass gave way to pavement, and terminal buildings evolved from simple structures to architectural statements of modernity.

Forward-thinking officials in Lexington were eager to bring commercial air service to central Kentucky.

On August 15, 1945, the U.S. Army presented the city with the opportunity to do just that, turning over airport operations to the local government. Community leaders wasted no time in taking full advantage. Plans were immediately made

> **" ONCE YOU HAVE TASTED FLIGHT, YOU WILL FOREVER WALK THE EARTH WITH YOUR EYES TURNED SKYWARD, FOR THERE YOU HAVE BEEN, AND THERE YOU WILL ALWAYS LONG TO RETURN. "**
>
> **— LEONARDO DA VINCI**

The terminal building is occupied in early 1946 despite being under construction. Progress on the terminal had been impeded by material shortages due to the war.

to build the region's first fully functional commercial terminal building. Lexington was about to become the "Air Crossroads of Kentucky."

Until that time, Blue Grass Field had been an active training facility for Army operations. In the fall of 1945, the first airline to begin operations at Blue Grass Field – locally owned Bluegrass Airlines – conducted its inaugural flight out of Lexington. But it wasn't until 1946 that Blue Grass Field's first state-of-the-art terminal became a reality, utilized by major airlines to serve central and eastern Kentucky travelers.

As early as 1940, Atlanta-based Delta Air Lines had expressed an interest in adding a Lexington stopover if a new terminal were built. In addition, Transcontinental, Western Airlines and Braniff Airways had applied to federal authorities for permission to inaugurate flying service at Lexington.

Previously, much smaller airlines provided short-haul service in and out of Lexington, but the opening of Blue Grass Field was key for major commercial airlines to begin operations at Lexington. As a result, central Kentucky businesses became increasingly dependent on the new airlines serving Lexington to transport their people and products (including horses) quickly to various locations across the country. Flying for business became standard operating procedure for many corporations and industries in the Bluegrass region.

After months of construction delays, Blue Grass Field's impressive new terminal building was finally completed in early October 1946. Only days later, two major airlines began regularly scheduled stops in Lexington, utilizing Douglas DC-3 aircraft.

In the spirit of friendly competition, Delta Air Lines and Eastern Air Lines had previously signed contracts to begin operations at Blue Grass Field on the same day – October 15. Blue Grass Field's first commercial flight, however, actually occured two days earlier than originally anticipated with Delta winning the race to be the first carrier to offer regularly scheduled commercial flights to Lexington, initiating its first stop at Blue Grass Field only a few hours prior to Eastern's first flight occurring on the same day.

Whether traveling north, south, east or west from central Kentucky, those seeking to travel by air now needed only to drive as far as Lexington's Blue Grass Field to begin their journey.

NOW BOARDING...

Delta Air Lines began serving Kentucky on October 13, 1946, offering twice-daily service at Blue Grass Field: Flights 20 and 21. The occasion marked the first interstate commercial flight for a city that had been preparing for the moment for nearly two decades.

Delta's first official passenger flight to Lexington was a 21-passenger Douglas DC-3, arriving in Lexington from Atlanta at 8:14 a.m. en route to Cincinnati. The plane had a top speed of 170 miles per hour.

According to airline records, Lexington was the 26th city and Kentucky the 12th state to be served

The first Delta Air Lines DC-3 lands at Blue Grass Field on October 13, 1946.

The first Eastern Air Lines flight lands within hours of the first Delta flight. It was en route to Louisville.

1946

Gas is 21 cents per gallon.

The first commercial flight departs from London's Heathrow Airport.

Frank Capra's *It's a Wonderful Life* is released.

The United Nations General Assembly holds its first meeting.

Winston Churchill warns of an "Iron Curtain" falling over Eastern Europe.

Tide detergent is introduced.

Using a B-29 Superfortress, the U.S. starts atomic tests on Bikini Atoll islands.

The French bikini appears in Parisian shops.

Minimum wage is 40 cents an hour.

Delta AIR LINES BRINGS AIR SERVICE TO
LEXINGTON

Typical Flight Times and Fares Via Delta

Here are typical flight times, and one-way fares, from Lexington to various key points on the Delta system. For departure times, also for flying time and fares to other points, call your Delta ticket office.

to:

ASHEVILLE
2 Hours, 31 Minutes . . $11.70
*CHICAGO
3 Hours, 16 Minutes . . $15.70
CINCINNATI
36 Minutes . . $ 3.25
KNOXVILLE
1 Hour, 04 Minutes . . $ 7.65
ATLANTA
2 Hours, 15 Minutes . . $14.85
*SAVANNAH
5 Hours 27 Minutes . . $22.60
CHARLESTON
4 Hours, 59 Minutes . . $ 21.35
COLUMBIA
4 Hours, 11 Minutes . . $ 17.85
*JACKSONVILLE
6 Hours, 28 Minutes . . $27.75
*MIAMI
8 Hours, 30 Minutes . . $44.00
All fares plus tax

*Substantial reductions in flight times and increase in frequency of service will be effective November 1.

Ticket Office: Blue Grass Airport.
Phone: 8881

FLIGHTS to and from Lexington in fast, 21-passenger luxury Deltaliners will begin next Sunday, October 13. Delta, the airline serving the South for eighteen years, is proud to link a key city of Kentucky with all the other points on its far-flung system.

Note the map, and the cities Delta serves, also the accompanying table of flight and low fares. Delta also offers economical Air Freight service on every scheduled flight.

A Delta office has been opened at the Blue Grass Airport. Telephone at any time or call in person for schedules, reservations and general information.

CHICAGO
MUNCIE
ANDERSON
NEW CASTLE
CINCINNATI
LEXINGTON
KNOXVILLE
ASHEVILLE
GREENVILLE
SPARTANBURG
COLUMBIA
CHARLESTON
FT. WORTH
DALLAS
SHREVEPORT
MONROE
JACKSON
TYLER
MERIDIAN
BIRMINGHAM
ATLANTA
AUGUSTA
ALEXANDRIA
BATON ROUGE
NEW ORLEANS
SAVANNAH
BRUNSWICK
JACKSONVILLE
MIAMI

Delta AIR LINES

by Delta. Service to Kentucky concentrated on north-south routes including two daily southbound flights – one to Atlanta with a stop in Knoxville and one to Miami with eight intermediate stops. There were also two daily northbound flights – one non-stop to Cincinnati and one to Chicago Midway with one stop in Cincinnati.

For those lucky enough to witness the celebrated event that early morning, watching the magnificent silver wings of the gleaming Delta DC-3 appear on the horizon in Lexington must certainly have been a thrill they would not soon forget.

News accounts of the historic flight were broadcast on all three of Lexington's radio stations: WKLX, WLAP and WLEX.

City and county officials including acting Mayor Edward S. Dabney and Gilmore Nunn, chairman of the Lexington-Fayette County Air Board, were among those on hand to proudly greet the arriving airplane – which was filled with other dignitaries, an assortment of U.S. air mail and miscellaneous freight. Later that same day, an Eastern Air Lines flight left Lexington bound for Washington, D.C.

It was official! Blue Grass Field was now a modern commercial airport.

A flight from Lexington to Chicago in 1946 aboard Delta cost $15.70 and took three hours and fifteen minutes. A flight from Lexington to Miami cost $44.00 and took eight hours and thirty minutes.

Eastern offered similar airfares and flight duration times for its Lexington service to Boston, Detroit, New York, St. Louis and Washington, D.C.

The number of seats available on Delta flights departing daily from Lexington totaled 84. By the end of 1946, Delta had enplaned 883 passengers at Blue Grass Field. By the end of 1947 – its first full

Passengers Len Shouse, Sr. and Gilmore Nunn fasten their seat belts on Delta Air Lines' inaugural flight from Lexington to Cincinnati.

year of service at Blue Grass Field – Delta had enplaned 5,708 passengers. That number would continue to grow with each passing year of service.

Clearly, civil aviation in central Kentucky and around the globe was becoming a way of life for more and more travelers from across the Commonwealth.

The Douglas DC-3, sometimes affectionately nicknamed "The Gooney Bird," was a low-wing, cantilever all-metal, propeller-driven monoplane. This eye-catching aircraft with retractable landing gear was considered the workhorse of the aviation world in the 1930s and 1940s. Its speed and range revolutionized air transportation.

The DC-3s designated for commercial passenger transport included a snack bar and hot food buffet to serve passengers. These aircraft incorporated the latest radio and navigational instruments including Bendix 10-channel radio transmitters and automatic radio compasses.

Print advertising from the era noted that Delta's flights featured "stewardess service, complimentary

Air Board and Board of Commerce representatives are among those joining special passengers on the first Delta flight from Lexington to Cincinnati.

it would begin offering stops at Blue Grass Field. The first Piedmont passenger flight at Blue Grass Field left Lexington bound for Cincinnati on February 20, 1948. A ticket for the flight cost $9.42, one-way.

Four months earlier, on October 14, 1947, Air Force captain and legendary pilot Charles "Chuck" Yeager, broke the sound barrier in the first manned supersonic flight – flying in the Bell X-1 rocket plane and reaching a speed of more than 700 miles per hour. News of Captain Yeager's phenomenal achievement only served to further the public's already rapidly increasing interest in aviation.

Air service at Blue Grass Field continued to grow and improve over the next decade. In 1948, Blue Grass Field's runways were certified to handle larger four-engine airplanes as airlines brought newer and larger planes into service. By 1950, a new control tower had been constructed and a Civil Aeronautics Administration communications station was now operating in new offices – part of a comprehensive program to provide aircraft utilizing Blue Grass Field with the finest and most modern air-ground communications available.

Delta also modified its DC-3s in 1950 to hold 28 passengers and boarding stairs were incorporated into the aircraft's doors. However, in the coming years, DC-3s would be gradually phased out of service.

By 1954, Blue Grass Field was offering travelers a total of 27 flights daily, served by Delta, Eastern and Piedmont.

BLUE GRASS FIELD: ONE OF THE NATION'S OUTSTANDING FIELDS

After months of planning, Blue Grass Field was officially dedicated on November 10, 1946, with remarkable pomp, ceremony and one of the greatest air shows that the city of Lexington had ever seen. Legions of local citizens turned out to participate in the festivities.

An estimated 10,000 people braved the wet weather to be present at the dedication of the community's new regional airport and to see the spectacular air show over

Eastern Air Lines President Eddie Rickenbacker arrives for the formal dedication of Blue Grass Field on November 10, 1946.

meals, courteous and efficient pilots and traditional southern hospitality."

Offerings included a choice of "fine cheeses, appetizers, potted meats and fish, relishes, sandwich spreads and accompanying condiments." Available beverages included coffee, tea, milk, hot chocolate, beef bouillon and bottles of Coca-Cola®.

In a marketing effort to persuade air travelers to fly Delta, the airlines gave its fastest flights bold, stirring names such as "The Rocket" (Chicago to Miami), "The Comet" (Fort Worth to Miami) and "The Meteor" (Fort Worth to Chicago).

Other airlines would also soon add service to Lexington. In May 1947, Piedmont Airlines announced

Lexington. The celebration turned into a full two-day commemoration as numerous dignitaries stepped forward to give speeches, citing Blue Grass Field over and over again as an exemplary airport.

According to a report in the *Lexington Leader*, the extensive air show began with an awe-inspiring parachute jump at approximately noon and included precision aerobatics and special aerial demonstrations by Civil Air Patrol men flying primary and advanced trainers and private craft.

Next up, Army aircraft crowded the sky for ninety minutes with impressive Boeing B-29 Superfortress strategic bombers and Douglas C-47 Skytrain mil-

Left: A young girl checks out the landing gear on her "nose-to-tail" tour at the 1946 air show. *Below:* A P-80 Shooting Star fighter jet gets a closer look from spectators attending the "biggest air show ever" in Kentucky.

itary transport aircraft, P-47 Thunderbolts, gliders, training planes and Lockheed P-80 Shooting Stars – the first fighter jet used operationally by the U.S. Army Air Forces.

The crowd of onlookers marveled as a P-80 Shooting Star performed overhead during the sky exhibition by the Army Air Forces (AAF) and Lexington Squadron of the Civil Air Patrol. Excited youngsters were among the interested spectators as inquisitive bystanders pressed closer and closer to personally inspect the various aircraft on display.

Spectators who studied the jet fighters as they sat on the ramp gaped in astonishment as the kerosene-burning planes soon zoomed across the field at a jaw-dropping speed officially clocked at 565 miles per hour.

Soon thereafter, the Shooting Stars flashed past Blue Grass Field's control tower on a speed run and went into a mesmerizing vertical climb to an altitude of 7,000 feet. People who looked through the jet flute while the planes were on the ground soon scurried for safety when the pilot reached for the ignition switch just before takeoff.

Lieutenant Colonel Dallas A. Clinger was the announcer for the dedication's air show and also flew a P-51 Mustang in a series of breathtaking aerobatic maneuvers.

Included in the AAF portion of the exhibition were low-altitude formation-flying maneuvers by B-29 Superfortresses, precision six-point slow rolls and other aerobatic maneuvers by P-47s, P-51s, and a C-47 Glider tow and glider "snatch pick-up."

Air show visitors, who crowded near the Army planes parked on the ramp, were able to take a "nose-to-tail tour" of both a B-29 and a C-54 Skymaster hospital ship. During World War II, C-54s were uti-

lized by Franklin D. Roosevelt, Douglas MacArthur and Winston Churchill.

Also included in the exhibition was the "AAF Caravan," a fleet of trailer trucks containing extensive displays of technical equipment. In addition to helping dedicate the new terminal, the air show was a patriotic effort to gain support for the advancement of aviation by giving the public a look at the planes that won the war.

A number of the officers and enlisted men participating in the air show called Blue Grass Field one of the nation's outstanding fields, according to the *Lexington Leader*. One of them commented, "We have been all over the country with this show, and Lexington has one of the best civilian airports I have seen."

Ceremonies also included the unveiling of a bronze plaque dedicated to the memory of Mayor T. Ward Havely, whose tireless energy made the $1 million city-county airport possible.

Captain Eddie Rickenbacker, president of Eastern Air Lines and keynote speaker at the dedication ceremony, remarked, "The citizens who are responsible for this airport should enjoy the prestige and appreciation of all the other citizens of this community."

Rickenbacker, a Medal of Honor recipient, was America's most successful fighter pilot in World War I with 26 aerial victories. An avid race-car driver with a strong entrepreneurial spirit, he owned the Indianapolis Motor Speedway before combining several small air carriers in 1938 to form what would eventually become Eastern Air Lines.

In his dedication, Rickenbacker noted that Blue Grass Field was "one of the finest" airports regardless of size and that it was a community project from which all citizens would profit. The importance to Lexington of its modern airway link was comparable to cities with access to waterways and railway links. Those cities that took earliest advantage of these resources grew fastest.

"You would be a wayside station as transportation

A crowd estimated at 10,000 turned out for the Blue Grass Field dedication and air show on November 10, 1946.

develops if you were not on the airway map of this land of ours. I congratulate you on having the foresight and conviction to put yourselves on the airways maps. Lexington will benefit by your foresight," Rickenbacker declared.

FINALLY, THE AIRPORT HAS A TERMINAL BUILDING

Thousands of first-time visitors to Blue Grass Field on that day agreed. The new three-story terminal, a stucco-covered masonry building complete with a rooftop control tower, provided a shining example of modern architecture associated with the recent developments in transportation, commerce and public works of the 1940s.

This building, with its distinctive semi-circular-front – the first purpose-built terminal for commercial passenger flight in Lexington – included a small restaurant and coffee shop on the ground level with circular glass windows where visitors to the airport could sit and enjoy a snack or hamburger and soda and watch the daily airplane activity. The building's walls were decorated with splendid scenes of central Kentucky's storied horse farms such as Calumet and Spendthrift.

The original terminal was small by today's standards but extremely efficient and convenient for its time. Thoroughbred horsemen could fly in to Blue Grass Field, park their airplane only a short distance away from the terminal and easily walk across Versailles Road to attend

Great view of the air show with landing marker in the foreground.

POWELL-WALTON-MILWARD
A Partnership Takes Flight

Maintaining a business relationship for more than 60 years is almost unheard of today, but that's how long Powell-Walton-Milward (PWM), a division of J. Smith Lanier & Co., has been handling the insurance and underwriting for Blue Grass Airport.

Samuel Walton and Hendree Milward look at a helicopter at Blue Grass Field with Logan Gray.

Yet, to this fourth generation family business, 60 years may seem like a flash because they have served the Lexington area since 1852. Originally owned by W. King & Son, Henry Milward purchased half interest in the agency for $10,000 in 1919. In the late 1940s, Milward's son Hendree purchased the W. King & Son agency and later joined forces with a friend, Samuel B. Walton, to form the Walton-Milward Agency.

In 1971, the Walton-Milward and Alfred G. Powell agencies merged to form Powell-Walton-Milward. Today, PWM is a division of J. Smith Lanier & Co., a fifth-generation company with roots going back to 1868. Brothers John and Greg Milward are the third generation in the family business, while John's son, Kav, and Greg's sons, Will and Jeff, are the fourth generation.

The Milward family's involvement in Lexington's aviation activities goes all the way back to the Halley Field days when Henry Milward, at the urging of friend Scott Breckinridge, brought his young son, Hendree, to the airfield to see Charles Lindbergh land for his "not-so-secret" visit to Lexington back in 1928.

The Walton-Milward agency began

The Milward family saw Lindbergh land at Halley Field in 1928.

An interest in aviation from the earliest days can be seen in a Milward family photo album. These remarkable images show the Goodyear Blimp Puritan at Halley Field c. 1930.

handling insurance matters for Blue Grass Field in the early days, when the terminal was little more than one room with passengers claiming baggage under an awning at the side of the building. The airport's insurance needs have grown much more complex over the years, and PWM has grown with them while retaining a strong focus on customer service. They have been onsite in the aftermath of incidents ranging from damage caused when a University of Kentucky basketball championship celebration got out of hand in 1978 to the monumental tragedy of Flight 5191 in 2006.

More than 50 seasoned professionals in the PWM office and the resources of J. Smith Lanier & Co., the nation's ninth largest privately held brokerage, give the firm the depth to handle underwriting for an airport with over a million passengers and thousands of aircraft landings each year. The people at PWM take pride in their long-standing relationship with Blue Grass Airport and in being an integral part of the central Kentucky community. To the airport, PWM is truly a partner with a purpose.

When the terminal building opened, it was considered state-of-the-art. A restaurant wing was soon added to the left side of the building. *Below:* The lobby of the original terminal at Blue Grass Field.

the popular horse races or auction sales at Keeneland.

Blue Grass Field's terminal would serve as the administration building for the airport and airline operations. It was home to the major airlines serving the community for the next three decades.

Surprisingly, however, almost from the day Blue Grass Field officially opened for commercial traffic, it was at a decided disadvantage. Civil Aeronautics Board guidelines of the day stated that an airport would not be certified for service of four-engine aircraft unless the main runway was at least 5,000 feet long. While twin-engine DC-3s currently served Lexington passengers using a 4,000 foot runway, larger, more comfortable and more efficient four-engine aircraft quickly became the standard of passenger travel elsewhere.

The airport board quickly recognized this shortfall, and one month after the new airport opened, it requested funding from the federal government to extend the runway by 1,500 feet for a total of 5,500 feet, and to install a security fence around the airport's grounds. That request, as many others that followed for similar runway improvements, was turned down by federal officials.

The government did, however, approve funding for other additions to the airport. A modern control tower was built and opened in January 1950 replacing the original rooftop tower. Construction of the two "wings" or concourses of the terminal continued through 1951, when the final addition to the airport – The Blue Grass Airport Dining Room – opened for business.

In the 1940s and 1950s, the public regarded air travel as exhilarating and glamorous – a perception that airline advertising executives seized upon and readily promoted. Going somewhere on an airplane was a momentous event in and of itself – the destination was almost secondary! Passengers wore tasteful suits and fashionable hats. It was a time when the world was vast and air travel was indeed grand.

This was partly because frequent air travel was generally the sanctuary of the rich and a tool of business executives, and partly due to the fact that prices on various routes were regulated by the government, meaning that airlines couldn't compete on price alone. Instead, they had to compete on standards of service, vying against

Top: Air travelers leaving Washington Airport during National Air Travel Week, October 2–9, 1938, are being given a special treat courtesy of Eastern Air Lines. Cakes baked from their favorite recipes are being put aboard each plane by chefs of the leading hotels in the D.C. area. *Bottom:* The first Piedmont passenger flight at Blue Grass Field was in February 1948.

Coffee is served in style with china cups and saucers.

the well-established railroad lines and passenger liners. Airlines operating during this period attempted to attract passengers with the sort of comfortable, elegant appointments of which today's occasional flier can only dream.

Routine travelers included those who worked for the government, large corporations or the military. During the 1940s, the male business traveler was every airline's main customer and the expectation of service was high. The fiercely competitive airlines were only too happy to try to meet the expectation.

There were no rigid security screening checkpoints to navigate before boarding. In fact, families often eagerly greeted their returning loved one on the airport's tarmac as passengers disembarked from arriving flights.

Passengers were personally welcomed aboard their flight by a friendly, smiling stewardess dressed in a crisp, freshly-pressed uniform and wearing pristine white gloves; her pillbox hat perched perfectly atop her neatly styled hair.

Splendor was the standard. There was more room, more comfort and more personal service; more of everything. By today's criteria, every passenger was traveling first-class. Luxurious silver service was available on many flights. The finest beef was cooked and carved onboard

TO PIKE OR NOT TO PIKE ...

The road on which the current airport is located was once called a "pike" and then later referred to as a "road."

Versailles Road, where Blue Grass Airport is located, was originally a toll road called Versailles pike. It was later referred to as Versailles Pike (note capital "P" on "pike") and ultimately as Versailles Road.

The word "pike" comes from "turnpike" or a road where tolls were collected. According to *Merriam-Webster*, the word *turnepike*, first noted in 1678, was a revolving frame bearing spikes and serving as a barrier (from *turnen* to turn + *pike*).

These roads were often privately maintained and a fee, or "toll," was charged to those traveling the road to cover the main-tenance costs and upkeep. Here in central Kentucky, a tollhouse was often built over the road. The toll-keeper would live in the house, collect the tolls and maintain the road, which gives one a fresh appreciation for Nestlé Toll House® cookies ...

A toll house on what was then Harrodsburg Pike

Above: Stewardesses first began flying on Delta airplanes in 1940. This photo was taken at the Atlanta Airport in 1945. *Right:* Early Eastern Air Lines stewardesses were registered nurses.

and passengers were served their meals on fine china accompanied by linen napkins and silver cutlery. Cabins were invitingly spacious and even had bars where passengers could leisurely smoke and drink as they desired.

EARLY FLIGHT ATTENDANTS

Stewardesses of the period were highly educated and extensively trained in charm, passenger service, airline safety, meteorology, operating routes and schedules, and the proper ticketing of passengers.

In the early 1940s, stewardesses were often required to be registered nurses, unmarried, between the ages of 21 and 26 and between five feet three and five feet five inches tall. Perfect 20/20 vision was mandatory. Typically, their weight also had to fall within a certain range and weigh-ins were part of their normal routine. They also were required to wear foundation garments (otherwise known as a corset or girdle) – no jiggle allowed!

Each applicant was asked to submit two recent photographs with her application – one head and shoulders

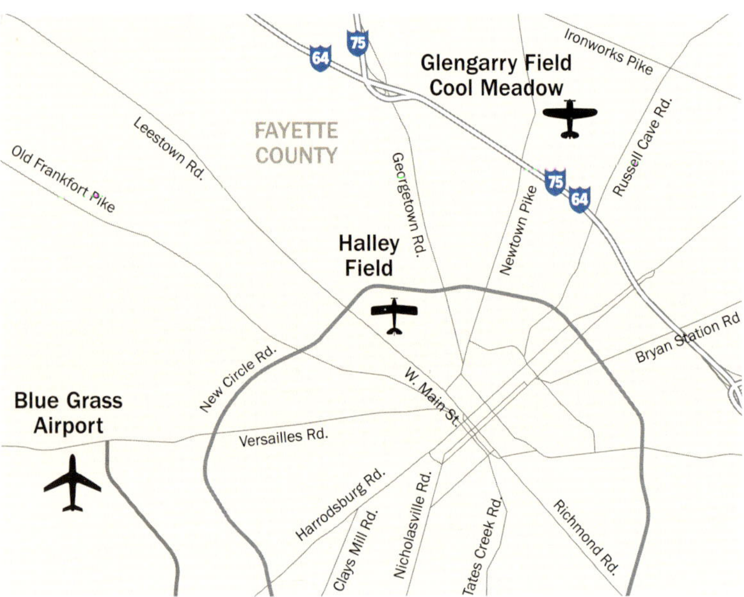

Map showing location of current airport and the two former airfields

1955

Gas is 23 cents per gallon.

Dwight D. Eisenhower is President of the U.S.

American Airlines, TWA and United Airlines create "Coach Class."

The United States Air Force Academy admits its first class.

Rosa Parks refuses to give up her seat on a bus in Montgomery, Alabama.

Dr. Jonas Salk develops a vaccine for polio.

Ray Kroc starts McDonald's chain of fast-food restaurants.

Disneyland opens in Anaheim, California.

photograph, one full-length photograph. During the six-month probationary period, salary for a new stewardess was approximately $110 per month.

After the start of World War II, when nurses were in high demand by the military, airlines opened their doors to the general female population. However, so many young women clamored for the chance to have a career in the friendly skies that acceptance to stewardess training school became next to impossible. For women seeking a professional career in the 1940s, flying was considered a very attractive alternative to secretarial school or teaching.

Stewardesses often took the necessary time to learn each passenger's name on a given flight and when not busy would sit and talk to passengers desiring a warm conversation or even play a game of cards on occasion. Stewardesses were also expected to light cigarettes for passengers who smoked on board.

An unforeseen increase in air travel near the end of the decade meant that many more stewardesses had to be hired and quickly trained. By 1951, there were 3,400 stewardesses flying the U.S. skies, and the number continued to increase as air service expanded.

The media ultimately helped create the larger-than-life persona of airline stewardesses – that of lovely young ladies flying to exotic locations around the world, leading exciting, adventurous, romantic lives. By the 1960s, the top three jobs that young American women aspired to were stewardess, actress and model.

The main attraction of air travel for many passengers during this glorious period of time, however, was simply the unmatched thrill of soaring high into the heavens and gazing down at the earth below; the unique opportunity to observe the rolling fields and pastures; and the chance to stare out of the plane's windows at the lines of the stately trees and towns extending for as far as the eye could see in any direction.

Flying in the 1940s and 1950s was indeed romantic, stirring and resplendent, and a reason to travel for those who could afford to take advantage.

CAR RENTALS

After World War II, the rental car industry also grew rapidly. As the number of airline passengers increased, so

In this different view of Blue Grass Field, Army Air Force airplanes can be seen in the foreground.

too did the need for more rental vehicles, and it wasn't long before rental car companies began opening rental locations inside major airports.

Hertz Rental Car Company, the nation's leader in rental car operations in the mid-1950s, is credited with opening the first airport rental car franchise in Lexington, providing travelers at Blue Grass Field with a selection of top-notch vehicles beginning in 1955.

The growing popularity of airlines for business travel meant that more people needed a car for their business trips, and Lexington was no exception.

Founded in 1946 with three cars, Avis Rent-A-Car was the first company to offer airport-focused car rentals. The company's founder, Warren Avis, was a former Army pilot. Avis became the second largest rental car company in the country by 1953 and began offering service at Blue Grass Field in 1956. Wendell Murphy, who launched the local Avis franchise, started by talking Charles Bohmer at Bohmer Flying Service into letting him take over the

airport car rentals that Bohmer occasionally offered. Bohmer later joked that giving Wendell the rental car operation was the worst business decision he ever made. The Avis franchise is still operated today by Murphy's wife, Betty.

The term "fly-drive" soon became popular among air travelers as rental car companies provided a much-needed service to businessmen and tourists alike.

National Car Rental would become the third major company to offer rental car service at Blue Grass Field, with Budget Rent A Car and Enterprise Rent-A-Car offering service in future years.

The walk to pick up your rental car

*The main attraction of
air travel for many passengers
during this glorious period of time
... was simply the unmatched thrill
of soaring high into the heavens
and gazing down at
the earth below.*

at modern-day Blue Grass Airport is easy and beautiful. Adjacent to the baggage claim area, a covered walkway takes the traveler past a scenic grouping of life-size bronze horses being led around by their grooms in a small paddock area. If one looks closely, one might see an uncanny resemblance – one of the grooms looks startlingly like James E. "Ted" Bassett III, former chairman of the board of Keeneland and president of Breeders' Cup. A coincidence? We don't think so... ✈

BLUE GRASS AIRMOTIVE
STANDARD OIL COMPANY PRODUCTS
BOHMER
FLYING SERVICE
BLUE G

"And Allah took a handful of southerly wind, blew His breath over it, and created the horse .... Thou shall fly without wings, and conquer without any sword. Oh, horse!"

— Bedouin Legend

EQUINE TRANSPORT:
When Horses Fly

BY MARYJEAN WALL

Air transport of horses is an important business in the heart of the historic Bluegrass region, long known for its champion equines. H.E. Sutton Forwarding Company – or simply Tex Sutton to most people – is central to this specialized niche. Tex Sutton provides service on a Boeing 727 dedicated exclusively to the business of flying horses.

Kentucky Derby winners, Breeders' Cup winners, show horses, the occasional pet accompanying these equine stars and at least two steers have flown in and out of Blue Grass Airport in the care of Tex Sutton.

Rob Clark of Naples, Florida, currently owns the company whose founder was the late Tex Sutton, a lifelong horseman who combined equine knowledge with years of experience in transporting horses by rail. Sutton was shipping horses on trains when the rising price of freight forced him to look skyward in 1969 and phase in a business model utilizing airplanes.

The company's logo could not be more appropriate. Pegasus, the mythical winged horse, takes flight straight out of the words "Tex Sutton." The logo holds pride of place on the tail of the company's Boeing 727-200 that it leases from Kalitta Charters II of Ypsilanti, Michigan. Painted along the length of the plane from the front door to the wing are words stating an important mission to horse owners: "First Class Equine Air Travel."

First-class is pretty much the way Pegasus winged his way through mythology. He so faithfully toted lightning bolts for Zeus, that Zeus rewarded him with a constellation of stars named "Pegasus." In modern times, mortal horses forgo a gift of stars and settle in for a first-class flight aboard a jetliner with "Air Horse One" painted on the side.

THE LOGISTICS

Horses adapt well to flying, according to Mike Payne, operations manager for Tex Sutton. In 2012, the company flew 591 horses out of Blue Grass Airport. A full load on this particular airplane usually numbers 21 horses, configured in seven rows of three horses abreast in individual stalls.

Crews generally place the tallest horses in the middle of each row because that is where the fuselage rounds to its highest arc. The shorter horses go into the outside stalls. And, yes, the horses wear "seat belts," which actually are straps fastened across their backs. The straps help keep the horses on their feet should the plane hit an air pocket during flight.

Horses usually fly facing forward. Room is saved for an aisle along the side so that attendants can move throughout the airplane.

These hooved passengers are actually ideal air travelers. They don't ask for peanuts or pretzels; they munch happily on hay that comes with the price of their plane fare. They slurp water served up in individual buckets. And, as an article on ESPN.com once pointed out, horses have it easier than human passengers since they don't have to remove their shoes for security checks.

Pilots take special care when flying horses so as not to throw them off balance. They make wide turns and smooth landings. The pilots begin their descent about 100 miles farther out than customary. This enables them to make a shallow descent to the runway. With live cargo whose value might run into the millions of dollars, they can't take chances that might lead to their passengers becoming injured.

PRECIOUS CARGO

"Everything is gradual," said Payne. "You don't want to do anything too quickly. You don't want to turn too sharply or nose the plane over too quickly or level it off too quickly because the horses could get floated up (vertically off their feet) before they even come in contact with the straps. And if they get floated, they're going to scramble trying to find the floor, and then they might fall down. Or, if you're descending and level off too quickly, their hind legs are going to slip out from under them."

"You have to be aware that those are precious animals," said Mike Hamdooni, the flight crew's captain.

The horses are precious indeed, and most of all

they are iconic to the Bluegrass region. With horses coming and going in and out of Lexington to race or compete in shows, to breed on Bluegrass farms, or even to make a trip to the Southern hemisphere during Kentucky's summer months for breeding in places like Australia, it's easy to understand why equine jet service is essential to the horse business.

The Tex Sutton plane is the only jet dedicated exclusively to horse flight working out of Lexington. For international flights, the company makes arrangements with shipping agents that specialize in sending horses overseas. Tex Sutton generally works in conjunction with Mersant International, Ltd., but other agents include Horse America, Inc., Equi Air Shipping Services and International Racehorse Transport. Horses leaving the country by air go through U.S. Department of Agriculture quarantine facilities at New York, Miami

A Boeing 727 cargo aircraft is used by H.E. Sutton Forwarding Company (Tex Sutton) to transport horses.

Frank Muth made front-page news when he accompanied the first horse traveling by air from Lexington in 1946.

or Los Angeles. Airlines which have their own stalls for shipping horses overseas include Air France, Asiana, Cargolux, FedEx, KLM, Korean, Lufthansa and Singapore. If they don't have their own stalls, they rent them from Instone Airlines or European Cargo Services.

The Boeing 727 that Tex Sutton leases not only presents a curiosity to casual travelers through this airport, but the unique maintenance routines this plane undergoes might surprise many of these travelers.

For example, the plane is checked regularly for spilled urine. Horses will be horses doing what they do, and they can't exactly climb over the passenger next to them to get to the restroom during flight. Every 100 flight-hours the crew removes the horse stalls from the plane to check the fuselage floor for corrosion, a real possibility if urine should leak onto the metal surface.

More often, the crew will find the floor clean and dry. The stalls are self-contained and are configured to catch spills. "If anything were to leak out there's a layer

of absorbent material under the stalls, and below that is a tarp and below that is a sheet of plastic," Payne said. The horses stand on wood shavings, superior to straw for absorbing waste.

AN HISTORIC PERSPECTIVE

Equine air travel has come a long way since the mid-1940s, when air freight service for the shipping of horses began to evolve as a commercial enterprise. A lone Thoroughbred had shipped by air in California as early as 1928 from San Diego to San Francisco. But, commercial air transportation of equines did not really get off the ground in the United States until October 22, 1945, when two Thoroughbreds went by air from Los Angeles to Bay Meadows racetrack near San Francisco. The Flying Tiger Line handled this historic shipment.

The year 1946 was auspicious for horses taking to the skies. Two American Saddlebred show horses flew from New York to Los Angeles on February 4 of that

This Seaboard & Western Airlines DC-4 Skymaster freight plane transported the first transatlantic shipment of horses in 1946.

Smouse flew to Italy on a DC-4 Skymaster freight plane belonging to Seaboard & Western Airlines. The plane made several stops along the way. In a recorded interview that resides in the Keeneland Association Library, Smouse told of his observations on the trip including haunting reminders of the recently fought war.

On the North American side of the Atlantic, civilian life had readjusted quickly from wartime, and civilians were benefiting from technology the military had developed for use during the year, with their flight possibly the first transcontinental air shipment of horses. Calumet Farm's Thoroughbred, Armed, flew cross-country that same year.

Also in 1946, the first transatlantic shipment of Thoroughbreds by air received great attention in the media. The flight originated in Milan, Italy at 8 p.m. on May 16, 1946 and arrived in Newark, New Jersey at 7:30 p.m. on May 17 after refueling stops in Shannon, Ireland, and Newfoundland. Three of the four Thoroughbreds on board were bound for Arizona and the racing operation of Rex Ellsworth. The fourth Thoroughbred, a stallion named Sirte, was headed for Walter J. Salmon's Mereworth Farm in Lexington.

The horses flew in the care of Cliff Smouse, a Lexington horseman. When the door closed on the aircraft in Milan and the plane prepared to take off, the Italians who had gathered to watch the departure wept. Not only were they saying goodbye to four valuable horses and their future contributions to Italian bloodstock, but it was also a poignant and monumental historic event.

World War II had ended only the previous year. Though the United States and Italy had fought on opposite sides, horse racing and breeding interests were helping to bring the two countries closer together.

war. Radar and improved air travel ranked high on this list. Emboldened by new technology, American entrepreneurs saw new horizons opening up in commercial air travel. It was not long before they began to envision an increasing need for transporting horses by air across the Atlantic. Smouse realized this when he made his historic crossing. They can "see a future," he said about this new horizon for equine transport.

Smouse had no idea how much of an understatement he had just made. Six months following that first flight from Italy, six racehorses left Ireland by air in November, traveling from Shannon to Burbank, California, in 29 hours. They flew on an American Overseas Airlines Skymaster air freighter named *Missouri American*. During the flight's one stop for refueling in Newark, New Jersey, a crowd of some 15,000 persons turned up at the airport to see this curiosity of a plane carrying horses. Sportsmen from various points in California went to Burbank to see the flight land.

SHIPPING OUT TAKES ON A NEW MEANING

Prior to the war, horses had traveled from North America to Europe in ships, the same method of transport that had been used for stock since the Spaniards arrived in the New World. By 1938, a year after World

War II had begun in Asia, transport of horses by ship from New York to Europe and other points had become state-of-the-art in its methods.

Vans would line up at New York's Pier 58 to load horses onto the ship at the noon hour, a time when most stevedores would have ceased work in order to eat their lunch. This was the only time of day when noise and activity on the docks stood at a low point, posing a greatly reduced risk of frightening the horses.

Vans carrying horses would pull into position at the pier. Workers would sprinkle sand on the ground to prepare a no-slip walkway for the horses all the way from the trucks to the ship's gangplank. They also lined the gangway in peat moss to help keep the horses from slipping and falling.

The run by steamship between New York and London took about 10 days. Kentucky Derby winners Reigh Count (1928) and Twenty Grand (1931) made this journey following their wins at Churchill Downs. Triple Crown winner Omaha likewise rode the high seas to England after winning the Kentucky Derby, Preakness and Belmont Stakes in 1935.

Illustrations of equine transport during the 16th century

When Omaha returned to New York in 1936, owner William Woodward set out to shield his valuable horse entirely from the commotion on the docks. Woodward arranged to have a railroad car placed on a float and brought alongside the pier so that Omaha only had to walk across the ship's deck and then across a special gangplank into the boxcar waiting for him on the float.

The price of a ticket for ship travel might seem ridiculously low to us when compared with prices for air

Olympia was the first horse to fly in for racing at Keeneland in 1948. Flying in via U.S. Airlines, Olympia went on to win the Breeders' Futurity at the October meet.

Horses were loaded and transported by ship during the early part of the 20th century.

travel in modern times: A stall on a ship cost $130 and upwards in 1938 ($2,138 in 2013 dollars). This was expensive when considering that the price for a human on the same ship was $105 ($1,721 in 2013 dollars).

For longer journeys of 18 to 20 days to Chile or Argentina, a ship carrying horses might be outfitted with a large sandbox on deck, so that the animals could take a roll once a day in order to have some exercise. Then, as now on planes, shipping horses by boat required a specialized crew familiar with horses. They were called sea-going grooms. These sea-going grooms would lead them from their shipboard stalls to the sandbox and keep an attentive hold on the horses' lead shanks while the animals enjoyed a good roll in their extra large sandbox.

Modern air carriers don't need to worry about exercising their equine passengers. Nor do they need to plan a feeding schedule to prevent the horses' gastric distress during what could be a 20-day journey by ship. Air travel is so fast and easy that the horse barely realizes it has left its own stall before it reaches new quarters. The Tex Sutton company calls this process "stall-to-stall" because the horses' feet never touch the ground throughout the journey.

TEX FINDS HIS NICHE

When he founded H.E. Sutton Forwarding Company in 1957, Sutton chose to leave the flying to others and stick with what he knew. Shipping horses by air was still somewhat a novelty, and Sutton perceived his niche on board trains. The business required a specialist who could deal both with horses and with the railroad companies, to make sure the horses did not end up sidelined on a spur. Shipping horses on the ground was as complicated a process as it was in the air, and horse racing professionals recognized that Sutton knew the business.

Most of his clients knew Sutton well, for the garrulous man from Texas spent a lot of time at the tracks, betting the races and socializing with fellow horsemen. Though they knew Sutton like an old friend, most never knew his real name. He was "Tex" to the racing world. The initials "H.E." in the company name would remain a mystery to most. Those initials actually stood for Halford Ewel, a name few knew and rarely used when speaking to Sutton.

Everyone had called him "Tex" from his earliest years. Mike Payne, operations manager for the company, believes Sutton "probably rolled over in his grave because his name is on our web site." Sutton's real name went up on the web site following his death at age 78 in 2000, a period that led to several changes of ownership for the company. The name remains in place on the web site as a nod to Sutton's historical role in founding the company. Still, Payne recalls that when he went to work for Sutton in 1990, "I was warned early on not even to ask him (his real name). He would never tell anyone."

Sutton was as unique as the name he chose to ignore. Born in Lamesa, Texas, he left home at age 11 in 1933, hopping on a freight train to find his fortune. His formal education had extended only to the fourth grade,

but this mattered little to Sutton. He soon acquired all the practical knowledge a young man needed during the Depression era.

The Great Depression was entering its fourth year when Sutton left home. People everywhere had lost their jobs, and many were also losing hope. Not so for young Sutton. He had found a place for himself

❝ *Tex is a horseman's horseman …*

He knows how to handle the horses

***… and the trainers.* ❞**

– Trainer Henry Moreno, *Spur* magazine

Right: Tex Sutton unloads John Henry, racing's all-time money winner as of 1985, as he arrives at Blue Grass Airport. *Above:* Governor Martha Layne Collins greets John Henry upon his arrival.

at the small, non-sanctioned racetracks throughout the Midwest and Southwest, many of them at county fairs.

Horse folk called these little holes-in-the-wall the "bush tracks" of racing, as in "bush leagues" – the lowest levels of the sport. Most of these tracks were less than a mile in circumference and one step away from the end of the line both for the horses and their caretakers. If you learned to make it in these places, you could survive anywhere.

An adventurous kid like Sutton would have thought he had found heaven knocking around these dirt-kicking tracks. They were like the circus, overrun with oddball characters, hard-knocking horses and horsemen who knew better than their counterparts in the major leagues how to keep a cheap horse in well-oiled running condition. Sutton must have absorbed every lesson these folks taught him. He became, by everyone's acknowledgment, a true horseman.

"Tex is a horseman's horseman," trainer Henry Moreno once told *Spur* magazine. "He knows how to handle the horses – and the trainers."

These qualities enabled Sutton to work his way up from the bush tracks into the mainstream of the sport. After

H.E. "Tex" Sutton (on left) and Mel Prince

World War II, which he spent stationed on a naval base in the United States, Sutton returned to what he knew best – horses. The horses brought him to Kentucky, to California and to other points of distinction in the racing world.

At one point Sutton managed the racing and breeding operation of Ralph Lowe on Lowe's properties in Kentucky and Texas. Lowe's most notorious moment in the sport occurred when jockey Bill Shoemaker lost the 1957 Kentucky Derby on Lowe's horse, Gallant Man, due to misjudging the finish line. Sutton, who enjoyed betting thousands of dollars on just about any

Above left: Horses were typically transported by rail from the 1800s to the mid-1900s. *Above right:* John J. McCabe Horse Transportation delivers a yearling to Blue Grass Field on this DC-3 for the 1952 July Sales at Keeneland.

race, may well have lost big on this Derby. We simply don't know whether he bet on his patron's horse this time – Sutton generally suffered his losses in silence.

AND THEN THERE WAS PRINCE

That same year, 1957, saw Sutton roll out his rail transportation business. In 1964 he made a fortuitous move, hiring a man named Mel Prince, who had once trained a horse for him in California. Prince would become as iconic to H.E. Sutton Forwarding as Sutton himself. Prince began with the company in the rail transportation days and transitioned with Sutton into the company's air transport era, which launched in 1969. Prince accompanied the horses on their flights and gained the trust of the trainers and owners of these valuable animals. Moreno, the California trainer, told *Spur*, "If Mel can't load a horse, no one can load it."

The evolution of the Tex Sutton company from rail to air occurred quite casually but with an astute eye to the future. Rail freight had become increasingly expensive, and Sutton began to believe he should pursue what was then a less expensive model. Ironically, that new model was the airplane, which today is not at all inexpensive. Sutton considered his prospects, and as Prince told the *Thoroughbred Times* in 2000, "One day we were sitting on a bale of hay in a railroad car talking, and Sutton said, 'What do you think about flying horses?'"

They thought it might make good business sense and also would be good for the horses, since air transport was faster. John J. McCabe had been among the pioneers of chartered equine air transport in the United States and founded the John J. McCabe Horse Transportation Company in 1949 at Garden City, New York. Sutton knew he could do the same – if he could put together the financial stake this would require.

In fact, air transport was beginning to change the face of horse racing. Flying was the move to make.

Long before the Breeders' Cup day of international racing began in 1984, Laurel Racetrack in Maryland inaugurated the Washington, D.C. International race in 1952. This event stood as the only international horse race in the United States and attracted entrants from around the world, including Soviet Russia even though the Cold War had escalated in the 1960s. The International would not

have been possible without improved air travel for horses.

Sutton did not care for McCabe, who died in 1994. Gail Prince (then Gail Cox), who joined Sutton during the company's transition to air transport, had managed McCabe's headquarters and recalled that the two men were not at all fond of each other. Nothing will drive

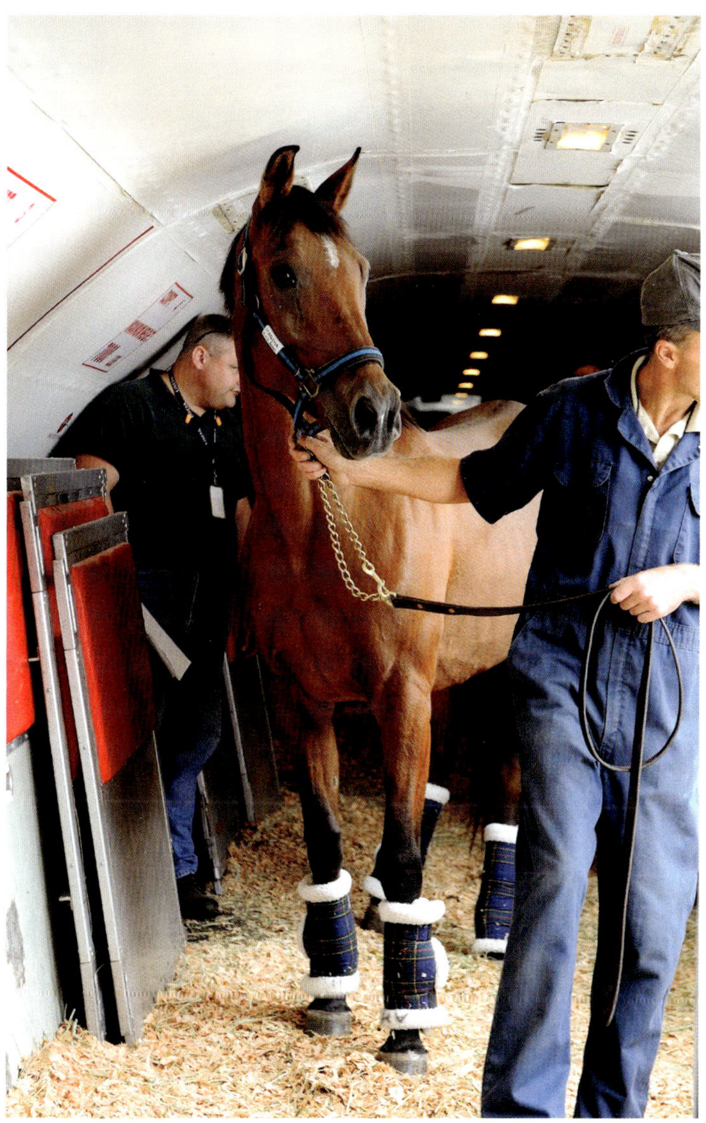

Even on modern aircraft, there is not a lot of headroom for horses.

the determination of business entrepreneurs like a professional rivalry. Sutton hired her away from McCabe and she, like Mel Prince (whom she later married), became an integral part of the Sutton operation.

Gail Prince remains with the company today and is responsible for booking the flights. All of the horsemen recognize her and share a respect for her work ethic. She

Moving off the runway at Blue Grass Field in April 1968 is Link, owned by Claiborne Farm. He was nominated to run in the Blue Grass Stakes and the Kentucky Derby.

goes nowhere without her loose leaf binder that she calls her "office." The binder contains pages of flight schedules, time conversions for each time zone, a rate sheet and records of flights booked.

With 43 years behind her at Tex Sutton, Prince is the repository of the company's institutional knowledge. "Our company was built by horsemen, for horsemen, and for the horse," she said.

Her memories range from horses shipped (Secretariat, Cigar, John Henry and Spectacular Bid, among them) to oddball facts that pop into her mind. Many are aware that Ricardo's, a restaurant in Versailles, Kentucky, was originally a train depot. Prince recalls that this depot was built so that Sutton could offload horses in Versailles.

"By the time they got it built, the trains became so expensive that Tex went to flying, and we didn't need it," she said about the depot. The irony, as she pointed out, is how expensive jet fuel has become. "I can remember when it was $625 to fly a horse from California to Kentucky," she said. "Now it's $4,650 one-way."

IT COSTS TO FLY FIRST-CLASS, ESPECIALLY FOR HORSES

The price of a 2013 ticket from Kentucky to New York is $3,250 for a single stall on a fully loaded plane. If a client wants the stall enlarged to the width of 1-1/2 stalls or wider, the client will pay more. If the client wishes to reserve the plane for use only of his horses, the price rises to about $50,000 roundtrip. Grooms and trainers fly free.

As anyone can imagine from filling an automobile tank with gas, the price of jet fuel has greatly increased the cost of flying horses by air. Operations Manager Payne said the company is trying to be more conservative and efficient in its operations in order to save on fuel. For example, all flights previously originated and terminated in Lexington. Now, they begin and end wherever the shipments dictate. This might mean a layover of a few days in California rather than returning the plane to Lexington and returning it to California for the next flight. "Jet fuel is our number one expense," Payne said. "I think it consumes about 40 percent of our revenue."

In another fuel-saving measure, the company planned to outfit the jet with winglets, those upright tips attached to the end of each wing and which are seen now on many planes. Payne said the winglets should save six percent on fuel burned. Another change brought by rising fuel prices has been in construction of the traveling stalls. The stalls formerly were constructed

Arriving at Blue Grass Field is Foggy Note, owned by Mrs. J. Potrykus. The three-year-old gray filly was nominated for the Ashland Stakes and the Kentucky Oaks.

THOROUGHBRED GREATS AND BLUE GRASS AIRPORT

There is a reason that Lexington is known as the Horse Capital of the World. The following horses are just a few of the many thousands that have flown in and out of Blue Grass Airport in the expert hands of H.E. Sutton Forwarding. While this is a list of famous Thoroughbreds, champion horses representing every equine discipline have been through Lexington's airport.

Affirmed

The last horse to win the Triple Crown (in 1978), he was the great-great grandson of War Admiral and the great-great-great grandson of the legendary Man o' War, considered by many to be the greatest Thoroughbred racehorse of all time.

Cigar

Cigar retired as the leading money earner in Thoroughbred racing history, winning $9,999,813 for his owners and breeders, Allen and Madeleine Paulson. Mr. Paulson, owner of Gulfstream Aerospace Corporation, named Cigar not for the stogie but for a five-letter aviation term given to intersections on aeronautical navigational charts.

John Henry

John Henry, a gelding, retired to the Kentucky Horse Park after winning 39 races and a record $6,591,860 in earnings. He was sold twice at Keeneland's Thoroughbred auction sales, once for $1,100 as a yearling and again as a two-year-old for $2,200.

Rachel Alexandra

The accomplishments of this popular filly earned her the 2009 Horse of the Year title. When she won the 2009 Preakness Stakes, the second leg of the Triple Crown, she became the first filly to win the race in 85 years.

Ruffian

She earned the name "Filly of the Century" after winning Eclipse Awards in 1974 and winning the Filly Triple Crown in 1975. She was undefeated in her first 10 races and set records in each of the eight stakes races in which she raced.

Seattle Slew

Winner of the Triple Crown in 1977, Seattle Slew remains the only horse to win the Triple Crown while undefeated.

Secretariat

In 1973, Secretariat became the first U.S. Triple Crown champion in 25 years, setting race records in all three events in the series.

Spectacular Bid

Spectacular Bid was the leading American two-year-old of 1978. In 1979, he won the first two legs of the Triple Crown – the Kentucky Derby and the Preakness.

Storm Cat

While his career earnings as a racehorse topped out at $570,610, Storm Cat's breeding career netted millions. Considered one of the greatest stallions of all time, Storm Cat's stud fee was $500,000 per cover for five consecutive years.

Zenyatta

Another popular filly known for her ability to connect with fans and for her distinctive prancing gait, this winner of 19 consecutive races in a 20-race career earned her Eclipse Awards in 2010 for top Older Female and Horse Of The Year.

John Henry

Affirmed

Secretariat

After a flight, horses are loaded onto waiting vans for transport to their final destination. It is not unusual to see a lineup of horse vans waiting on the tarmac during peak equine event seasons.

of steel and wood, which were extremely heavy. The stalls currently consist of a core of honeycomb aluminum covered with a fiberglass skin. These stalls weigh about 1,200 pounds less than the older stalls, which each weighed 2,300 pounds.

Trending now is the increasing number of show horses the company ships. Payne said this has represented a big change in the business over the past five years. The loads "used to be probably 95 percent Thoroughbreds," he said, "and now we're closer to 70 percent Thoroughbreds and the rest are event horses, dressage horses and jumpers. We probably took 39 or 40 horses to Mexico for the Pan American Games and brought them back. We took the U.S. team, the Canadian team and a few of the Argentinian horses that were here in the States."

Tex Sutton also transported a number of horses to the Alltech FEI World Equestrian Games, held in 2010 at the Kentucky Horse Park in Lexington. The company brought in a charter from California carrying horses from Australia and New Zealand, as well as many American horses on scheduled service.

SHIPPING SEASONS

The company's busiest times of the year revolve around two seasons. The first season is the buildup to the Kentucky Derby, which includes spring racing at Keeneland. The second is the buildup to the Breeders' Cup, including fall racing at Keeneland.

According to Gail Prince, the calls to book begin early in the spring perhaps a month or two before the Derby, which always falls on the first Saturday in May. "As soon as their horses cross the finish line (for example, in a stakes race during the winter in Florida), they start making plans for the Derby," she said. "Or we're heading to the Breeders' Cup. And then the following week to ten days after each of those big races, we're getting them back where they came from."

Tex Sutton keeps a crew of five on each flight for the purpose of loading the animals, caring for them during flight and unloading them at their destination. Kalitta Charters II provides two pilots, a flight engineer and a mechanic for every flight. Spare parts are kept in the plane's belly for the mechanic's use. The idea is to repair any mechanical problems without having to depend on airport maintenance providers, who might be busy, or on trying to find spare parts from outside sources. The goal is to resume the flight as quickly as possible. If horses have to stand on a plane for a long time, they can become adversely affected by heat. They also might become agitated.

PERFECT PASSENGERS

Regardless of horses' particular needs, the pilots say they enjoy flying the animals to their destinations. "I prefer flying them rather than people because the horses don't complain," said the captain, Mike Hamdooni. He keeps his own American Quarter Horse and a half-Arabian at home in Dallas, Texas. Hamdooni flies with First Officer Rod Maragh of Fort Lauderdale, Florida, and Second Officer Amand Nair of New York.

The pilots laugh about the way their passengers sometimes behave. "Once in a while we hear them talking," said Hamdooni. Nair added, "They whinney. They stomp their feet."

Occasionally the pilots do feel this foot-stomping up front. "But not a lot," Hamdooni said.

Some international flights combine cargo with human passengers. If that cargo happens to be horses, it can make for a rather memorable flight.

"You wouldn't know the horses are on board un-

The trip isn't over until the horses are safely off-loaded into a waiting van. Coordinating all of the details involved when transporting horses is a fine art better left to experts – in the air and on the ground.

less they started neighing halfway across the Atlantic. Sometimes, the captain may announce there are horses on board so they don't startle people in flight," the *Chicago Tribune* once quoted Simon Glennie, president of International Racehorse Transport USA. Glennie oversaw shipment of two European horses in 2004 to the Arlington Million race at Arlington Park, near Chicago. The horses arrived at Chicago O'Hare International Airport on a KLM flight carrying dozens of people.

Like human passengers, horses are limited in the amount of luggage brought aboard. Since a net of hay for snacking is provided free, stables may not send individual hay bales on a Tex Sutton flight. With the company trying to save on jet fuel, the extra weight of hay bales is frowned upon. Besides, hay bales loaded into the plane's belly can be hazardous, according to Payne.

"We've never had anything catch on fire," he said, "but we've had the dust out of the hay set the smoke alarms off and make the airplane think it's on fire. This creates a major problem that you have to deal with: You have to land."

When Sutton reconfigured his shipping operations from rail to air, he took a client base with him that grew in lockstep with the growth of horse racing. He changed with the times, but surprisingly he never lost a fondness for his origins in traveling by train.

"There was a romance in the trains, but I can't tell you what it was," Sutton told *Spur*. "It was dirty, cold, miserable – and you loved it."

Sutton might have looked with fond nostalgia on the good old days of train travel, but he is remembered most for taking to the air. The company he founded continues to provide a service that might be little known to casual travelers through Blue Grass Airport but is of great importance to Kentucky's worldwide horse business. Pegasus does indeed fly – on the broad wings of this Boeing 727 that has forged a myth of its own in the equine world. 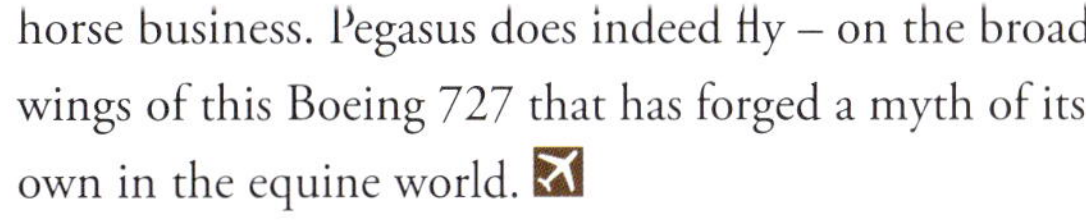

THE ULTRAMODERN AND GORGEOUS CONCORDE HAD TOUCHED DOWN

IN LEXINGTON NEARLY 24 YEARS AFTER THE FIRST PIEDMONT AIRLINES 727

JETLINER MADE ITS TEST LANDING AND TAKEOFF AT BLUE GRASS FIELD ... LEXINGTON

AND ITS PROUD AIRPORT HAD COME A LONG WAY SINCE 1965.

THE JET AGE:
Dawn of a Modern Airport

BY DAN DICKSON

If you had driven along Versailles Pike past Keeneland Race Course at about 3:30 p.m. on Thursday, October 7, 1965, you might have glanced up and noticed an aircraft coming in for a landing at Blue Grass Field. Nothing new there, happens all the time, drivers might have thought. But the arrival of that Piedmont Airlines Boeing 727 jetliner was more symbolic than most Lexington-area residents out and about the city that autumn afternoon realized. In that moment, they had witnessed the dawn of the jet age in Lexington.

On the ground, about 100 people, definitely more attuned to the significance of the occasion, greeted the jetliner's arrival. Onboard were several Piedmont executives, who were flying test runs in and out of several cities where Piedmont planned to provide jet service in the South and Southeast. But how many of those onlookers actually realized how the new generation of jetliners would profoundly change the airport, city, state, region and nation forever?

Soon, central Kentuckians would be able to board jets in the Commonwealth's second largest city and more easily and quickly fly off to visit relatives in Chicago for Thanksgiving, head to a vacation spot in Florida or conclude a business deal in New York. Almost overnight, travel speeds would more than double.

Because of jets, the entire world would open up to local passengers and the phrase "it's a small world" had new relevance. Lexington residents were now in the same league as "big-city" travelers who could jet across the oceans at incredible speeds to destinations that before seemed too far away and inconvenient to visit. Travelers would marvel at how much bigger, faster and more comfortable jet aircraft were than their predecessors.

American Gemini astronauts were routinely orbiting the earth, and NASA was planning to send a crew to the moon in just a few short years. Kentuckians on the ground also wanted to go, in the words of the Fifth Dimension's 1967 hit song, "Up, Up and Away." It seemed anything was possible in the new, feel-good jet age.

A decade before the first jet arrived at Blue Grass Field, International Business Machines (IBM) had broken ground for a new typewriter manufacturing facility in Lexington. Typewriter ribbon and carbon paper production were added the next year. IBM's plant and campus employed nearly 2,000 workers with good pay and benefits. As the dominant employer of that era, IBM helped boost Lexington's economy and strengthen its middle class.

Lexington's time had come. The city, with a population in 1965 of about 151,000, was growing up, ready to become a major regional and economic player. The arrival of IBM and jets were clear evidence of that.

JET AGE A LITTLE SLOW TO TAKE OFF

The advent of jet travel in Lexington came in fits and starts. Although Piedmont had demonstrated that a commercial jetliner could safely land and take off at Blue Grass Field, most airlines still deferred jet service to other airports with longer runways and more aircraft services than Blue Grass could offer. The lack of advanced safety equipment and emergency personnel on site was also considered a drawback to securing additional jet service. It would take several more years for Lexington to fully get into the jet business.

In 1965, the airport was doing its best to attract more jets to the Bluegrass region. The airport board applied for federal funding for a 700-foot extension of Runway 4-22 for a total of 6,000 feet. Also, several additional inches of asphalt would be applied to the entire runway to accommodate the higher weights and speeds of the jetliners. If the federal government approved the funding request, Lexington and Fayette County would have to come up with the rest.

Airport General Manager Logan Gray often reminded news reporters that Runway 4-22 was the airport's only commercial runway and that the region's economic future depended on it joining the jet age. A sales engineer at

Above: An aerial view of Blue Grass Field in 1964. *Below:* A coat of blue paint and new awnings freshen up the exterior of the Blue Grass Field terminal building.

Douglas Aircraft had told him a 6,000-foot runway, at minimum, was necessary to safely bring in the DC-9 jets his company was building.

Soon, a new airport beacon, said to be one of the largest in the country, was installed on the roof of the control tower at Blue Grass Field. The beacon rotated six times per minute and reportedly could be seen from as far away as a few miles south of Berea – approximately 40 miles south of Lexington.

More powerful ramp lights were ordered, too. They boosted light intensity by three to four times, it was reported. Gray cited increased night air traffic as the reason for boosting the lighting. Also late in 1965, Lexington Air Taxi Company started a 24-hour air taxi service at Blue Grass Field, providing charter

service, pilot training and additional hangar space for private aviation.

SOME PERSONAL PERSPECTIVES

Jim Graybill was a local boy who fulfilled his dream of becoming an Eastern Air Lines pilot in 1961. He called flying one of the most addictive experiences a person could have, having soloed for the first time at Blue Grass Field as a 16-year-old in 1949. Graybill flew a dozen different planes for Eastern over a 28-year career and loved every minute of it. It was all he ever wanted to do, and he never considered it work. It was a sad moment for Graybill and Blue Grass Field when, after almost 35 years, Eastern Air Lines stopped service to Lexington in 1980 – an after-effect of airline deregulation.

Another perspective comes from Gene Van Meter, a local contractor often hired to handle projects at Blue Grass Field, who recalled working around the busy airport in the mid to late 1960s. Though a runway might be closed if a crew was working close to it, other times it would remain open and workers would get a thrill, or for some a scare, as incoming and outgoing flights would roar directly overhead. The men could look up and see the bellies of the great birds.

Van Meter said he never knew what celebrity would appear next at the airport, both two- and four-legged varieties. There were movie stars, television personalities, University of Kentucky star athletes and politicians, including governors, senators, and even a president or two.

As the jet age progressed, Logan Gray would quite literally roll out the red carpet when VIPs and Hollywood stars arrived at Blue Grass Field. This was such a hit that it ultimately became standard operating procedure for all flights coming into the airport, and Lexington became known for its red-carpet treatment for deplaning passengers.

Of course, leading Thoroughbreds of the era, along with their famous owners and trainers, would fly in from both coasts to prepare for spring and fall meets at Keeneland, including the Blue Grass Stakes in April (a race that Delta Air Lines would later sponsor). Some of those horses won the Kentucky Derby a few weeks later in Louisville or the Preakness or Belmont Stakes after that. Van Meter recalled how the horses were often pam-

An aerial view from the early 1960s showing Keeneland Race Course, which is conveniently located across Versailles Road from Blue Grass Field.

1965

Gas is 31 cents per gallon.

The McDonnell Douglas DC-9 makes its first flight.

Warren Buffet gains controlling interest in Berkshire Hathaway (at $18 per share).

United Airlines places orders for $750 million in new aircraft.

Astronaut Edward Higgins White makes the first U.S. space walk aboard Gemini 4.

A Boeing 707 makes the first polar circumnavigation of the world.

The Pillsbury Doughboy first appears.

First-class postage stamps are 5 cents.

A special crane was brought in to install the new beacon on top of the tower at Blue Grass Field in October 1965.

vice featured four-engine prop-jet Lockheed Electras seating 22 in first-class and 60 in coach. Prior to this breakthrough, Lexington-area residents had to drive to Standiford Field in Louisville or Cincinnati/Northern Kentucky Airport in Hebron, Kentucky, to get a non-stop flight to the Big Apple or plan on a short trip from Lexington by air to reach these departure points.

Gray called Eastern's direct service to New York the biggest development for Lexington in the last 20 years, saying passengers would no longer be considered "second-class citizens" because they had to drive to other airports. Local aviation experts agreed direct service to New York City was a good start, but direct flights to Washington, D.C. and Chicago were necessary, too.

Gray wasn't stopping there. He wanted better service from all the airlines and as soon as possible. He cited one estimate that said as many as 55 percent of potential airline passengers in central Kentucky drove to either Louisville or the Cincinnati area to catch flights. That had to stop, he admonished.

Fares on the early jetliners were not yet affordable to the masses. It would take airline deregulation in 1978 for fares to become more competitive and less costly. So, in the mid 1960s, mostly upper middle class and well-to-do travelers bought commercial jet tickets.

pered and treated more gingerly than the human cargo.

Van Meter was proud of Lexington and enjoyed telling fellow passengers about his hometown as they made their final approach to Blue Grass Field. As the airplane descended over the remarkable landscape, he'd tip off out-of-towners to glance left or right out the windows to catch a glimpse of the scenery below. There was famed Calumet Farm, with its barns trimmed in "devil red" and surrounded by gleaming white fences, or Manchester Farm with its distinctive cupolas. Another treat was pointing out beautiful Keeneland Race Course.

EASTERN PLAYS A ROLE

In October 1966, exactly one year after Piedmont's historic jet landing, another milestone was reached when Eastern Air Lines announced it would launch non-stop jet flights between Blue Grass Field and John F. Kennedy Airport in New York City. The ser-

LOGAN GRAY HAS A VISION

An announcement in May 1966 may have caused Lexington aviation officials to wonder about the future of general aviation at Blue Grass Field with possible competition coming from within its own market. A "baby airport," as it was referred to, was being considered for Scott County. Four possible sites were in the running, according to Harold Prather, chairman of the Scott County Airport Board. All were "within range of Lexington businesses and private pilots." It would be decades before that airport was ultimately built. The Georgetown-Scott County Regional Airport began operations in 1993.

Prior to this announcement, Blue Grass Field's Gray had proposed tentative plans for what was labeled an "annex" airfield in Lexington. Three potential sites were targeted off Richmond Road about two miles south of New Circle Road. Gray envisioned 3,000 feet of hard surface runway, return taxi strips from each end of the main runway and ground facilities for maintenance and refueling. The goal was to relieve growing congestion at Blue Grass Field. But nothing came of the idea. Two decades later, subdivisions sprouted where some had imagined airplanes taking off in southeast Lexington.

Throughout this time, Gray kept lobbying for further improvements at Blue Grass Field. A still longer runway, maybe even a parallel one, and a new and larger terminal were clearly in his sights. Now that jet travel was becoming more common across the U.S., Gray must have believed the chances of getting these upgrades were improving.

Gray was Blue Grass Field's undisputed hands-on leader. He was considered by some to be an intense person who stayed on top of every detail at the airport. During the previous year he had asked the media to cooperate during airport emergencies, of which there had been several in recent years, some involving crashes and deaths. Gray asked reporters not to jam phone lines to the control tower during such incidents, to wait at least eight minutes before announcing an emergency on radio or television and to urge a curious public to please stay away from the airport.

In contrast to Logan Gray's intensity, Jack Adams, the airport's maintenance supervisor, was seen as a more calm and low-key figure. Though quite different in nature, the pair complemented each other and made an effective team.

Gray's vision for the future of midsize city airports like Blue Grass Field caught the attention of officials with the Lewiston-Auburn Municipal Airport in Maine. In November 1967, Gray was invited to tour the airport, provide consulting services and give a speech before the local aviation committee. While there, Gray encouraged the Maine community to pressure Northeast Airlines to improve its service. Gray had occasionally used that tactic successfully with Eastern, Delta and Piedmont airlines. He also urged the creation of an independent airport authority and the hiring of a professional airport manager at the Maine airfield.

During his Maine airport visit, Gray recommended many cosmetic improvements on the property, such as installing a new electric airport sign, removing old fencing, improving landscaping and erecting flagpoles with the State of Maine and American flags at the entrance. In all this, Gray was drawing upon his experience at Blue Grass Field, which he noted was in poor condition when he arrived four years earlier but now was clean and attractive, though still a small municipal airport.

WITH THE JET AGE COMES A PRICE – NOISE

The downside of jets flying in and out of Blue Grass Field during this era was the noise factor. People living

Above left: Officials of Eastern Air Lines, members of the airport board and local business leaders attend a luncheon at the Continental Inn to announce the inauguration of non-stop Electra service to New York. *Above right:* Passengers board the first Eastern Air Lines Lockheed Electra non-stop flight to New York.

Above: The lobby of the original terminal at Blue Grass Field in 1974, with large images of horse farms around its perimeter. *Below:* Baggage claim was located outside in all weather. Employee David Plummer unloads bags on a cold day.

and working in surrounding neighborhoods and on adjoining farms noticed the difference in the sound that jets made during takeoff and landing versus that of propeller planes. The airports in New York, Chicago, Atlanta, Dallas and other big cities often faced the same dilemma. These airports utilized bigger jets – often 747s – because they made it possible to fly coast-to-coast or internationally. Airport noise was becoming a national issue.

In later years, the local airport board commissioned a noise study to determine what actions might be necessary to make the airport a quieter neighbor to residents living, working or worshipping nearby.

The FAA approved operational and land management strategies to mitigate the impact of jet noise at Blue Grass, should the airport board decide to implement them. These included accelerating conversion to quieter jets and soundproofing or acquiring homes and other buildings in the flight paths immediately off the ends of the runway.

The airport identified 17 residences and a church along Parkers Mill Road and Dedman Lane at the south end of Runway 4 and two homes north of the airport for possible soundproofing or acquisition. Ultimately, compromises would be reached and agreed upon.

GROWING PAINS AND SOLUTIONS

In January 1967, a new development plan included an airport terminal and a 1,000-foot runway extension for a total of 6,500 feet to accommodate the newer smaller jets (300 feet longer than announced a year earlier). The airport board and the Lexington-Fayette County Planning Commission approved the recommendation. Several architectural firms familiar with airport terminals were selected to submit designs for the new Blue Grass terminal. The location was expected to be southeast of the existing airport parking lot. The completion date was vague: 1971 or 1972. The plan also called for the three sections of Runway 15 closest to

REPUBLIC PARKING
Taking Customer Service To Another Level

If you fly in and out of Blue Grass Airport regularly, you may begin to take for granted how stress-free the entire experience is when compared to larger airports. Getting there is simple, especially if you live in Lexington – it's a straight shot from downtown or a loop around the beltway.

And parking? With more than 1,900 parking spaces and a spacious 1,025-car parking garage just steps from the main lobby, plus options of valet parking and short- and long-term parking just a stone's throw away, parking is easy. Even economy parking is located onsite for maximum convenience.

Customer-friendly parking doesn't just happen. It is meticulously planned, built and maintained. The success of Blue Grass Airport's parking facilities and services owes much to its partnership with Republic Parking System.

This long partnership got its start through an introduction of Edward Scrivner, Jr. and Winn Turney, Commissioner of the Kentucky Department of Aviation, who were airport board members at the time the new terminal was being contemplated in the mid 1970s. To solve the funding puzzle necessary to finish terminal construction, Scrivner and Turney negotiated an agreement between Blue Grass Airport and Republic. That was in 1975, and Blue Grass Airport and Republic Parking System have been working together ever since.

Like some other long-term partners of the airport, Republic is a family-owned business. This professional parking management firm based in Chattanooga, Tennessee, opened its doors in 1966 and is one of the largest privately held providers of parking management services in the U.S.

> *Over 65 airport contracts worldwide and Blue Grass Airport was one of the first.*

Just because they are from a neighboring state doesn't mean that they are regional in scope. With over 65 airport contracts worldwide, Republic is the industry leader in onsite airport parking operations, and it started with Blue Grass Airport as one of its first airport clients. Perhaps Republic's best selling point is its strong focus on creating partnerships with airports to deliver superior customer service and stringent revenue controls.

They feel a strong sense of responsibility to ensure that the airport parking facilities they operate reflect the same high degree of quality as the airport itself. They focus on providing services (even operating the luggage cart program) and managing growth for small and midsize airports. Forging a partnership dedicated to total airport success is Republic's goal. They recognize that everyone wins when an airport succeeds.

And Republic offers parking with benefits: Did you know that you can leave your car at airport valet parking and have it washed, detailed and ready to go when you return from your trip? Imagine how great it would be to drive home in a sparkling clean vehicle. Now, that's the perfect ending to any travel story!

Clean, well-designed parking facilities and services like valet parking and auto detailing make Republic Parking an industry leader.

Airport letterhead from 1967

Versailles Pike to be closed and used as a taxiway.

How a new terminal would be financed was still up in the air, but the official declaration that such major upgrades were necessary for a modern city airport was a clear and positive signal to the community.

Present needs, however, still had to be addressed, and stopgap measures would be required. Better use of space was desperately needed to extend the life of the old terminal until a new one could be built in the early 1970s. Work completed in April 1967 to the existing terminal improved the overall flow by separating departing and arriving passengers and their baggage and simplifying ground transportation. Canopies were provided over select entryways to protect passengers in bad weather – a temporary solution that some found quaint but most

recognized as inadequate as a permanent fix.

On April 1, 1968, the first commercial jetliner, a Delta DC-9, took off with paying passengers on a flight to Detroit. This came two and a half years after the first jetliner landing and takeoff test was conducted. The pace of progress in this new jet age clearly needed to be accelerated.

In July, ground was broken for the 1,000-foot extension of Blue Grass Field's Runway 4-22. Work was completed in late 1969. The $1.24 million project also included construction of a 78-foot FAA control tower with adjoining equipment and office space. It was to be located on 1.7 acres of land across from the airport access road and would be twice the height of the old tower, which sat on top of the existing terminal first

This DC-9 was the first Delta jet to be in service at Blue Grass Field.

opened in 1946 when the airport basically had three World War II-era runways.

More activity was coming to the airport property. In August 1968, Governor Louie B. Nunn announced that the airport board had agreed to lease a 28-acre tract of land at the southwest corner of Blue Grass Field to the state at no cost for 50 years. The property was for a new National Guard Armory, with an estimated building cost of $515,000.

In September 1969, the Air Line Pilots Association identified Blue Grass Field as "dangerous" due to inadequate fire and rescue equipment on-site and because of a sharp drop-off at the end of the main runway. Two months later, airport General Manager Logan Gray appointed Edward Hammel as the airport's first chief of rescue operations. Soon after, funding was approved for four firefighting vehicles and a heated garage to house them. Plans were in place to create a full-time fire department.

Later that spring, the Blue Grass Field Fire and Rescue squad conducted its first firefighting drill demonstrating how the combination of a flame retar-

Major General Larry C. Dawson, Logan Gray and Colonel James W. Stocker participate in a 1970 groundbreaking ceremony for the new armory.

dant and water could suppress a fire long enough to possibly rescue passengers.

In slow, measured steps, Lexington was beginning to move forward with the creation of a modern airport.

CONTROVERSY AND DELAY

Despite the hoopla over jet travel, not everyone in the Bluegrass favored longer runways for jetliners, or even a second parallel runway, which was a long-term goal for some airport planners. The airport's growing pains were creating an uncomfortable situation for Dr. George Gumbert, a member of the airport board

Above: Blue Grass Field firefighters demonstrate a truck that dispenses fire-smoldering chemicals from twin turrets atop the cab. *Right:* Construction is underway on the new FAA control tower in 1968.

The caption for this September 30, 1973 *Herald-Leader* photo reads: "Mob scene might accurately describe the conditions on any given day at the Blue Grass Field terminal building, where increased flight schedules have increased passenger boarding considerably."

for 22 years, later becoming its chairman. For many years, Gumbert, a licensed pilot, received pushback and vocal opposition from horse farm owners and land preservationists.

Raised on a farm himself, Gumbert understood agriculture. But his role at the airport and his in-depth understanding of aviation compelled him to find a way to balance the safety and physical needs of the airport with the desires of those who sincerely wanted to save Lexington's precious green space. Both sides would have to compromise.

The *Lexington Herald* and the *Lexington Leader*,

the city's daily newspapers, were regularly calling for construction of a new terminal building and for other improvements at the airport. That pleased Gumbert and Gray, who needed all of the support the community could give them to upgrade Blue Grass Field thoroughly.

In September 1973, the airport board announced yet another expansion plan. Estimated at $4.3 million, this one included a new terminal and parking lot, expansion of an air freight building, a new entrance road and extension of one runway. The new terminal would

BLUE GRASS AIRPORT

The final loan agreement for the construction of the new terminal at Blue Grass Field is signed in 1973. Reviewing the agreement are (from left) A. Clay Stewart, airport board chairman; Weldon Shouse, board attorney; Dr. George Gumbert, airport board member and Roy B. White, Jr., airport board vice-chairman.

increases in jet fuel prices were the result of the Middle East oil embargo. The Organization of Arab Petroleum Exporting Countries or OAPEC (Arab members of OPEC plus Egypt, Syria and Tunisia) decided to "punish" the United States for its military support of Israel. The impact was felt in every American airport. Eastern, Piedmont and Allegheny airlines were among those that reduced service to Lexington for several months. The embargo was lifted the following March, but the economic damage had already been done. The embargo combined with the effects of airline deregulation in 1978 were a one-two punch. Eastern announced plans to pull all service to Lexington by 1980, despite having served the area since 1946.

FINALLY, A NEW TERMINAL IS IN SIGHT

On Christmas Eve 1974, Lexington aviation enthusiasts got a welcome Christmas gift. The airport board voted unanimously to execute a $5.3 million loan agreement with seven local banks (about $2 million more than was announced the year before) to build the new terminal and make other improvements. The winning bid came from general contractor White and Congleton Company, but not without some controversy. Its bid was not quite the lowest, but was the bid the board favored. White and Congleton predicted it would begin excavation work

be 70,000 square feet – almost five times more area than the existing 27-year-old terminal. The announcement said seven local banks had approved the board's loan application for $3.25 million. In addition, the plan anticipated funding of $650,000 from the Federal Aviation Administration and $500,000 from the Commonwealth of Kentucky.

However, the bidding process to secure a contractor for the airport project and final details concerning the local bank loan would take another 15 months to complete.

An international crisis had its effects on Blue Grass Field beginning in the fall of 1973. Steep

for the new terminal within 10 days and expected to begin erecting steel by April.

The financing package the airport board had negotiated through local banks had an unexpected impact on the board itself. Five of the six board members resigned after receiving a legal opinion that their positions as shareholders, directors, officers or employees at some of the seven participating banks suggested, if not constituted, a conflict of interest. Chairman George Gumbert remained on the board.

On January 22, 1975, ground was broken for the

A. Clay Stewart, Mayor Foster Pettit, County Judge Robert Stephens and Dr. George Gumbert officially break ground for the new passenger terminal on January 22, 1975.

new terminal. Work was progressing as expected when six months later the aviation community was shocked by the unexpected death after a short illness of airport General Manager Logan Gray at age 59. He had managed the airport for 12 years, leading it through many changes including construction of a new control tower, radar installation, runway extension and much more.

For months, Gray had been beating the bushes in his usual passionate way – promoting the airport and the new terminal to every civic organization that would host him. Sadly, he would

Construction of the new terminal moves forward while the airport operates without delays.

not live to see it completed and open for service. For a time, the airport board considered naming the terminal after Gray, but it decided to build upon the value of the region's brand identity by keeping the name Blue Grass Field. A few months later, the airport board named James Brough the new general manager.

As 1976 dawned, the new terminal was nearing completion. Just in time, the airport unveiled a new logo that was the work of a University of Kentucky graphic arts class. Sophomore art major Jill Reiling's design was chosen. The red, white and blue artwork captured the essence of the local equine industry and featured a race day bugler whose white jacket is emblazoned with blue stars. The logo, with only minor modifications and a change in name (from Blue Grass Field to Blue Grass Airport), has remained essentially the same decades later.

ALL THE MODERN CONVENIENCES

On April 28, 1976, the new terminal officially opened following a ribbon-cutting ceremony. It contained 70,000 square feet, nearly five times the size of the old building. Some recalled Thanksgiving, Christmas and Easter holiday periods when the old terminal was so jammed that people could hardly move.

Terminal building is under roof and on its way to completion in these 1975 photos.

Above: A jet bridge in use. *Below:* The official unveiling of the new Delta Air Lines jet bridge in December 1977.

a modern airport. Some called the airport the "front door and back door of the city." Brough said the terminal was built with future expansion in mind and would serve the city "well into the 1980s."

Maryellen Buxton, manager of the insurance information desk, said transferring from the old terminal to the new one was like "moving from a little town to a big city." Buxton said one thing the new terminal wouldn't have that the old one did have was "coziness."

Down the road, another welcome airport feature was the addition of a jet bridge. Also known as a jetway or jetport, it is the enclosed, movable connector that extends accordion-style from the terminal gate to an airplane, allowing passengers to board and disembark from an airplane without going outside.

This terminal seemed cavernous by comparison.

When the new terminal opened, five commercial airlines served Lexington: Allegheny, Delta, Eastern and Piedmont, as well as a "feeder" airline, Air Kentucky. Air Kentucky did the "short hops" flying between Lexington, Louisville, Nashville, Owensboro and Bowling Green. There were also counters assigned to rental car companies Avis, Budget, Hertz and National.

The new terminal had an indoor baggage claim area so passengers no longer had to brave the elements as they waited for their bags to be delivered outside under the old striped awnings.

Some 467,000 passengers were predicted to use the airport in 1976. The new terminal was expected to boost the local economy because businesses might want to expand or move to Lexington now that the city had

Mary Jo Maloney, daughter of long-time Airport Board Member and Chairman George Gumbert, recalls her dad bringing the family to the airport for a test ride on Delta's new device. "You would have thought the family had a new Ferrari," she laughingly recalled. When her family stepped inside, it was as if they were on an amusement park ride – as the jetport was raised and lowered to the delight of the kids. The Gumberts

weren't the only ones captivated by the new terminal; the public seemed to love it too, especially those who had endured the older, cramped terminal.

In June 1976, the airport board voted to raze the old structure. After evaluating the cost to re-purpose the old terminal, they opted to construct a memorial plaza that would include a public viewing site. However, the lowest bid for that project came in 30 percent over the original budget and the project was scrapped. Before it was completely gone, Gumbert and his wife and daughter took to the air to catch a rare and final sight – the contrast of a shiny new terminal located next to the half-demolished old one. Pictures were snapped from the plane to capture and preserve this important transition.

FAST-FORWARD

Streaking down the runway of Blue Grass Airport (the name changed in 1984) was perhaps the most spectacular commercial jetliner in aviation history – the Concorde Supersonic Transport (SST). The world's fastest plane traveled at 1,350 miles per hour, twice the speed of sound.

Through special arrangement with British Airways and sufficient advance bookings, the Concorde visited Lexington to pick up 98 passengers for a flight to London. There, passengers had options to board the Orient Express for a train excursion through Great Britain or to board the *Queen Elizabeth II* and sail to New York. Depending on the choices, ticket prices for the package ranged from $3,995 to $9,064 per person.

With the proper ramp pass (prior to September 11, 2001), people actually walked around the parked Concorde, taking pictures and enjoying a tour inside. Private planes even taxied up nearby for a closer look or to have their photo taken alongside the sleek and elegant Concorde. Thousands of fascinated people from across the region flocked to the airport to get a glimpse of the dazzling aircraft. Traffic clogged Versailles Road as drivers pulled over, got out and peered through the fence at the famous aircraft.

Lexington, through active and engaged local travel agents, was able to draw enough local interest to book the Concorde. Neighboring cities like Louisville, Cincinnati, Indianapolis and Knoxville didn't generate the same interest to attract the soaring white Concorde.

The ultramodern and gorgeous Concorde had touched down in Lexington nearly 24 years after the first Piedmont Airlines 727 jetliner made its test landing and takeoff at Blue Grass Field.

Lexington and its proud airport had come a long way since 1965. Arriving, you might say – in style. ✈

Above: A rare photo of the new and old terminals at Blue Grass Field. The old terminal, located on the left, was demolished in 1977.

Above left: Local pilots Betty and Kent Moseley stand on the wing of their Piper PA-28 with the SST Concorde in the background.
Above right: Lexington's Laura Combs waves from an EA-18G Growler which she has flown in to Blue Grass Airport on training missions for the Navy.

TIMELINE

A Look Back at Aviation in the Bluegrass
1907 – 2013

1907

Roy Knabenshue of Toledo, Ohio, brings his powered-balloon airship to the Blue Grass Fair.

1910

On August 6 and 7, Canadian aviator J.A.D. McCurdy flies his Curtiss biplane at the Blue Grass Fair. He performs again in August 1911.

Berger aviator Paul Peck - 1912

1912

The Aviation Meet and Automobile Races event featuring Berger's aviators is held on June 3 at the Kentucky Association racetrack in Blue Grass Park at 5th and Race Streets. Crowds are thrilled as four "aeroplanes" fly above the racetrack simultaneously.

1914 - 1917

Coinciding with WWI, several airplanes are based at a landing field off Richmond Road, beyond the city limits. They operate from an open pasture, landing and taking off into the wind.

1919

The U.S. Army brings a flying circus to the Bluegrass to promote the sale of Victory Bonds using surplus planes from the French, Italian, German and American air forces. It stages sham battles, aerobatics and stunts for the public. In Lexington, the circus operates during April from Hinata Farm, owned by Clarence LeBus, on Russell Cave Road.

1921

WWI flying ace, former Lieutenant Jesse O. Creech flies from Chicago to Lexington on June 18 as part of a publicity stunt originally conceived to bring a live pig as a passenger and present it to Lexington Mayor T. C. Bradley. The pig doesn't make the flight, but Creech arrives in four hours, averaging 75 miles per hour with one stop at the Indianapolis Speedway. Creech lands in the field of Dr. Samuel T. Halley's farm on Leestown Pike. A new Avro three-seat aircraft is used for the flight, which promotes the beginning of the Lexington Aviation Company, with Creech serving as general manager and chief pilot.

1924

In the Aeronautical Bulletin detailing state-by-state landing facilities published by the Air Service Office in Washington D.C., Lexington's Halley

Field is listed as follows: 900 feet east and west by 1,200 feet north and south; surface rough in places; southwest prevailing winds; supplies in town; located two miles west of Lexington; north of Old Frankfort Pike; slopes down on north; barn on northwest; trees in southeast corner; house on northeast; available indefinitely. This information is dated April 1, 1922. The bulletin included all known landing strips in each state.

1925

The Roscoe Turner Flying Circus arrives in Lexington on June 4 for a stunt over the University of Kentucky football stadium.

1927

Dr. Samuel Halley officially opens a field on the western side of his farm on May 28 for aviation use … Lexington Municipal Airport at Halley Field is dedicated on June 11 and WWI flying ace Ted Kincannon of Dallas, Texas, is named manager. Lexington Airways Company, operated by Kincannon, will fly passengers in five commercial airplanes … Roscoe Turner lands at Halley Field to give passenger rides over the city for a fee.

1928

Colonel Charles A. Lindbergh lands at Halley Field on March 28 on what is supposed to be a secret visit to Lexington and stays at the home of Dr. Scott Breckinridge, brother of Colonel Henry Breckinridge, who is legal advisor to Lindbergh. The next day nearly 3,000 people come to see him off at the field. His airplane narrowly misses hitting a row of trees as it takes flight.

1929

The *Lexington Leader* headlines on October 31 read, "Ten Airplanes Bought, New Field is Planned By Lexington Airways, Inc./Local Group to Build New Landing Field/Harkness Edwards, one of the incorporators, says work to start in 30 days." This ambitious undertaking, announced ironically on Black Tuesday – the ruinous event associated with the start of The Great Depression – shows huge optimism by Edwards and his partners. They are negotiating to purchase a 125-acre tract and launch a general aviation, passenger-carrying and pilot-training operation. Harkness Edwards

is president of Edwards Motors Incorporated (on Vine Street Extended) and the son of Dr. Ogden Edwards, owner of the great Standardbred operation, Walnut Hall Farm. The tract they ultimately purchase is on Newtown Pike.

1930

The Kentucky State Air Board is created to make flying safer and to promote the establishment of adequate airports across the state … On February 28, local newspapers announce the lease of 250 acres of J. Blythe Anderson's farm on Newtown Pike, five miles from the city. The lease for this new airfield is ratified on March 3; however, the field will not be suitable for use for an extended period of time. Halley Field continues to operate … The lease on Halley Field expires on April 15. On May 1, a new one-year lease is signed by a group of fliers … In June, inspectors from the Mason-Dixon Airline Company and the All-Metal Airline Company declare Halley Field inadequate to handle aircraft landing during inclement weather and eliminate it as a possible site for airmail and passenger service. They indicate that the proposed airfield at J. Blythe Anderson's farm on Newtown Pike would meet their needs … The Goodyear blimp, *Vigilant*, visits Halley Field on November 18. The Goodyear blimp, *Puritan*, had preceded it earlier in the year.

1931

In March, the Lexington Cab Company, owned by Norman and Leroy Smith, expands its transportation operations to include aviation, offering "air service to any place at any time" from

Air circuses were popular in the 1930s.

Glengarry Field (later renamed Cool Meadow Airport) in the mid 1930s

Halley Field. A special "night flight" service is established and sightseeing trips over the city are offered for $1.50 per person ... An autogyro plane owned by John Hancock of Wilkes-Barre, Pennsylvania, lands at Halley Field in May after stopping in Cincinnati. Hancock is visiting friends in Lexington because of Kentucky Derby festivities. Also, two parachutists land at Halley Field as part of the dedication celebration of the new veterans hospital on Leestown Pike ... The licensing of pilots and their aircraft in Kentucky begins in earnest in September with 91 pilots and 65 airplane owners paying the $5 registration fee to become licensed in Kentucky... An air meet and races are held at Halley Field, October 2-4. One nationally known stunt pilot, Freddie Lund, dies and another, Scotty Burmood, escapes injury when their airplanes collide during an air race.

1932

On August 1, Halley Field shuts down after Lexington's Board of Commerce withdraws support following two fatal accidents and a number of injuries. After new manager Woodford Baxter is hired, Halley Field reopens within the month.

1934

On May 14, the city takes an option on a portion of the J. Blythe Anderson farm on Newtown Pike. The 100-acre site is chosen after inspectors with the Federal Bureau of Aeronautics find it meets federal government specifications. The city leases the property for five years with an option to purchase the land for $300 per acre ... Although the airport is far from complete, a Curtiss Fledgling flown

Amelia Earhart - 1936

by G.W. Salmons lands on August 3. Construction is plagued by delays but continues slowly for several more months ... In October, it is noted that the new airport is beginning to draw business despite being under construction. City manager Paul Morton bans all flights from using the new field, particularly

those carrying passengers, due to liability issues ... Halley Field closes after the property changes hands. The field is plowed as it reverts from airstrip to farmland ... In November, numerous complaints from pilots and then one pilot's emergency landing on a farm field west of Lexington result in the placement of additional airport directional markers on rooftops around Lexington the following month. These markers will help pilots find Lexington's new airport. More will be added in coming years.

TRAVEL BY AIR
Anywhere — Any Time

LEXINGTON AIR TAXI SERVICE CO., Inc.
1412 First National Bank Bldg.   Phones 855 or 7280.

1935

In a report of city accomplishments released in January, the progress of the airport is described as being "in good condition except for spring seeding." The need for lights and a hangar were also mentioned ... On July 21, Lexington's new airport is christened "Glengarry Field" after the name of the farm of J. Blythe Anderson. Glengarry's 165 acres of fields and wooded hills and its stately historic home overlooking the new airfield were where Union troops encamped during the Civil War. Celebrations for the opening include a two-day air circus. Bad weather postpones the second day of the event to the following weekend and more than 3,500 people witness the festivities ...

Lexington Air Taxi Service is incorporated on August 9 and begins operations on September 1, despite the lack of lighting and a hangar ... On September 29, construction begins on a hangar at Glengarry Field and on October 10, Admiral Byrd's world-famous Antarctic expedition plane, *The Stars and Stripes*, arrives at the field for exhibition and passenger flights ... The Board of Commissioners pass Resolution 165 on December 9 stating that the airport operated by the city be designated and known as "Lexington Municipal Airport, Glengarry Field." It is later renamed Cool Meadow Airport.

1936

On January 14, the *Lexington Herald* publishes an announcement by Dr. J. Farra Van Meter, president of the Lexington Public

Forum Association, that pioneering aviator and "Queen of the Air" Amelia Earhart will be the guest speaker at its meeting on Sunday afternoon at the Henry Clay High School auditorium … It is announced on March 26 that Glengarry Field will be leased by the city to the Lexington Air Taxi Service under terms of an ordinance given first reading by the board of city commissioners … Daily flights between Lexington and Louisville begin April 20 … On August 6, a scathing report on Glengarry Field's condition is front-page news in the *Lexington Herald*. Numerous photos accompany the article … The tradition of flying in for Keeneland begins – albeit at Glengarry Field – as the Thoroughbred racecourse opens its doors for the first time on October 15.

Early airmail postmarks - 1937

1938

Airmail is officially flown from Glengarry Field on May 19, although its route would not be considered approved by the Civil Aeronautics Board until February 28, 1941. Also in May, a demonstration is given in Lexington of an autogyro being used to deliver mail in Chicago … A formal announcement is made on June 24 of the city leasing Glengarry Field and naming Lexington Flying Service as the lessee.

1940

Due to the shortcomings of Glengarry Field and the opportunity to attract major funding, Mayor T. Ward Havely and County Judge W.E. Nichols sign an application for federal aid for a municipal airport for Fayette County and the city of Lexington at a cost of approximately $1

Franklin Delano Roosevelt

million. On June 1, a survey is started by the city's engineering department to find the most suitable site for an airport … On June 6, Senator A.B. Chandler places an application by Lexington, Fayette County and the Lexington Air Board for financial and technical assistance in construction of a $1,150,000 commercial and military airport before the War Department and the Civil Aeronautics Authority in Washington … On August 16, immediate action toward obtaining a site for an adequate airport is recommended at a joint meeting of city and county commissioners by Gilmore Nunn, chairman of the Lexington and Fayette County Board of Aviation … On December 16, President Franklin D. Roosevelt approves an allotment of $138,829 for construction of the airport. These funds are for building the airport but cannot be used to purchase the site. Local authorities say they will need $700,000 for the project, but these funds would be enough to get started … In late December, with the help of local bankers, attorneys and businessmen, Fayette County Fiscal Court works out a finance plan to match funds from the city of Lexington to purchase an airport site. Lexington banks will advance the $80,000 the county needs, taking a mortgage on the outlying parts of the 600-acre proposed airport site and on a county-owned sanitarium property to be sold on Leestown Pike … On December 29, the front page of the *Lexington Herald-Leader* features an artist's rendering of what the airport might look like and the accompanying article outlines the chances of procuring the necessary property. The tract considered most favorable is Shenandoah Farm owned by Mrs. Frances McChesney Van Meter across from Keeneland on Versailles Pike, six miles west of downtown Lexington. The Civil Aeronautics Authority grants approval of the 593-acre tract of land as a prospective location for Lexington's commercial airport. The property will be deeded jointly to the city and county after the fiscal court completes payment of its share of the site cost within five years.

On December 16, 1940, President Roosevelt approves an allotment of $138,829 for construction of the airport.

1941

On January 24, Mayor Havely and County Judge Nichols announce the appointment of the first Airport Advisory Committee to include: L.B. Shouse (president of the Lafayette Hotel Company, as a citizen member), four city commissioners, Mayor Havely, Judge Nichols and three county commissioners … The city of

Lexington enters into a written agreement on February 6 with the federal government to acquire fee-simple title to that portion of the land on which the construction would take place … On March 6, a petition signed by 14 property owners in close proximity to the airport's proposed location is

Warren Wright, Sr. - 1941

presented to Mayor Havely in an effort to halt the approval of the new airport location. Included in the names are some of the most influential businessmen and farm owners in Lexington: Warren Wright, Sr., Leslie Combs II, L.R. Cooke, James Alexander and Peter A.B. Widener II. The petitioners cite traffic from Keeneland and the airport, noise and the potential construction of roadside taverns that may become "eyesores." Havely quickly rebuts and addresses their concerns effectively enough that the Board of City Commissioners meet that evening and unanimously approve the purchase of the 593-acre parcel for the proposed $750,000 city-county commercial airport … On April 1, in a shocking development, Alex Fugette, a tenant on the 593-acre tract of the airport site, is granted a temporary restraining order prohibiting work on the new airport. Mr. Fugette contends he holds a verbal contract with the former owner of the property through the 1941 crop year. Robert M. Odear, attorney for the city of Lexington, asks for an immediate hearing before Fayette Circuit Judge Chester D. Adams to dissolve the restraining order … Judge Adams denies Fugette a temporary injunction on April 11 stating insufficient proof of a verbal contract … On April 28, counsel for Fugette files an amended petition asking the court to issue a permanent injunction that

would prevent construction work on the project … The Board of City Commissioners adopts a resolution on May 1 that would evict Fugette. The city is concerned that prolonged litigation may result in the loss of the entire airport project due to federal funding deadlines and states it is a national defense necessity to move forward on construction … May 20 is a banner day – Federal officials approve final plans for the airport and release $201,000 in federal funds to finance the first phase of construction. The *Lexington Leader* reports that designation of the new airport on Versailles Pike as a "national defense necessity" served to remove obstacles set up through litigation to block the project. Early the next morning, 50 Works Progress Administration (WPA) workers begin grubbing the land and clearing it of brush and trees. Delta Air Lines

announces it will serve Lexington as soon as the airport is ready … Later in May, Warren Wright, Sr., owner of Calumet Farm, offers his services in connection with construction of the new airport. Mayor Havely appoints Wright as a member of the advisory committee of the airport board … On May 28, zoning restrictions are proposed and a resolution is adopted by the Fayette County Fiscal Court prohibiting certain types of businesses (e.g., roadhouses, dance halls, liquor stores, tourist camps and restaurants) in the area around the new airport. The county judge is empowered to refuse

Sign directs WPA workers at airport entrance - 1941

issuance of license to any entity that might adversely affect the "morals, health, welfare, peace and tranquility of the zone" … In July, Fayette Circuit Judge Adams rules that the county and city are entitled to immediate possession of Fugette's farmhouse, outbuildings and fields. Adams includes a provision allowing Fugette to harvest his final crops provided he does not interfere with work on the airport … On July 31, Governor Keen Johnson, Senator A.B. Chandler, Mayor Havely and others dedicate the new airport site … Lexington and Fayette County take undisputed possession of the new airport property on August 21 as a result of a $1,815 settlement of a 20-week, court-fought controversy with Fugette … On September 25, the Civil Aeronautics Authority (CAA) allocates $235,000 for the second phase of construction of the new airport. Phase II includes paving of the three principal runways, paving of taxiways and lighting of boundaries and landing strips. A third phase of construction includes plans for a terminal building and hangars.

1942

The first aircraft, an Army Air Corps B-25 bomber, officially lands on the new airfield on June 11 … In December, Mayor Havely and County Judge Nichols announce they have leased the airfield on Versailles Pike to the U.S. Army for $1 per year with the understanding that the Army obtain "priorities for lighting equipment." They have included the lighting provision in the contract as their best hope of getting lights for the field due to wartime restrictions.

1943

The U.S. Army's use of the airport is minimal due to lack of facilities and lighting. However, it is used for glider training exercises and testing parachutes produced by Irving Air Chute in Lexington. Irving's federal contract stipulates that one out of four parachutes purchased for the military be tested from a height of 500 feet. Dummies, rather than people, are used to test the chutes as they are dropped over the airfield … Mayor Havely dies on March 22 at St. Joseph Hospital after a brief illness.

1944

The first runway lighting system is installed … On August 22, the *Lexington Herald* front page reports that Blue Grass Field is the name chosen for Lexington's new million-dollar airport. Peter Powell, Lexington oilman, is appointed as manager.

1945

Robert D. Short and Company is awarded a nearly $65,000 contract to construct the airport terminal building with wings to be added later … On September 20, Circuit Court Judge Adams

Weather Bureau station construction is well under way in 1944.

rules in favor of the city of Lexington to relocate a hangar from Glengarry Field/Cool Meadow to the new airport … The city of Lexington passes an ordinance on December 27 creating an airport board to be known as the "City of Lexington-Fayette County Airport Board" to take charge of the management of Blue Grass Field. The board shall consist of six members, three of whom will be appointed by the city and three by the county. The city members shall be appointed by the city manager and the first members appointed shall serve for terms of one, two and three years, respectively. Upon the expiration of the first terms, successors shall be appointed for three-year terms. Members of the airport board shall serve without compensation except for the secretary-treasurer, who may or may not be a member of the board, who can receive a salary of $500 per year.

1946

The newly appointed airport board meets for its initial session on February 11. The members of the first board include Gilmore N. Nunn, F.H. Wright, L.B. Shouse, Sr., Washington Reed, Fred Bryant and J.A. Middleton … Minutes of the airport board meeting on March 15 report that the hangar currently located at Glengarry Field/Cool Meadow Airport has finally become the property of the city of Lexington and that all litigation over ownership has ended. The old hangar, which is already being dismantled, is to be moved to Blue Grass Field. It was also decided that henceforth the board would meet each Friday at noon at the Lafayette Hotel. Board minutes from March 29 report that a tractor and a manure spreader are badly needed for maintenance of the fields around the site. Bluegrass Airlines'

Eddie Rickenbacker dedicates Blue Grass Field in 1946.

Airmail postmark - 1946

new lease becomes effective April 15, 1946 … On September 6, the airport board accepts a bid from Jerome Lederer of the White Tavern Shops for the first restaurant concession at Blue Grass Field … In September, board minutes note that Carey Construction and Lehman-Roberts are awarded a joint contract to construct a roadway from Versailles Pike to the terminal building. It is expected to be complete by November 10 for the formal opening of the field … On October 13, Atlanta-based air carrier Delta Air Lines begins serving Kentucky, offering twice-daily service at Blue Grass Field. Delta's first official flight to Lexington is aboard a 21-passenger Douglas DC-3, arriving in Lexington from Atlanta at 8:14 a.m. en route to Cincinnati … The first Eastern Air Lines flight lands within hours of the first Delta flight. It is en route to Louisville … Blue Grass Field is officially dedicated on November 10 with 10,000 people attending the two-day celebration. A bronze plaque is placed at Blue Grass Field in memory of the late Mayor T. Ward Havely whose tireless energy made possible the $1 million city-county airport.

Plaque commemorates the late Mayor T. Ward Havely.

1947

In February, teletypes are installed in the Weather Bureau Office … Airport Manager Powell reports at a February airport board meeting that he has been contacted by Jerome Lederer, lessee of the restaurant concession, who complained that under the terms of his contract he is unable at this time of year to cover expenses and he desires to install pinball machines, which will substantially increase his revenue. The board votes to permit the installation.

1948

On May 12, the Goodyear blimp makes its first visit to Blue Grass Field … Later in July, the airport board gives permission to Bohmer Flying Service, the fixed-base operator, to manage a rental car operation for the benefit of its patrons. Board minutes also reflect that a "Gentlemen's Agreement" with several neighboring property owners would prohibit construction of commercial enterprises on airport property adjacent to Versailles Pike, thereby ending discussion about the building of a motel on airport property. Airport

Hangar under construction in 1948.

Manager Powell brought up the point that without auxiliary business ventures the airport would probably never become a "paying proposition." County Judge Nichols and Mayor Thomas Mooney say that this is satisfactory to them … In November, Blue Grass Airmotive, the second general aviation service to offer charter flights and airplane repair, constructs a new hangar … Powell reports to the airport board in early December that the Communications Branch of the CAA now has seven employees on duty at Blue Grass Field who are temporarily housed in the Weather Bureau Office until more space can be provided by constructing an addition to the terminal building.

1949

Contracts authorizing Bohmer Flying Service and Blue Grass Airmotive's purchase of gasoline and oil from different dealers, with the airport's interests fully protected, are given approval at the March 11 airport board meeting. Also, a contract with an insurance company leasing space for use of the trip insurance policy machine in the lobby is approved … On April 19, the airport board votes to prohibit commercial advertising of any kind on any part of the field adjacent to Versailles Pike frontage … Chamber of Commerce President A.E. Oram and Secretary Ed Wilder together

William Harrison flies a Piper J-3 Cub over Cool Meadow in 1949.

with that body's Agricultural Committee, L.C. Brewer, John Clark and Colonel Thomas J. Johnson, meet with the airport board on July 26 and request that their organization be permitted to establish a riding academy on a portion of Blue Grass Field not presently being used. John Clark, spokesman for the group, advises that they would like to erect a stable and stake out bridle paths in areas not directly adjacent to runways or taxiways.

1950

A new mark in Lexington's aviation progress is made in mid January when the new $28,000 control tower at Blue Grass Field is put into operation … An article appearing in the *Lexington Leader's* Blue Grass Review states that Blue Grass Field channels $500,000 into the area and is growing in airline passenger and freight service. The airport currently has three concrete runways – one that is 4,000 feet in length and two that are 3,500 feet in length. Light planes use grassy strips along the main runways. The article reports that few people realize the airport is capable of handling four-engine airliners

Control tower employee Joe Hayden adjusts new equipment - 1950

with ease … On February 8, Fayette Fiscal Court members voice opposition to the plan to build a 190-acre park and playground at Blue Grass Field because a system of small neighborhood parks has yet to be built in Fayette County … A Chamber of Commerce committee tours the new airport park site in May to make preliminary surveys for bridle paths and for cleaning and grading the property. A 10-member committee of the Lexington Junior League, headed by Mrs. John A. Bell III, will handle details of a campaign to promote the Chamber of Commerce's new airport park … In early June, Robert D. Short and Company are notified by Powell to begin work on a $60,000 addition to the administration building at Blue Grass Field … Manager Powell resigns from his position effective August 1 … Oscar Parks, former manager of Greater Cincinnati Airport in Boone County, succeeds Peter Powell as manager of Blue Grass Field … On November 10, the CAA announces that it will put up $50,000 to match a similar local appropriation for a $100,000 project to lengthen runways and taxiways at the airport … An early winter

Holes are drilled for neon lights in new airport sign - 1951

storm leaves 11 airport and airline personnel snowbound at Blue Grass Field for two days and nights in late November.

1951

The Lexington-Fayette County Airport Board and the Lexington Chamber of Commerce petition the Civil Aeronautics Board in early March for permission to intervene in two route-extension applications of Eastern Air Lines. Eastern wants inclusion of Paducah on its present route from St. Louis to Nashville and rearrangement of another route from Louisville to Memphis … On October 6, the *Lexington Leader* reports that the airport dining room will need a new roof after 75-miles-per-hour winds and heavy rains wreak havoc on the structure.

1952

Representatives of Blue Grass Field meet with representatives of the CAA on March 24 to talk about safety and noise abatement at the airport. This meeting is an outgrowth of

the appointment of a committee by President Harry Truman to investigate airports after a series of tragic airplane crashes in

Blue Grass Field - 1952

TIMELINE

Elizabeth, New Jersey … On March 31, the *Lexington Leader* announces that a new 40-passenger, twin-engine airplane will make its debut at Blue Grass Field when Eastern Air Lines puts its new Martin Silver Falcon into service on April 7 … Airport employee William D. Steele is struck by lightning and killed at Blue Grass Field on June 13 … It is announced in late July that the longest runway at the airport will be extended from 4,000 feet to 5,000 feet in length to permit four-engine planes to operate more safely … On September 24, local Eastern Air Lines Manager C.E. Buxton announces additional air service linking New York and the East with Lexington.

1953

Airport Manager Parks announces on March 10 that landing planes will soon have an electronic guide straight to Runway 4. He also announces that preliminary work is underway to lengthen that runway from 4,000 to 5,000 feet … On June 3, Airport Board Chairman Gilmore Nunn announces that construction is expected to begin in about two weeks on a 1,000-foot extension of one of the runways … A mother so excited and happy that she can't speak and a father who believes that prayer is responsible for their boy's safe return, greet their son, Corporal Elmer Frost, at Blue Grass Field on August 31. He had been a prisoner of war for more than 33 months … Four-engine service from the newly lengthened main runway is inaugurated before noon on October 16 when the University of Kentucky football team boards a Capital Airlines plane to go to Baton Rouge for the Louisiana State University game … Airport Board Chairman

POW Corporal Elmer Frost returns in 1953.

Nunn announces that Blue Grass Airport is now prepared to handle with maximum safety, any type of commercial airplane now in service.

1954

President Dwight Eisenhower flies into Blue Grass Field on April 24 for a visit to Lexington … On April 29, a five-member commission visits Blue Grass Field to consider it as a possible location for an Air Force Academy … According to the November 19 airport board minutes, it is understood that Keeneland Association is now having a hydraulic loading ramp built which they desire to use at the field for the handling of horses to and from planes … Airport Manager Oscar Parks dies from a heart attack on November 28 after a two-year illness. Frank W. Phillips commences work on January 4, 1955, succeeding Parks.

> *On April 29, 1954, a five-member commission visits Blue Grass Field to consider it as a possible location for an Air Force Academy.*

1955

On January 12, Mr. and Mrs. Frederick L. Van Lennep, prominent Lexington horse owners, are waiting at Blue Grass Field for the arrival of their private DC-3, which is en route, when word comes that the aircraft has collided with a TWA twin-engine Martin 202 over Limaburg, Kentucky, killing a total of 15 passengers and crew … The May 31 minutes of the airport board indicate that commitments have now been made by both the city and county whereby each will furnish an additional $2,500 to defray the expense of installing high intensity runway lighting, which will be used in connection with the Instrument Landing System (ILS). Airport Manager Phillips advises that CAA surveyors and construction workforce have already started on this important project and that a completion date may be expected by January 1, 1956 … The Joe E. Mellen, Inc., Hertz Rent a Car concession lease is presented to the airport board on July 18 to be authorized and signed … Regarding previous airport board discussion

An overflow crowd leaves after President Eisenhower's arrival in 1956.

over furnishing a horse-loading ramp for use in loading and unloading livestock, it is now understood that Cromwell Bloodstock Agency intends to purchase this equipment and make it available. An agreement will be worked out at a later date as to charges to be assessed for the ramp.

1956

Airport board minutes from May 4 show that an old fire truck, formerly owned by Fayette County, has been given to the airport and has been reconditioned and prepared for active service by the maintenance crew … President Dwight Eisenhower returns to Lexington on October 1 … Later in October, Airport Manager Phillips advises the airport board that the lease with Hertz Rent a Car has expired and that they are anxious to renew and to obtain an exclusive concession. He also advises that Avis is anxious to obtain a similar concession, and it was agreed that identical leases would be offered to both parties … Blue Grass Field employee Alonzo Lowry is the first of three persons to spot the "Truth or Consequences" air defense test plane at the airport.

1957

An agreement is signed on May 31 between Keeneland Association and the airport board acknowledging that

the racecourse may be asked in the future to remove trees on the grounds obstructing the approach to Runway 15 and to lower the infield flagpole if deemed necessary for safety purposes … The Instrument Landing System (ILS) is commissioned on July 17 with costs borne by the CAA and U.S. Department of Com-

merce because ILS is considered an integral part of the federal airway system. The ILS provides precision guidance for a safe aproach and landing on the runway, especially when visibility is reduced during inclement weather conditions … The airport board adopts a motion opposing the location of a motel on Versailles Pike within 1.5 miles of the airport.

1958

Plans for expansion of the airport in anticipation of turbo-prop jets are presented to the airport board; two of three runways must be extended by 500 feet each to accommodate these jets – a $1.5 million development that will be paid for with federal, state and local funds … A Piedmont plane carrying 12 passengers and a three-man crew is delayed three hours due to an anonymous bomb threat … Gilmore Nunn announces his resignation of the airport board chairmanship … H.C. Adams' bid for a 10-year lease for a pay parking area at Blue Grass Field is approved by the board. Plans call for the present 180 spaces to be increased to 240 spaces, with the first 20 minutes of parking at no charge.

1959

Gene Sims, the first female controller at Blue Grass Field, is assigned to the Federal Aviation Agency (later renamed the Federal Aviation Administration) control tower … On April 26, Eastern Air Lines launches Golden Falcon service with champagne to New York and stops in Charleston and Washington … In May, Keeneland Association is given notice to lower its infield flag pole pursuant to an agreement signed in 1957.

First female controller - 1959

Senator John F. Kennedy at the airport in 1960.

1960

On the recommendation of J.S. Watkins Engineers, it is unanimously voted by the airport board on June 15 to accept the bid of Carey Construction Company and H.C. Adams for a 500-foot extension of Runway 22 and an extension of runway lighting and markings in the amount of $89,472 … The board votes at the November 15 board meeting to offer J.A. Patterson the sum of $21,500 for the purchase of 43 acres lying adjacent to the southeast end of Runway 15-33. This amount will also compensate the owner for the right to remove all trees upon his property which will obstruct the approach to Runway 33 when extended 500 feet southeast. This amount is also to purchase a "Right of Flight" and the future right to enter and lower, or light, any obstructions which might be allowed to grow or be erected upon the Patterson property … The board also votes to proceed with negotiations with Mr. and Mrs. H.C. Adams for an easement permitting the board to lower trees; maintain the trees at the level of the approach surface leading to Runway 22; to light any obstruction remaining; and for an avigation easement over the property.

1961

A motion is passed by the airport board that the request of Blue Grass Airmotive, Inc., for a jet fuel installation be approved as

recommended by Manager Phillips … Phillips announces the board's plan to ask for federal funds to carry out an improvement program outlined in a budget request to the city last November. Plans call for spending a maximum of $500,000 during fiscal years

1962-63. The airport board is invited by the federal government to participate in the Airport Aid Program passed by Congress … Phillips warns that Blue Grass Field may go out of business unless some entity comes up with money to solve immediate problems; $100,000 is needed to clear obstructions at the ends of the auxiliary runways and $40,000 is needed for other issues … An Approach Lighting System (ALS) is commissioned in December.

1962

Piedmont Airlines flies the last scheduled DC-3 from Blue Grass Field on March 14 … Fred L. Bailey is named airport manager on October 26 and starts November 15 … The federal government will fund a $230,000 project to install a new approach lighting system to guide pilots in poor visibility.

1963

New Airport Manager Bailey requests a leave of absence effective April 1 to take care of business at an airport in Akron, Ohio. Logan Gray, assistant manager at Greater Cincinnati Airport in Boone County, becomes the airport manager on July 14. He states that his goal is to make the airport comfortable, convenient and expressive of Lexington's character … The restaurant at the airport is renamed the Skyline Room.

New airport limousine – 1963

1964

In January, Airport Manager Gray sharply criticizes the quality of service offered by Eastern Air Lines, Delta Air Lines and Piedmont Airlines. Fifty-five percent of Lexington's potential air traffic drives to either Louisville

Logan Gray with Powder Puff Derby survey team – 1964

or Cincinnati. In the following days and months, those carriers announce added service for Lexington including flights to Chicago, New York, Washington, D.C., and Cincinnati … In the hit 1964 movie *Goldfinger*, Blue Grass Field is mentioned as the destination for James Bond's nemesis Auric Goldfinger … On May 21, Lady

Bird Johnson arrives at Blue Grass Field to begin her visit to eastern Kentucky and to speak to the Kentucky Federation of Women's Clubs … Approximately 1,500 people gather to greet Senator Hubert H. Humphrey, a vice presidential candidate, when he lands at midnight on October 28.

1965

In January, a bomb scare from an anonymous caller ties up traffic while a search of baggage is made … On October 7, Piedmont Airlines flies the first passenger jet, a Boeing 727, into Blue Grass Field. The landing and takeoff are witnessed by 100 people … In November, a new cargo building opens … On November 7, a light plane, flown by student pilot Odell Stewart Blankenship, snaps 69,000-volt power lines while landing safely at Blue Grass Field. Several sections of Lexington and Versailles lose power for less than one hour; the airport is on emergency power for almost five hours after the incident … In December, a plan for a 200-acre Blue Grass Airport Park is presented. The Community Recreation Association would operate the park.

Weather Bureau open house - 1966

1966

In March, a new firefighting and rescue truck is placed into service … It is announced in July that a $1 million project intended to bring jet service to Blue Grass Field will focus on Runway 4-22, which will be overlaid with several inches of asphalt and lengthened by 700 feet. To prevent closing the runway to commercial air traffic, the work will be done in the evenings, from 11 p.m. to 7 a.m., for at least 20 nights and will be observed by the Federal Aviation Administration (FAA) for possible use at other airports. An FAA spokesman says he believes that this night

project is the first of its kind in the United States … In October, Allegheny Airlines announces proposals for direct flights linking Lexington with Nashville, Pittsburgh, Cleveland and Detroit … A daily one-stop flight, from Lexington to John F. Kennedy Airport in New York connecting through Cincinnati, begins on October 30 … Julia Allen Short, a prominent Lexington sportswoman, civic and political leader, dies while landing the light helicopter she is piloting at Blue Grass Field on October 28. It crashes when the helicopter's skids hook power lines and snap the tail rotor. Short was among only 30 women in the world licensed as a helicopter pilot.

Vocalist Ethel Waters - 1967

1967

A new terminal and 1,000-foot runway extension are proposed in an airport development plan. The recommendation is approved by the airport board and adopted by the City-County Planning Commission … Nine men, including four University of Kentucky professors, die in the crash of their chartered twin-engine plane approximately 1.75 miles from the end of the runway. It is the worst aviation disaster to-date in central Kentucky … Construction of a new FAA control tower utilizing radar is expected to begin in mid November and take about one year to complete. The control tower will have adjoining equipment and office buildings and will be located on 1.7 acres across from the airport entrance road.

1968

Allegheny Airlines is welcomed as a new airline in March with non-stop service to Pittsburgh and Nashville. Construction of the new FAA control tower starts in July … Delta Air Lines begins jet service in April with

DC-9 aircraft weight restrictions because of shorter runways; its non-stop jet service to Chicago is announced in October … Jet service to New York aboard Eastern Air Lines begins in December.

1969

Vice President Spiro Agnew visits in May to speak at the spring meeting of the Republican Governors Conference … In August, Governor Louie B. Nunn announces the airport board will lease a 28-acre tract of land located at the southwest corner of Blue Grass Field to the Commonwealth of Kentucky at no charge for 50 years for a new National Guard Armory … In September, Blue Grass Field commissions a survey of the airport's firefighting needs with recommendations to be made for equipment and manpower. The Air Line Pilots Association had listed Blue Grass Field as among those airports "pilots believe to be dangerous at least some of the time" because of what they deem inadequate fire and rescue equipment. The report said Blue Grass Field "operates with a team of volunteer firemen, a small supply of extinguishing agent and one crash-rescue truck." … In October, Airport Manager Gray defends the airport's safety record and explains the many improvements made over the last several years to enhance safety. He also explains that to resolve criticism of the airport not having "proper" crash-rescue equipment, it would be necessary to purchase $250,000 in equipment, construct a $250,000 firehouse and employ a staff of approximately 12 people … On October 23, the Goodyear blimp flies over Lexington … The airport board authorizes the purchase of $70,000 of crash-rescue equipment including a crash-rescue truck, a dry chemical sprayer, firefighter entry suits and various pieces of smaller equipment in November. The airport also appoints a chief of crash-rescue operations … Members of the airport board formally dedicate the runway and taxiway extension on November 14. Extending the runway from 5,550 to 6,500 feet took approximately one-and-a-half years to build at a cost of $1.3 million. Following the ribbon-cutting ceremony, Delta Air Lines Flight 761 officially uses the runway for the first time.

Lunch counter …

and restaurant in the late 1960s.

1970

On March 3, First Lady Pat Nixon arrives at Blue Grass Field for a five-hour visit to Lexington, the second of five stops in as many states on a tour of student volunteer projects. Several thousand Kentuckians, University of Kentucky student hosts and Governor Louie B. Nunn are among the state and local dignitaries welcoming Mrs. Nixon to Kentucky … Blue Grass Field's crash-rescue team participates in its first full-scale training exercise by extinguishing a fire and rescuing a dummy from inside a burning automobile. The March 17 exercise acquaints the public and crash-rescue team with the operation of the airport's recently purchased $38,000 fire truck … In spring 1970, a new 78-foot FAA control tower replaces the previous tower located on the top of the terminal building. The federal government paid for the $634,000 project … The October 15 open house and dedication of the FAA tower is canceled because of a bomb threat … A twin-engine Aerojet Commander with two people aboard crashes on November 15 while attempting to land in rain and sleet at night at Blue Grass Field. The pilot, Wally Neal of Columbus, Georgia, and co-pilot, Robert Cordoso of Atlanta, are killed; a chartered plane carrying the University of Kentucky football team landed safely minutes earlier.

Judith Ford, Miss America 1969, poses with young friend – 1970

1971

Buckeye Air Service, a charter company, announces it will increase its fleet by two aircraft for a total of 20 … Governor Louie B. Nunn and a crowd of about 500 people greet President and Mrs. Richard M. Nixon as they disembark from Air Force One at Blue Grass Field before motoring to the burial of civil-rights leader Whitney M. Young, Jr. … In June, Keeneland offers to rebuild the concrete steps on the airport property, which lead to Keeneland, at no cost to the airport … Betty Moseley and Virginia Chamberlain are Kentucky's first representatives in a decade in the 1971 All-Woman Transcontinental Air Race (Powder Puff Derby) – the largest women's airplane race in the world. The duo will fly Moseley's plane, *Smitten Kitten* … After vandals steal six runway globe lights,

First Chamber Leadership Visit – 1971

Airport Manager Gray gives airport security orders to shoot anyone tampering with runway and taxi lights because of the hazardous conditions caused … On December 21, the FAA's second highest award for distinguished service is presented to Betty Moseley during ceremonies at Blue Grass Field. The award is given for her assistance in saving a fellow competitor during the Powder Puff Derby. While Moseley was competing, she heard a distress call over her radio from another contestant who was low on fuel, lost and unable to make contact with the FAA control tower. Mosely relayed the emergency situation to the tower and for the next 20 minutes served as an intermediary between air traffic controllers and the lost pilot, who eventually landed safely at a nearby Air Force base.

1972

In March, the FAA announces the installation and operation of airport surveillance radar, which provides 24-hour service for aircraft arriving and departing within a 40-mile radius … In a document released by the Lexington-Fayette County Merger Commission on June 20 outlining the charter of the newly formed Lexington-Fayette Urban County Government (the city and county were previously separate entities), Section 7.18 pertaining to the airport board renames it as the "Lexington-Fayette Urban County Airport Board." It retains all of the powers, duties and functions previously held, including the appointment of an airport manager and staff as prescribed by law. All vacancies on the board are to be appointed by the mayor subject to the provisions of Section 7.02 of the new charter … On November 10, a Southern Airways jetliner carrying 31 passengers departs from Alabama and is hijacked by three men. At one point during the 30-hour ordeal, the plane is diverted to Blue Grass Field for refueling. Ground crewman Darrell Melton refuels the

plane while the engines are running. After receiving $2 million in ransom and assurances of safety, the hijacked plane lands at Havana's airport where the hijackers are promptly arrested … In December, new security measures take effect at Blue Grass Field, two months before being required under a new federal law. Every person traveling will pass through metal detectors or be searched with a wand and then their carry-on luggage will be searched. The new measures are aimed at thwarting the increase in hijacking. Blue Grass Field is the first airport in the southeast FAA division to be FAA-approved on the security portion of the new regulations.

1973

Former President Lyndon B. Johnson lands at Blue Grass Field in January heavily guarded by Secret Service agents and an Army detachment from Fort Campbell. Johnson will be the guest of honor at the Centennial Founder's Day Convocation of the University of Kentucky, the 100th anniversary of the founding of the university … Runway 33-15, built in 1942 as part of President Franklin D. Roosevelt's WPA program, permanently closes in March. The closing of the runway will permit the airport to use about 30 acres of land beside Runway 33-15 and allow for improved facilities for both private and commercial aviation … On June 9 and 10, the Lexington Jaycees sponsor an airshow at Blue Grass Field, which includes a number of aerobatic performers and displays of aircraft and aerospace items. This is the first airshow to be held in the area since the late 1940s … In September, Blue Grass Field announces

Passengers offer a not-so-fiery protest against airport security - 1973

Secretariat's arrival – 1973

a $4.3 million expansion plan to include a new terminal and new parking area tripling present capacity. An additional 36 acres is being purchased from Headley Shouse for expansion of the terminal, air freight building, a new entrance road and extension of one runway. Bohmer Flying Service will be moved across the field to the southwest area and modernized. The new terminal will be 70,000 square feet compared to the 15,000 square feet of the existing terminal. Seven local banks approved the board's application for $3.25 million in loans; the state is contributing $500,000 and the FAA is contributing between $600,000 and $700,000 toward the project … Triple Crown winner Secretariat flies into Blue Grass Airport on November 11 to take up residence at Claiborne Farm. Although Secretariat owner Penny Chenery, trainer Lucien Laurin and representatives of Claiborne Farm try to keep the horse's arrival a secret, approximately 150 people who learned of the flight wait by the landing strip for the plane's arrival.

1974

Princess Margaret and Lord Snowden arrive in Lexington in May to attend the 100th running of the Kentucky Derby in Louisville. A crowd of 50 spectators greet the royal couple at the airport. They will be guests of Mr. and Mrs. C.V. Whitney, and they will tour Bluegrass horse farms while visiting … Bohmer Flying Service's hangar is moved 2,400 feet to the southern tip of the airport to make way for construction of the new terminal.

Construction begins on new airport terminal in 1974.

The hangar is known as "The Spirit of St. Louis" because it once housed Charles Lindbergh's airplane … On December 24, the airport board votes unanimously to execute a $5.3 million loan agreement with seven local banks and formally awards the construction contract for the new terminal to White and Congleton, Co. The firm is expected to begin excavation for the terminal foundation in about 10 days, with erection of structural steel projected in early April 1975.

1975

Superior Flying Service purchases Bohmer Flying Service in February … On July 11, Logan Gray dies at his home after a short illness at age 59. He managed the airport for 12 years, supervising construction of a new control tower, radar installa-

James Brough - 1975

tion and runway extension. He was unable to see the completion of his latest project – the multi-million dollar terminal, scheduled to open in April 1976. Gray was known for his "red-carpet" welcome of special airport visitors … James Obermiller is named acting airport manager upon Gray's death, and James A. Brough, airport manager in LaCrosse, Wisconsin, since 1973, is named executive director in November … The airport board awards the contract for parking operations to Chattanooga-based Air Terminal Parking Company, later to be known as Republic Parking System, Inc.

1976

In March, just prior to the grand opening of the new airport terminal, airport management announces a new red-white-and-blue logo emphasizing the Bluegrass

Thoroughbred industry by incorporating a bugler whose jacket is a pattern of blue stars while the rest of the figure is red and white. A University of Kentucky graphic arts class of nine students produced the new logo. Sophomore art major Jill Reiling's design was accepted and will be used on airport stationery, publications and visual displays … The new multi-million dollar terminal opens to the public on April 25 in advance of the official ribbon-cutting ceremony.

The new facility contains 70,000 square feet and costs approximately $10 million, including relocation of hangars, utilities and taxiway improvements … The new terminal officially opens on April 28 … Republican Presidential Candidate Ronald Reagan arrives in Lexington on May 13 for a campaign visit. Jimmy Carter, the front-runner for the Democratic presidential nomination, arrives at Blue Grass Field on May 18 … In June, Norwood Construction Company is selected for the demolition of the old terminal building … The airport board approves the lease of Superior Flying Service to be passed to Air Associates, Inc. in October … On November 28, four members of a Lexington family are killed and two others injured when their twin-engine plane crashes short of the runway during an attempted landing in heavy fog and freezing rain.

1977

The year begins with the Lexington Women's Club demanding a traffic light at the entrance to Blue Grass Field … Former President Gerald Ford arrives at Blue Grass Field on April 11 and is greeted by Lexington Mayor Foster Pettit and Dr. Vincent Davis from the University of Kentucky's Patterson School of Diplomacy. This was Ford's first visit to Lexington in 25 years … The airport board requests Executive Director Brough to contact Keeneland and the Fire Department to investigate the possibility

Demolition of terminal – 1977

of constructing a fire station near Keeneland and the airport … The board approves the dates of June 11 and 12 for the 1977 Jaycees Air Show … Delta's new jetway is dedicated on December 19 with a ribbon-cutting ceremony.

1978

More than 7,000 University of Kentucky basketball fans swarm the terminal on March 27 to catch a glimpse of the Wildcats, who defeated Duke, for Kentucky's fifth national championship. The damage to the terminal may total $30,000 … Two days after a

third meeting with groups expressing vigorous opposition to an expansion proposal, Executive Director Brough announces in July that the airport board will take more time and gather additional information to study its proposed master plan update. Prepared by a Chicago airport consulting firm, the plan calls for expansion of the parking, passenger terminal and general aviation facilities; however, the most controversial part is a new $19 million, 8,000-foot main runway parallel to the existing 6,500-foot runway … In September, Prince Philip, husband of Queen Elizabeth, arrives for the World Three-Day Event Championships at the Kentucky Horse Park. Mayor Jim Amato welcomes him to Lexington … The Airline Deregulation Act of 1978 is passed, eliminating government control over the launch of new airlines, fares and routes. This legislation allows market forces to drive the airline industry and will have a dramatic impact on commercial aviation.

1979

In a special meeting called in April, the airport board unanimously adopts a

Coach Hall addresses fans in 1978.

plan calling for construction of a new $24.4 million, 8,000-foot runway between Versailles Road and Parkers Mill Road, crossing Parkers Mill Road west of Little Georgetown. The runway will be built northwest of the present runway, instead of southeast as originally recommended by the airport's consultants. The airport board votes to locate the new runway on the opposite side of the present runway; however, this plan would ultimately be derailed due to public controversy … A new public safety facility is dedicated in October. The centrally located firehouse has quick access to all runways, taxiways and ramps. Fire and rescue vehicles can get to the farthest point on a runway within three minutes after an alarm sounds.

1980

Frontier Airlines begins service to St. Louis and Denver on February 1 … Also in February, Eastern Air Lines, serving Lexington since 1946, announces it will cease operations in Lexington effective June 1 … Later in the month, a single-engine Comanche 260 crashes while attempting to land. The injured pilot and passenger survive thanks to the efforts of

Public Safety Officers Curtis Taylor and Joseph Weis, who remove their outer garments in sub-zero temperatures to warm the victims of the crash … US Airways and Piedmont Airlines begin new flights on June 1 to Washington, D.C. and New York City, effectively nullifying Eastern Air Line's recent announced pullout from the Lexington market … The airport board takes out a three-year note in July for $436,300 at eight percent to replace the leaking roof of the terminal building. The note is payable semi-annually to First Security National Bank & Trust Company of Lexington, acting for and on behalf of itself and

> *In February 1980, Eastern Air Lines, serving Lexington since 1946, announces it will cease operations in Lexington.*

Central Bank & Trust Company, Citizens Union National Bank & Trust Company, Second National Bank & Trust Company, Bank of Commerce & Trust Company, Bank of Lexington and Bank of the Bluegrass … Tennessee Airways begins offering commuter flights to Knoxville.

1981

In late summer, a six-week air traffic controller strike forces airlines to drop many of their small flights and funnel more flights through major hub airports instead. The airport responds by hiring MER & Associates to orchestrate a public service advertising campaign promoting the airport. The project involves local travel agencies and incentives to travelers. MER's cost estimate for the multi-faceted, six-month campaign is $8,400. The theme of the new campaign: "You Can Get There From Here."

1982

Blue Grass Field receives a $1.1 million two-year federal grant to construct a 10-acre general aviation area … The airport board adopts a resolution restricting ultra-light aircraft from using the airfield … Representatives from Delta Air Lines, Frontier Airlines and Piedmont Airlines report that business could be better. Frontier lowered ticket prices in March and April and although volume increased, they lost $1.6 million with the reduced fares … In July, the airport board adopts a resolution to offer more favorable terms to its commercial airlines recognizing that the changed federal regulatory atmosphere, slow economic business conditions, inflation and escalating costs have impaired the airlines and operations at the airport.

1983

At the January airport board meeting, Delta Air Lines reports that the company had the best December ever, while the other airlines report that they are still struggling. John Jenks, representing Van Dusen Air Inc., reports that its figures are also down and that they are looking forward to the January horse sales for a boost … In February, the Flight History Museum, precursor to the Aviation Museum of Kentucky, has a quiet takeoff as it opens its doors to the public … It is reported in May that the airport will add 550 feet to the main runway rather than constructing a second runway … Construction begins on the runway extension in September.

1984

On March 28, the airport name changes from Blue Grass Field to Blue Grass Airport … The first United Airlines flight arrives on June 1. United is offering three non-stop flights a day to Chicago … Former President Gerald Ford arrives at Blue Grass Airport on May 3 to inaugurate an educational program

Former President Gerald Ford - 1984

at the University of Kentucky … Queen Elizabeth II visits central Kentucky in early October for a private six-day visit. As the guest of Will and Sarah Farish at Lane's End Farm, she will tour local horse farms and attend her first American horse race at Keeneland. The airport is the site of a brief reception for the Queen, who is greeted by Governor Martha Layne Collins, Mayor Scotty Baesler, Woodford County Judge-Executive Jenny Sue Given, Versailles Mayor Paul Noel and the Farishes. Approximately 120 U.S. and foreign

The first United Airlines flight arrives on June 1, 1984.

journalists are present. A crowd of 600 turns out on the rainy day to watch the Queen's arrival.

1985

Johnson Romanowitz architectural firm orchestrates a major expansion and redesign of the terminal building. Enhancements include switching the location of the baggage and arrival areas, additional windows and skylights, and a second floor mezzanine suitable for jet bridge access to airplanes … In June, the airport announces that it will spend $1.5 million to repair and improve intersection designs

Governor Collins greets John Henry - 1985

of roads leading into the airport … John Henry, horse racing's all-time money winner, returns to his old Kentucky home in August. Governor Martha Layne Collins, trainer Ron McAnally and Keeneland President James E. "Ted" Bassett III are on hand to greet him … Eastern Metro Express announces four daily flights to Atlanta starting in December.

1986

American Eagle, a commuter airline, begins service on April 15 with three daily flights from Blue Grass Airport to the American Airlines hub in Nashville … In April, the airport board unveils a model of how the terminal could look in the year 2000, possibly doubling in size … Queen Elizabeth II arrives in Lexington in May for her second tour of world-renowned Bluegrass horse farms, inspecting stallions as possible mates for her broodmares and visiting the mares she owns and boards in Kentucky. During her private five-day visit, the

Queen will stay at Lane's End Farm in Woodford County … In July, the royal family of Dubai arrives in the first Boeing 747 to land at the airport.

1987

Mike Flack - 1987

Acting Director Mike Flack is named the new executive director of Blue Grass Airport on February 11, succeeding James Brough, who resigned in December 1986 to assume a similar position in Birmingham, Alabama … In June, Trans World Airlines (TWA) begins service at Blue Grass Airport with four daily flights – two non-stop flights to St. Louis and two connecting flights to St. Louis with stops in Louisville. Governor Martha Layne Collins cuts the ribbon as passengers board the inaugural flight on a DC-9. The U.S. Postal Service offers special cancellations, with the St. Louis-to-Lexington and the Lexington-to-St. Louis postmark, for TWA's inaugural flights … On December 5, a private twin-engine plane tries to make an emergency landing but crashes about 400 yards short of the runway, after the pilot reported an engine on fire. The pilot and co-pilot were killed and two others were injured.

1988

In March, responses to invitations to bid for a second fixed-base operator are received. It is announced that the successful bidder is Sprite Flite Jets, Inc. Jack Baugh, owner of Almahurst Farm, represents Sprite Flite and will ask for assistance with a bond issue later in the year to help finance the proposed $1.5 million facility … The airport board hears a brief update in July on the application for U.S. Customs Port of Entry status for the airport. There have been many inquiries and much support pledged. The expense for the first year is estimated to be approximately $85,000, with expense in subsequent years of less than $60,000. It would be located in the air freight building … In August, staff

Expansion work begins in the fall of 1988 that will double the size of the airport terminal.

recommends to the airport board that a separate entrance for general aviation and air freight traffic off of Man o' War Boulevard be approved and that the Urban County Government will pay at least $100,000 toward this project … Expansion work begins in the fall that will double the airport's terminal, create a 150-seat restaurant and lounge, more than quadruple the baggage claim area and create an observation deck. According to Executive Director Flack, these improvements and expanded rental car availability will enhance customer service.

1989

Queen Elizabeth II begins her third visit to the Bluegrass when the Royal Air Force VC-10 touches down at Blue Grass Airport in May. She again stays with Will and Sarah Farish at Lane's End Farm in Woodford County during her five-day private visit … The world's fastest airliner, the Concorde SST, visits Blue Grass Airport in early August. The supersonic Concorde, which travels at 1,350 mph, twice the speed of sound, lands at the airport on August 9 and departs August 10 with 98 passengers who paid a minimum of $4,000 each. The no-jet-lag, 10-day excursion is from Lexington to London on the Concorde with a return trip to New York City on the *Queen Elizabeth II* cruise ship. A Delta flight will carry passengers from New York back to Lexington. Versailles Road is jammed with vehicles, some double-parked, in order to get a glimpse of the Concorde … In December, Phase I of the terminal expansion adds 80,000 square feet of space – double its previous size. The new baggage claim area is four times larger and the car rental area has been expanded. Phase II will be completed within the next two to three months … The U.S. Customs Service opens a permanent office at Blue Grass Airport in late December. Shipments from foreign countries can now be flown directly to Lexington rather than landing in Louisville or Cincinnati, then shipped to Lexington. Also, private aircraft from foreign countries can now fly directly to Lexington.

1990

As part of the grand opening ceremonies for Phase II of the airport's $12 million expansion project, the Blue Grass Aviation Show and Armed Forces Day Celebration draws huge crowds to Blue Grass Airport  in May to see jet flyovers, parachute jumps, a helicopter rappelling demonstration and more than 50 aircraft on display. Visitors can also tour the newly completed airport terminal during its grand opening on Saturday … Enacted by the U.S. Congress, the Americans with Disabilities Act of 1990 (ADA) is signed into law on July 26. It is a wide-ranging law that prohibits discrimination based on disability for programs, services, facilities and accommodations. Blue Grass Airport is able to incorporate necessary accessibility changes into its new terminal expansion and update existing facilities at the same time.

1991

In April, Lexington residents are among the last to see the Goodyear blimp *Enterprise* on its way to company headquarters in Akron, Ohio, where it will be retired after more than 10 years of service. The blimp, which cruises at about 30 mph, will spend the night in Lexington, then Columbus, before it arrives in Akron. *The Spirit of Akron* will replace the airship, which is 193 feet long and 50 feet wide … A ceremony in October marks the completion of the upgraded Low Level Wind Shear Alert System (LLWAS) at all 110 airports designated to receive it. The new and improved LLWAS is an upgrade from the standard six-sensor unit version to a system with full microburst detection capability and other improved features.

1992

Airport officials create an ADA Advisory Committee in August to guide efforts in improving accessibility to the public. At monthly meetings, the

Goodyear blimp *Enterprise* visits Lexington - 1991

committee will take one section of the airport at a time and make recommendations on needed improvements … On July 23, Vice President Dan Quayle greets supporters at Blue Grass Airport as he arrives in Lexington to raise money for the U.S. Senate

candidacy of David Williams, who is running against incumbent Democrat Wendell Ford … In September, U.S. Senator Al Gore arrives for a brief visit to Lexington as he campaigns for the vice presidency. Within hours of Gore leaving the airport, First Lady Barbara Bush arrives in Lexington to boost literacy efforts in the

Commonwealth … On October 24, President Bush arrives at the airport via Air Force One. Bush greets a crowd of more than 1,500 people and speaks briefly before boarding a marine helicopter to attend a rally in London, Kentucky … On December 2, US Airways resumes service from Blue Grass Airport to New York's LaGuardia Airport via a Pittsburgh stopover. On December 15, Delta inaugurates direct service from Blue Grass Airport to LaGuardia with a brief stop in Cincinnati.

1993

The airport expansion is dedicated during a brief ceremony attended by Mayor Scotty Baesler, who proclaims May 13-19 as Aviation Week in the Bluegrass, and Governor Wallace Wilkinson presents a check for $260,000, the final installment of a $2 million economic development grant for the expansion program … Over 10,000 people visit Blue Grass Airport for the 1993 Navy League Blue Grass Air Show on May 15 and 16. Over 50 military and other aircraft are on-site for

personal tours and aerial demonstrations during the two-day show … Comair introduces the Canadair Regional Jet in an inaugural jet service to Lexington from Cincinnati in July … After 20 years of planning and three years of construction, the Georgetown-Scott County Regional Airport, officially opens on October 22. The $7.5 million project is supported by the airport board and is intended to relieve the growing general aviation traffic load … President Bill Clinton arrives in Lexington on *Air Force One* on November 4 and is welcomed at Blue Grass Airport by Governor Brereton Jones. The president is visiting the Lexmark printer and typewriter plant in Lexington to promote the North American Free Trade Agreement. The U.S. House of Representatives is scheduled to vote on the agreement the following week.

1994

The air traffic control tower at Blue Grass Airport begins 24-hour operation in February. The tower had previously been operating between 6 a.m. to

midnight. Prior to the change in hours, aircraft flying overnight relied on Indianapolis for air traffic control assistance … In March, Blue Grass Airport's newsletter, *Air Mail*, reports that the airport and specifically flight school Aero-Tech, Inc., will be the site of a Federal Aviation Administration Resource Center. The center will provide career information, educational programs, statistical information, historical data and other aviation-related material to the public.

1995

The airport board votes to ban smoking in all public spaces in the terminal in February. Smoking will be permitted in designated sections of restaurants, lounges and at curbside check-in areas

Continental Express begins service - 1995

outside the terminal … Members of General Jimmy Doolittle's Raiders hold their 53rd reunion in Lexington to coincide with the ribbon-cutting ceremony to open the Aviation Museum of Kentucky on April 15. The museum features a research library, gift shop and Kentucky's official aviation Hall of Fame. Also included are nine planes, historic uniforms and memorabilia collected by more than 170 aviation volunteers … In July, Blue Grass Airport completes a $4.5 million ramp expansion that increases aircraft parking by 25 percent. The project includes 19,130 square yards of concrete pavement, 18,200 tons of stone, 1,900 feet of storm sewers and 28 acres of seeding. Installation of an in-pavement lighting system improves visibility for incoming pilots during inclement weather … The first Continental Express flight, offering non-stop service to Cleveland, arrives at Blue Grass Airport on December 1.

Fans await the return of the 1996 NCAA Men's Basketball Champs.

1996

More than 1,500 fans, who couldn't make it to the planned rally in Rupp Arena, line the fences at Blue Grass Airport on April 2 to greet the NCAA Men's Basketball National Champions, the University of Kentucky Wildcats … As

Couple ties the knot at airport - 1996

hurrying travelers race toward their gates, Gayle Ray and Bruce Lewis take their marriage vows just after 6 a.m. on April 6. Minutes later, the Nicholasville newlyweds board a US Airways flight to Pittsburgh, on their way to a honeymoon cruise in the Caribbean. The name of their ship: *The Love Boat*. Due to a last-minute glitch in their wedding plans and early morning departure time, the couple was left with few alternatives other than an airport wedding. It's thought to be the first wedding at the airport … In June, Blue Grass Airport announces the addition of a $4 million fire training facility that could make Lexington one of the leading regional sites for training airport safety crews. In addition, the facility can train local firefighters and volunteer groups from Kentucky and surrounding counties. Scheduled for completion in 1997, the FAA will pay 90 percent of the center's cost … In July, runway expansion at Blue Grass Airport may be years away, but it's already stirring up controversy. The FAA requires airports to begin planning for expansion when 65-70 percent capacity for number of flights is reached. Airport officials say they have reached that capacity and will eventually need an $80 million, 9,000-foot runway if they're going to serve the growing region. In order to expand, the airport would need to buy at least part of six farms, most of them horse farms … Airport expansion opponents rally their forces under the aegis Airport Watch in September. Its leaders say the group has 1,700 members, comprised of people who signed petitions and received the group's mailings. The group, formed three weeks prior, has launched a campaign to convince politicians and the public that the expansion is a bad idea

… In October, Lexington Mayor Pam Miller says that Blue Grass Airport should get an outside opinion before building a new runway and proposes a study to help determine whether there is a real need for a bigger airport. Work on the assessment will not begin until after the FAA completes its environmental impact study. Airport Executive Director Flack says the report isn't expected until 1998 at the earliest. At least 10 of 15 council members have voiced opposition to the airport's expansion plan … On November 12, Mayor Miller states that if she had to vote today, she would vote against the proposed runway expansion. The mayor says that airport officials have not made a convincing argument … On November 21, Urban County Council votes 9-4 in favor of a nonbinding resolution that calls on the airport to look at options other than adding a new runway to expand Blue Grass Airport. The council also votes to establish a 12-member task force made up of members on both sides of the debate to continue examining issues related to airport expansion.

1997

In February, Blue Grass Airport moves ahead with plans to build a $9 million, three-level parking garage. The airport intends to issue a $9 million bond for the project. Passengers could be using the structure by early to mid 1998 … For the second time in six months, the Urban County Council approves a resolution in May to withdraw virtually all city support for the proposed 9,000-foot parallel runway. The vote is 11-2 … The airport signs a $1.1 million contract in July with URS Greiner Inc., a consulting firm based in Tampa, Florida, that will lead the two-year study of the proposed parallel runway and other expansion options … The ongoing battle between the city and Blue Grass Airport over a second commercial runway reaches a boiling point in mid November as two Urban County Council members, Gloria Martin and Al Mitchell, investigate whether the council can take control of the airport itself. Both sides cite state attorney general's opinions to support their opposing views. The previous month the council agreed to finance a $10.5 million parking garage at the airport but added the stipulation that the airport board limit its debt for fear the board would use the money to finance a new runway without the council's consent. The airport board denies the accusation and contends that the council has no right to impose such restrictions … The Urban County Council votes 10-3 in early December to approve an agreement worked out by Mayor Pam Miller, Airport Board Chairman Foster Ockerman and Vice Mayor Teresa Isaac for a parking garage at Blue Grass Airport that also allows the city to maintain some control over the airport's purse strings. The agreement would authorize city-backed bonds

for the $10.5 million garage without altering the financial relationship between the city and airport … On December 2, a much delayed parking garage at Blue Grass Airport moves forward as the airport board approves a compromised funding plan with the city.

1998

Michael Gobb - 1998

On February 9, U.S. Senator Wendell Ford announces FAA grants of $1.6 million to Blue Grass Airport for safety improvements. The airport will build a taxiway to accommodate more hangars in the general aviation area. It also will expand and renovate the aircraft rescue and firefighting building, purchase snow removal equipment and construct a building to house it. The grant will also fund a project to clear areas adjacent to the primary runway to reduce hazards from wildlife … The airport board briefly discusses legislation being considered by the state legislature on February 25, including the expansion of the Lexington-Fayette Urban County Airport Board from six to 10 members, a restriction on financing capital improvements exceeding $1 million without the state's approval and the use of aviation fuel taxes to create a state aviation trust fund … Mike Flack is named executive director at Columbia Metropolitan Airport in Columbia, South Carolina, in March … On April 15, Airport Board Member Jon Zachem is appointed as interim director for a three-month period while the board conducts a search for a new executive director … In June, Blue Grass Airport begins construction of a three-level parking garage to add 550 new public spaces and 68 rental car spaces … In July,

the airport board is expanded from six to 10 members. One member of the airport board is to be a representative of Lexington-Fayette Urban County Government designated by the mayor and the nine other members, two of whom must live within a three-mile radius of the airport, are to be appointed by the mayor and approved by Urban County Council … Blue Grass Airport officials announce the hiring of Michael A. Gobb as executive director in August. Gobb was most recently director of Bradley International Airport near Hartford, Connecticut.

1999

FAA officials expect a $1.2 million study of runway expansion at Blue Grass Airport to be completed by January 1, 2000. Officials say the consultants have narrowed the 13 runway proposals to four alternatives … The first level of the three-story parking garage is scheduled to open on July 30 … On October 20, the new garage is formally dedicated. By building a garage and revamping surface lots, the $10.5 million project has increased parking to 1,926 spaces, an increase of more than 60 percent.

2000

In mid December, after two days of talking about airport expansion, a divided airport board cuts the field of potential runway improvements to two options – extending the existing

7,000-foot runway or building a new runway parallel to Versailles Road. Although it has flown under the radar the last few years, the runway option parallel to Versailles Road appears to be a slight favorite. The airport's current main runway doesn't have 1,000-foot safety areas on each end as required by the FAA. Because it was built before the FAA established current standards, the airport doesn't have to meet the new requirements until it does major reconstruction; a pavement study shows that some reconstruction will be required in six years or less … On December 20, confronted by worried homeowners and citing the need to gather more information and public input, the airport board postpones a vote on runway expansion. "There are a lot of people who don't feel they have all the information they should have," Chairwoman Fernita Wallace said. Board members say they have to submit a runway choice to the FAA by February. "We have come to the end of the path," Board Member Natalie Wilson said. "We need to vote in January."

2001

On January 23, the airport board meets to discuss its surprise decision made the previous week to build a new runway parallel to the current runway – a decision that draws much controversy. The special meeting comes amid criticisms and concerns raised by Lexington officials and the FAA. The board's decision takes most people by surprise because that runway option had seemed to be off the table … On January 29, the airport board reverses course, opting to expand the existing runway at an estimated cost of $28 million, rather than build a new $80 million parallel runway. The expansion would rehabilitate the existing runway and lengthen it to achieve 600-foot safety zones at each end … In February, an economic impact study conducted by University of Kentucky researchers shows that although the airport generates $132 million in revenue annually and adds 1,760 jobs to the local economy, it loses about 41 percent of its potential passengers to cheaper, more numerous flights out of Louisville and Cincinnati … On May 15, the FAA signs off on a runway extension for Blue Grass Airport, effectively ending a long debate over the airport's future … US Airways announces daily non-stop service between Lexington and Reagan National Airport in Washington, D.C., beginning October 22, and Continental Express announces daily non-stop service from Lexington to LaGuardia Airport. Both are later canceled due to the events of September 11 … On September 11 at 9:45 a.m., the FAA orders all aircraft to land at the nearest airport as soon as practical due to terrorist attacks on the World Trade Center in

> *On May 15, 2001, the Federal Aviation Administration signs off on a runway extension for Blue Grass Airport, effectively ending a long debate over the airport's future.*

New York and the Pentagon in Washington, D.C. At this time, there are more than 4,500 aircraft in the air on Instrument Flight Rules (IFR) flight plans. It is the first unplanned shutdown of U.S. airspace. It is estimated that by 12:15 p.m. the airspace over the 48 contiguous states is clear of all commercial and private flights. Blue Grass Airport, Louisville International Airport and Cincinnati/Northern Kentucky International Airport are evacuated for security sweeps. Airplanes remain grounded for two days as Blue Grass Airport works on completing a FAA checklist imposing tougher security requirements. On September 13, Blue Grass Airport receives clearance for arrivals and departures shortly after noon, and the first flight leaves Lexington for Atlanta at 12:50 p.m. By September 18, about 20 percent of flights to and from Lexington have been canceled since the terrorist attacks, and airlines are announcing massive cutbacks to stem their losses … On September 29, Continental announces that it is dropping plans for non-stop service from Blue Grass Airport to LaGuardia Airport. The company had announced twice-daily flights on September 5, less than one week before the terrorist strikes. The ban on air travel, and low traffic after it was lifted, forced the already ailing industry to cut flights and lay off employees … In October, 35 National Guardsmen are stationed at five Kentucky airports, including three guardsmen at Blue Grass Airport. Guards will be stationed at the airport's security checkpoint and will be on duty any time there is a departing flight … Airline passengers are limited to bringing a single piece of carry-on luggage, rather than two, in addition to another small bag, such as a purse or briefcase, under new federal security rules issued in October … Following the September 11 attacks, the FAA eliminated all parking within 300 feet of terminals across the country as a safeguard against car bombings, eliminating 30 percent of Blue Grass Airport's parking. The airport parking garage regains use of approximately 500 parking spaces on November 17, but all cars parking in the previously restricted area are to be inspected … The Transportation Security Administration is established on November 19 to secure the nation's airports and the traveling public.

2002

Airlines across the country begin inspecting all checked luggage in January. The security act passed by Congress in the previous year gave the airlines 60 days to come up with a system to screen checked bags. Initially, the airlines will be in charge of screening all baggage. Responsibility will eventually shift to the federal government once new equipment is installed to scan additional luggage. Only a handful of the nation's 420 airports have that equipment. The rest will have to purchase the equipment as it becomes available. Only two companies in the U.S. manufacture the machines at a cost of about $1 million each … The federal government announces in February that it will take over checkpoints at Blue Grass Airport when agents from a new division of the U.S. Department of Transportation

American Trans Air (ATA) begins service to Chicago in 2002.

begin overseeing security. All screeners and bag checkers now employed by a private company will be replaced with federal agents by the government-set deadline of November 19 … National Guardsmen watching over security at Kentucky's airports will be replaced with local police by June. According to a Kentucky National Guard spokesman, it has cost the U.S. Department of Defense $1.9 million to station troops in Kentucky's airports … For the first time in 20 years, Kentuckians can enjoy non-stop service from Lexington to New York (Newark) as Continental Airlines kicks off service in June … American Trans Air (ATA) begins offering four daily non-stop flights between Chicago Midway International Airport and Blue Grass Airport in August … US Airways enters Chapter 11 bankruptcy reorganization on August 11, with the stated goal to emerge as a leaner, more competitive airline in March 2003

> *United Airlines files for Chapter 11 in early December 2002, the biggest bankruptcy in aviation history.*

… An elderly woman, Louise Babb, dies, and four other people suffer injuries when a Learjet air ambulance runs off the runway on August 30 while landing, clipping an airport navigational tower and skidding across Versailles Road through lunchtime traffic … As the nation's commercial airports celebrate meeting the November 19 deadline for having federal employees screen passengers, officials at Blue Grass Airport continue to make improvements to minimize the security effect on passengers. The airport plans to open a second passenger checkpoint station in December to reduce long lines during peak travel times … United Airlines files for Chapter 11 in early December, the biggest bankruptcy in aviation history, and vows to keep its jets flying while it tries to straighten out a business that is hemorrhaging as much as $22 million a day. The bankruptcy filing is the sixth largest in U.S. history, covering $22.8 billion in assets … December 31 is the federal deadline for the screening of all checked baggage, and Blue Grass Airport is ready. It has constructed a state-of-the-art system to screen baggage at a cost of $3.5 million, plus $1.6 million worth of explosive detection equipment.

2003

In April, Blue Grass Airport announces that it has seen a rebound in passengers during the past six months and reports that it has set a record for boardings during the period. From October 2002 to March 2003, 519,251 passengers boarded flights from the airport – an increase of 23 percent from the same period in 2002. It is attributed to adding five new destinations and a new airline since September 11, 2001 … In August, U.S. Senator Jim Bunning announces that the U.S. Department of Transportation has awarded $8.6 million in federal funding to Blue Grass Airport. The money will be used to help pay for the initial phases of a $35.5 million runway safety area improvement project now in design. Runway safety areas will meet FAA guidelines by adding 600 feet of safety area to each end of the runway. Construction is scheduled to begin by the end of the year … The Urban County Council unanimously approves a proposal to back expansion at Blue Grass Airport in October. The airport will issue $34.3 million in city-backed bonds to help fund a $66.5 million airport expansion. The rest of the financing will come from the federal government, passenger charges and rental car fees. Many of the changes will make flying easier. In addition to constructing runway safety areas, the airport will add a third security checkpoint lane, a business lounge, a larger rental car lot and six additional gate areas to reduce the inconvenience of passengers boarding and deplaning outside.

2004

In June, Blue Grass Airport is ranked as one of the nation's fastest-growing airports in 2003, ranking seventh in North America and fifth in the U.S. in passenger growth, according to Airports

Council International-North America. The airport had a nearly 19 percent increase in passenger activity last year … Delta Air Lines announces it will offer one flight a day between Blue Grass Airport and Reagan Washington National Airport in Washington, D.C., via a 50-seat regional jet beginning on June 15. Washington is the seventh most-popular destination for Blue Grass Airport customers … In September, US Airways files for Chapter 11 bankruptcy for the second time in the airline's history, seeking to restructure operating costs in light of ever-increasing fuel prices and intense industry competition. Blue Grass Airport gains two non-stop US Airways flights to Charlotte, North Carolina, to replace four flights to Pittsburgh it loses later in the year. Lexington is one of 35 cities to lose non-stop service to Pittsburgh as US Airways works to cut costs by $1.5 billion a year. The airline eventually emerges from bankruptcy protection in 2005 in conjunction with its merger with America West Airlines. … The runway safety area project necessitates the construction of a large embankment and a 30-foot-by-800-foot retaining wall along Versailles Road. To support the equine context of this corridor, the airport commissions a trompe l'oeil mural by internationally recognized artist Eric Henn depicting a stone bridge, federal-style house and images from Kentucky horse farms.

2005

Delta Air Lines inaugurates new service to Orlando, Florida, on January 31 … Blue Grass Airport can claim one of the most modern, efficient and effective baggage-screening operations in the U.S. The airport adds a mechanized system that carries luggage from check-in counters through bomb-detection machines in a back room, without human handling. The airport persuaded the Transportation Security Administration (TSA) to let it build the conveyor system with funding obtained through a $3.6 million grant from the FAA shortly before the FAA barred airports from using FAA money for security. The TSA paid the $1.6 million cost of two bomb-detection machines, and it received the FAA grant to fund the new system … Blue Grass Airport is selected by the Department of Homeland Security as

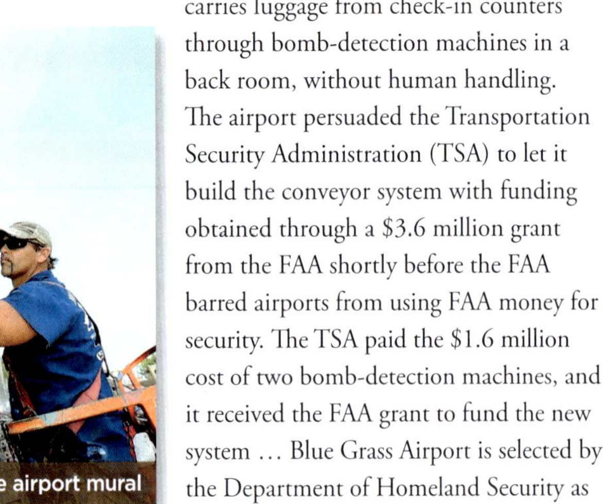

Artist Eric Henn working on the airport mural

one of only 12 airports nationwide to serve as a security hub for general aviation aircraft seeking to fly into Reagan Washington National Airport in Washington, D.C. General aviation aircraft have been prohibited from flying into this airport since the terrorist attacks of September 11 … American Eagle arrives at Blue Grass Airport in May with its distinctive red, white and blue 50-seat regional jets and access to American's hubs at Dallas/Fort Worth and Chicago O'Hare International airports … On June 16, the airport board unanimously votes to begin work on six additional gates for commercial jets, four new jet bridges to protect airline passengers from inclement weather and two new concession shops at a cost of $15.5 million … Delta Air Lines begins new non-stop flights from Blue Grass Airport to the Florida leisure destinations of Tampa and Fort Lauderdale. Lexington also will receive a second daily flight to Orlando. In the last five years, the airport has increased its non-stop destinations from seven to 15 … The first *New York Times* Bookstore in the nation opens in October and occupies 1,738 square feet in Concourse B … Blue

New York Times Bookstore - 2005

American Eagle arrives - 2005

Grass Airport provides 30 minutes of free parking beginning in November. The airport also recently added a cell phone waiting lot where drivers may wait in their vehicles until arriving passengers reach the terminal curb … The Club at Blue Grass, a unique airport-operated business lounge as opposed to an airline-operated lounge, opens in mid November. Located in Concourse B, it's geared to business travelers with amenities such as conference facilities, comfortable seating areas, computer work stations, complimentary high-speed wireless internet, business services and complimentary snacks and beverages … In December, Blue Grass Airport is awarded the Jay Hollingsworth Speas Airport Award for the landscaping project that includes the horse farm-themed mural.

2006

On August 10, federal security officials ban aviation passengers from carrying liquid and gel items onto airplanes after news of a terrorist plot to blow up planes headed to the United States from Great Britain … The airport's main runway closes to all air traffic for 48 hours starting August 18 as it is resurfaced. The paving will take about 24 hours and the remaining time will be spent placing new runway markings and signs. During the closure, approximately 120 trucks will haul 33,000 tons of asphalt to resurface the 7,000-by-150-foot runway … Forty-nine of 50 people died at 6:07 a.m. on August 27 as Delta Comair Flight 5191 crashes during takeoff from Blue Grass Airport. The lone survivor, First Officer James Polehinke, 44, is in critical condition and rushed to University of Kentucky Hospital. The plane crashed in a hilly, heavily wooded area on a neighboring farm after attempting takeoff from the wrong runway. National Transportation Safety Board (NTSB) officials arrive on the scene to investigate the accident. A temporary memorial is set up at the airport immediately following the accident for family and friends to leave flowers, wreaths, notes and mementos of those lost in the crash.

2007

In April, Blue Grass Airport opens its $16.9 million terminal addition. The newly expanded Concourse B features six additional passenger boarding gates, jet bridges for three of those gates, modern seating areas for passengers, a new food and beverage facility and additional restrooms. With this addition, the airport

Concourse B gate area - 2007

now has a total of 13 gates … On May 4, Queen Elizabeth II and Prince Philip arrive for a private visit in Kentucky … In late July, after a nine-hour hearing, the NTSB unanimously finds the pilots at fault for the crash of Delta Comair Flight 5191 in 2006. The NTSB rules the pilots overlooked numerous signs that should have prevented the accident, including runways and taxiways marked with large, lighted signs, runway numbers painted on the ground and that the short runway they used was closed and completely dark, in contrast to the correct runway nearby, which was lit.

Northwest Airlines merges with Delta - 2008

2008

Three new restaurant facilities open on March 27 including Quiznos sandwich shop, Knob Creek Bourbon Lounge and Caffè Ritazza gourmet coffee shop … Northwest Airlines announces in April that it will be merging with Delta Air Lines to form the world's largest airline. The combined airline will retain the Delta name and branding. The airline intends to integrate the operation of the two carriers in January 2010 … Governor Steve Beshear announces in July that Blue Grass Airport will receive $586,233 in Transportation Enhancement program funding toward a new front entryway that will be reflective of the region and increase the visibility of the airport … The American Bonanza Society selects Lexington as the host of its annual convention and fly-in. In September 2008, this association of more than 10,000 aircraft owners and aviation enthusiasts travels to Lexington and lines

the airport's ramp with dozens of aircraft … On September 23, the World Equestrian Games 2010 Foundation announces Blue Grass Airport as the Official Airport of the 2010 Alltech FEI World Equestrian Games … Well-known airport retailer, The Paradies Shops, opens a three-concept Blue Grass MarketPlace on October 15 that includes a Keeneland Shop, Paddock Shop and convenience store – all representing the flavor of the Bluegrass region … In partnership with The Triangle Foundation and Keeneland, Blue Grass Airport unveils a "paddock" area on October 21 with bronze equine sculptures created by world-renowned artist Gwen

Blue Grass MarketPlace - 2008

Reardon … Blue Grass Airport welcomes low-fare carrier Allegiant Air to Lexington with non-stop jet service beginning November 6 to Orlando and St. Petersburg/Clearwater … In December, upon allegations of inappropriate expenditures by the airport's management team, the Commonwealth's Auditor of Public Accounts Crit Luallen begins conducting an audit of the airport. Findings of the audit are expected to be released in several months.

2009

On January 2, Executive Director Gobb resigns his position upon accusations of inappropriate expenditures. Three members of his executive team resign their positions several weeks later. The airport board selects Eric Frankl, who previously served as director of airports for the Toledo-Lucas County Port Authority, as interim executive director on January 30 … In a letter to the community, Airport Board Chairman J. Robert Owens reassures the public that the board has taken decisive action to rebuild the public's trust. "With the help of experienced internationally recognized consultants, good solid financial controls and procedures are being designed and implemented to correct the abuses of the past. It is a new dawn at the airport and the public can rest assured that all airport funds will be spent wisely and prudently" …

Airport entrance - 2009

On February 20, the airport board issues a progress report stating it has moved swiftly to implement a sweeping series of reforms, including approval of whistleblower, code of ethics and travel/business expense policies, review of staff organizational structure and salaries, and future implementation of new purchasing and recordkeeping policies … Auditor of Public Accounts Crit Luallen releases the findings of the airport audit on February 25. The audit proposes recommendations to strengthen the airport's oversight procedures, many of which have already been implemented by the board. In the months and years to

Eric Frankl - 2009

follow, Luallen publicly praises the airport board for its quick and serious response to implementing the audit recommendations … Blue Grass Airport permanently closes its 3,500-foot runway (Runway 8-26) in February to begin construction on a $27 million relocated and realigned crosswind runway (Runway 9-27). The 4,000-foot runway will be relocated to better allow for future development and will no longer intersect with the airport's main 7,000-foot commercial runway … On June 9, the FAA recognizes Blue Grass Airport with the national 2009 Disadvantaged Business Enterprise (DBE) Advocate and Partner Award. This award is given to an airport that has demonstrated excellence in meeting the letter and spirit of the DBE program in the past federal fiscal year … The airport board unveils a new main entrance to the airport on September 17 that is reflective of the Bluegrass region. Designed to resemble the region's horse farm entrances, the entryway incorporates brick masonry walls, limestone capping, stone walls, landscaping and signature lighting fixtures … After serving eight months as interim director, Eric Frankl is named executive director on October 21, following a nationwide search by the airport board.

2010

In early February, Blue Grass Airport and elected officials unveil the latest renovations to the terminal's lobby level including the terrazzo floor in front of the security check-point that charts the sire lineage of the Thoroughbred. In addition to this tribute to the Thoroughbred, the Kentucky theme throughout the first level of the terminal includes limestone facings at all entryways. Renovations also include new airline ticket counters conforming to Americans with Disabilities Act guidelines, replacement of the ceiling system, updated signage, relocation of the Information Center and new floor and wall finishes … Low-cost airline AirTran Airways begins service on February 11 with non-stop flights to Orlando and Fort Lauderdale, Florida … United Airlines and Continental Airlines

TAC Air cuts the ribbon on July 28, 2010 to open a new 12,000 square foot executive terminal.

announce their intent to merge in May. The airline will operate under the United Airlines name upon approval of the merger … Airport officials invite the general public onto its 4,000-foot runway for a unique opportunity to walk, run, bike and stay active as part of the 2nd Sunday exercise initiative. The event not only promotes health and wellness, but also showcases the construction of the new runway … TAC Air cuts the ribbon on July 28 to open a new 12,000-square-foot executive terminal, which includes a high-definition movie theater, exercise facilities, wireless printing from laptops and smart phones, and a pilot lounge with private sleeping rooms and showers. In addition to pilot amenities, the terminal also has conference rooms and an art gallery featuring works by local artisans … Governor Steve Beshear, Mayor Jim Newberry, Department of Aviation Commissioner Winn Turney and FAA Administrator Doug Murphy join airport officials for a ribbon-cutting ceremony for the new crosswind runway, Runway 9-27 … Families of victims of Delta Comair Flight 5191 break ground on August 27 for a memorial at the Arboretum on the University of Kentucky campus … In November, airport officials report one of the busiest months in its history – partially attributable to the 2010 Alltech FEI World Equestrian Games – as more than 56,000 passengers departed from the airport during the previous month. Boardings increased more than 39 percent,

compared to 2009, and passenger traffic for October increased by more than 35 percent. The airport and its partners hosted more than 700 private and corporate airplanes, provided security for international dignitaries, welcomed more than 460 international athletes and facilitated 18 special event charter flights … Allegiant inaugurates low-cost, non-stop service between Lexington and Fort Myers/Southwest Florida on November 18 … A new

5191 Memorial - 2011

electrical vault replaces a WWII-era underground facility and controls more than 800 lights on the airfield. It includes touch screen technology to control all airfield lighting components and digital monitoring for lighting circuits.

2011

In January, the FAA awards Blue Grass Airport its Airport Safety Mark of Distinction Award for construction of the airport's new crosswind runway and associated taxiways and for the development of an operations department. The new 4,000-foot runway was completed in August 2010 and is used by private and corporate general aviation aircraft, which accounts for 65 percent of total operations at the airport … Eric Frankl is named the 2010 Air Carrier Airport Manager of the Year in April by the Federal Aviation Admin-

istration Southern Region … The second annual 2nd Sunday exercise and fitness event is held on June 12. The airport closes its 4,000-foot runway and associated taxiway for the day so that people can exercise on it … The 5191 Memorial Commission unveils a sculpture on August 27 to honor the 49 lives lost five years earlier as a result of the Delta Comair Flight 5191 accident. Created by renowned artist and Kentucky resident Douwe Blumberg, the 17-foot tall metal sculpture resides in the Arboretum in Lexington and includes 49 aluminum alloy birds in flight and a granite base inscribed with the names of those who were lost that day … On October 13, Blue Grass Airport celebrates 65 years of partnership with Delta Air Lines and the opening of the airport's first terminal … Allegiant begins non-stop service to Fort Lauderdale, Florida, on November 17. American Airlines files for Chapter 11 reorganization in the U.S. Bankruptcy Court on November 29. The airline states it is taking this action to achieve a competitive cost and debt structure and assure its long-term viability.

2012

Advanced imaging technology scanners are installed by the Transportation Security Administration at security checkpoint in March. The scanners detect concealed metallic and nonmetallic items using millimeter wave technology. The machines are outfitted

United Way 5k on the Runway - 2012

2013

In February, American Airlines and US Airways announce their intent to merge into one airline, retaining the American Airlines name. Upon approval from the Department of Justice and the Department of Transportation, the combined airline will create the country's biggest airline by total passengers served … First Lady Michelle Obama arrives at Blue Grass Airport on May 11 to speak with approximately 2,500 students at Eastern Kentucky University's graduation ceremony. Mrs. Obama selects this university in Richmond, Kentucky, because of its often-celebrated work with veterans … Passenger options expand with the addition of Dunkin' Donuts opening in the terminal concourse in November and Pepper's Mexican Grill planned for 2014. … The airport board completes its 2013 Master Plan Update, which launches the airport into a $60 million taxiway safety improvement program over the next decade. This project includes the realignment of the primary taxiway and the relocation of two key support buildings.

with software designed to enhance passenger privacy … Airlines transport the team, band, alumni and fans from Blue Grass Airport to the SEC tournament, NCAA Elite Eight and NCAA Championship. Congratulations are in order for the University of Kentucky men's basketball team when it returns from the

Vice Presidential Debate media - 2012

Final Four in New Orleans as NCAA National Champions. More than 2,500 fans gather at the airport to celebrate the arrival of the UK Wildcats as they return from the championship … The third annual 2nd Sunday on June 11 draws thousands to exercise, be active and play on the 4,000-foot general aviation runway. This year's event is also the torch-lighting kickoff for the upcoming Bluegrass

Kentucky Ale Taproom opens - 2012

State Games and an early morning 5K run around the runway in partnership with United Way of the Bluegrass … On June 12, in partnership with Creative Food Group and Alltech, the full-service restaurant at Blue Grass Airport re-opens as the Kentucky Ale Taproom …Vice President Joe Biden and U.S. Representative Paul Ryan arrive at Blue Grass Airport on October 10 and 11 to participate in the Vice Presidential Debate held at Centre College.

Red-tailed horse inspired by Tuskegee Airmen P-51 Mustang – 2013

THE FAMOUS
and Infamous

BY AVE LAWYER

Our story begins with University of Kentucky (UK) basketball, as does pretty much everything (okay, other than horses and bourbon) that really matters in the Bluegrass. More UK basketball players and coaches have achieved permanent celebrity status in Lexington than any number of world-class and bona fide moguls, idols and stars that have come through Blue Grass Airport.

When the UK Wildcats win the Big Dance (NCAA Basketball Championship), celebrations in normally sedate Lexington generate the kind of noise that makes national news. The final whistle blows and the UK campus erupts into a cacophony of horns, hoots and fireworks, accompanied by college kids cavorting on cars and the inexplicable torching of sofas. Equally mysterious, the nexus of the celebration inevitably shifts of its own accord to Blue Grass Airport. Chants of "Go Big Blue!" morph into "Go to the airport!" and the "Big Blue Nation" flocks to hail its conquering heroes.

With NCAA Men's Basketball Championship victories in 1948, 1949, 1951 and 1958, one would have thought that by 1978 UK fans might be fairly blasé about winning another one.

However, no one was prepared for the over-the-top reaction of UK fans for their "Big Blue" NCAA champs in 1978. Thousands upon thousands of fans descended on the pristine new terminal at what was then Blue Grass Field and proceeded to gather in the terminal. If there is such a thing as a "happy riot" – this surely would have qualified.

The next morning's *Lexington Herald* painted a vivid picture of the wild night. It was chaotic with Big Blue fans in a frenzy of gratitude after UK dispelled a 20-year drought by dispensing with archrival Duke in the final game. Blue Grass Airport public safety officers recall coming upon awed fans trying to chip up pieces of the terrazzo tile floor across which the team had walked.

Fans seeking a higher vantage point clambered atop a freestanding car rental kiosk, which promptly collapsed under their weight. Floors, including carpeting that would ultimately have to be replaced, were inadvertently doused in soft drinks and beer as thousands of elbows jostled for a view.

Normally undemonstrative Head Coach Joe B. Hall, puffing on a victory cigar, addressed the crowd from an upper level balcony. "People have accused us of not having fun this season," he said. "We didn't go to St. Louis to have fun. We went to win a championship!" At which point he ripped open his coat to reveal a 1978

Above: Adolph Rupp and his 1946 UK basketball team.
Right: The airport following the 1978 NCAA Men's Basketball Championship and 2011 NCAA Elite Eight.

> **" PEOPLE HAVE ACCUSED US OF NOT HAVING FUN THIS SEASON. WE DIDN'T GO TO ST. LOUIS TO HAVE FUN. WE WENT TO WIN A CHAMPIONSHIP! "**
>
> – JOE B. HALL ON THE 1978 MEN'S NCAA BASKETBALL CHAMPIONSHIP

National Champion T-shirt. You can imagine the effect that had on the crowd.

Dr. George Gumbert was chair of the airport board at that time, and he raced to the airport after getting a call about the unprecedented gathering of more than 7,000 fans at the terminal. "When the team arrived, they were met by thousands of fans that just descended upon this building [the terminal]. It was a sea of humanity," he later told his family. The take-away? "Clearly an unexpected moment in airport history and one that has not been repeated. We all learned a lot from it."

The airport was far better prepared when Coach Rick Pitino's national championship team flew in from East Rutherford, New Jersey, in 1996 and Tubby Smith's from San Antonio in 1998. The terminal was strictly off-limits, and a sturdy security fence barred fans' access to the ramp. There was a curious moment of indecision when the team got off the airplane with all the fans on one side of the fence and the players on the other. The fans wanted to touch their idols, and the team, no doubt, was ready to be loved. Realizing that the fence was probably in everyone's best interest, they did the next best thing – signing autographs and shaking hands through the fence.

Each time a Final Four team returned victoriously,

Clockwise from top left: The crowd gathers in the terminal awaiting the return of the 1978 NCAA Men's Basketball Championship team; Player Jack "Goose" Givens; Coach Joe B. Hall and player Rick Robey; Coach Hall being interviewed by media; Terminal is standing room only!

1978

the airport learned from the experience. Those key learnings culminated in 2012.

An internal committee was created to prepare for the return of John Calipari's national champions from New Orleans. The security fencing around the ramp was reconfigured with open chain link to allow the 2,500 fans, waving pom-poms supplied by the airport, an unobstructed view of their hoops heroes. Fans remember basketball player Darius Miller holding the championship trophy aloft as the team bus crept in extreme slow motion through a sea of hands, all reaching out to touch it as it inched by.

The airport's public safety team orchestrated a water cannon salute that greeted the arriving charter plane carrying the victorious UK basketball team. The longstanding aviation industry practice of "wetting the plane" with two firefighter's trucks on either side of the plane is used to mark special occasions. The shot of the charter plane taxiing slowly through glittering streams of water became the exclamation point on an undeniably unforgettable season.

Clockwise from top left: Coach John Calipari waves to the crowd as the ultimate 2012 NCAA Men's Basketball Champs return from the NCAA Elite Eight; UK men's basketball team bus makes its way through the crowd upon picking up the championship team; Players Anthony Davis and Darius Miller with the NCAA trophy; Crowd gathers; Water cannon salute for the returning champions.

2012

Top to bottom: Coach Rupp's 700 wins are celebrated; SEC basketball champs come home in 1969; Alabama Football Coach (and former UK Coach) Paul "Bear" Bryant arrives in 1973; banner predicts 1964 UK – Detroit football score.

THE QUEEN

Turning attention from those whose blood runs blue to actual bluebloods, Queen Elizabeth II, a noted breeder of Thoroughbred horses in Britain and winner of the 2013 Gold Cup at Royal Ascot, has flown in and out of Blue Grass Airport on four of her five visits to Kentucky.

A fascinating insight into the Queen's air transport has to do with what some call the "Queen Package." Since the United Kingdom does not have a jet dedicated to transporting the head of state and the head of government, when the Queen takes flight, a regular jet is pulled from the British Airways fleet, the seats are whisked out, and it is outfitted with furnishings and equipment "fit for a queen." At journey's end, the reverse occurs and the plane is released back to its duties as a commercial carrier.

Protocol stipulates very specific meeting and greeting etiquette. When the monarch's airplane landed at Blue Grass Airport on October 7, 1984, for her first visit, protocol was strictly observed right down to offering Her Majesty flowers. It had to be a child of a certain age or under, and certainly that child would be impeccably dressed for the occasion. One onlooker recalled that when the child came out bearing flowers, there were a couple of people not sure whether she was dressed impeccably enough. But the consensus was that she looked darling, and all in attendance wished they had been lucky enough to present a bouquet to the Queen.

Her Majesty wasn't the only one to experience true Bluegrass hospitality. Dismayed to learn that the Queen's pilots typically twiddle their thumbs in a hotel during the monarch's visit, Airport Board

Queen Elizabeth II on her third Lexington visit in 1989.

Above: Queen Elizabeth II gives a friendly wave. *Above right:* Flowers are traditionally presented to the Queen. *Bottom right:* The Royal Standard flies on the British Airways jet when the Queen arrives.

Chairman George Gumbert and his wife Skip did what good Bluegrass hosts always do: They threw a party, complete with Kentucky barbeque and invited all the fun people they knew – in this case local pilots – since both Gumberts were pilots. The air crew from the first royal visit had so much fun they told the second crew that they should hopefully expect to have that same party. Much goodwill and warm Kentucky hospitality were extended during the Queen's visits – and not just to the Queen.

POLITICS AS USUAL

In addition to crowned rulers, heads of state, including U.S. Presidents, Vice Presidents, First Ladies and presidential hopefuls, have typically visited Blue Grass Airport, at one stage or another in their political or private lives. Often, even before they are declared as candidates for office, their political parties make sure that their arrivals are "on the radar" and that supporters are there to greet them.

Senator John F. Kennedy addressed the graduating classes of the University of Kentucky and Transylvania University on October 8, 1960, a month before he became president. He was scheduled to return in December 1963 but, tragically, was assassinated the previous month. In a historical side note, President George H.W. Bush traveled to Lexington in October 1992 in the same Boeing 707 that had been designated *Air Force One* for JFK's ill-fated trip to Dallas in November 1963.

Robert F. Kennedy landed at Blue Grass Field on February 13, 1968, and traveled more than 200 miles on a two-day bus tour of Appalachia. Onlookers at Kennedy's arrival in Lexington would later tell of him spontaneously jumping up on a baggage cart to address the crowd gathered at the old terminal. The following week he announced his candidacy for president, but he died from an assassin's bullet some three months later. Senator Ted Kennedy would also visit in later years, and the focus was still on the grinding poverty of Appalachia, a troubling fact of life for many eastern Kentucky communities. Even the matriarch of the Kennedy clan, Rose Kennedy, came to Lexington with Lady Bird Johnson for a Democratic Party event.

A frequent visitor to Kentucky, the notoriously press-shy Richard Nixon kept members of the media at arm's

President Richard M. Nixon (center) arrives in 1971 to attend the funeral of Whitney Young, Jr., executive director of the National Urban League.

length. Locals still smile at the memory of a television news reporter, obviously denied all access to the great man, deciding to make Air Force One the story. Reporting live from the airport, he intoned slowly and dramatically, with the air of one covering an event of earth-shattering significance, "Air Force One is taxiing down the runway … and … we … have … lift-off!"

Some politicians attract less attention. An airport security official remembers asking himself, "Who is this?" as he escorted the gover-

Above left: Senator John F. Kennedy visits in 1960 shortly before becoming president. *Above right:* Senator Robert F. Kennedy visits in 1968. *Bottom left:* Senator Ted Kennedy is interviewed at the airport in 1969. *Bottom right:* Rose Kennedy (in white hat and sunglasses) visits for a Democratic fundraiser in the 1960s.

Above: President George H.W. Bush (waving) with Senator Mitch McConnell (far left). *Right:* President William Jefferson Clinton and First Lady Hillary Rodham Clinton.

nor of a small southern state arriving with little fanfare and an entourage of four to a waiting car. Months later, one William Jefferson Clinton was elected the 42nd President of the United States, thereby answering his question. It was the man who would be president.

THE RED-CARPET TREATMENT

When Airport Manager Logan Gray came to Blue Grass Field in 1963, he was full of ideas to make the airport more customer-friendly and to better reflect the warm hospitality and character of Lexington to the flying public. He was very enthusiastic and within the first few months had completed a number of relatively inexpensive but well-received changes ranging from new lobby décor, a "Welcome to the Home of the Wildcats" sign for UK fans, a new cocktail lounge and renovated restrooms (including a full-length mirror in the ladies room so women could "check their hemlines").

One of the most popular ideas Gray came up with was the idea of rolling out "the red carpet" for dignitaries. He planned to kick it off when hundreds of people came through the airport in August 1963 for a large

Senator and Mrs. John Glenn are accompanied by W.T. Young (middle) after receiving their Red-Carpet certificate in 1967.

Clockwise from top: Adlai Stevenson on a campaign stop in 1956; Crowds approach Eisenhower plane in 1956; Eisenhower motorcade leaves the airport for downtown Lexington; Governor Happy Chandler greets President and Mrs. Eisenhower; President and Mrs. Eisenhower are greeted by young ladies in "IKE" dresses and parasols.

Clockwise from top: John F. Kennedy (JFK), holding an official proclamation, arrives to campaign in October 1960; JFK deplanes upon arrival; JFK flanked by police officers; Robert F. Kennedy (RFK) greets well wishers in February 1968; RFK next to John Sherman Cooper (with hat in hand).

Clockwise from top: Governor Louie Nunn (left) with President and Mrs. Nixon in 1971; Lady Bird Johnson deplanes in 1964; Vice President Spiro Agnew in 1969; Alabama Governor George Wallace campaigns for president in 1968; Vice President hopeful Edmund Muskie with Lieutenant Governor Wendell Ford in 1968.

distillery meeting in Frankfort. His plan was to meet each of the big, chartered United Airlines DC-7s and assorted private planes with the roll out of a red carpet as passengers prepared to deplane. He also planned to have "a couple of girls in riding habits plus horses on the ramp" as visitors unloaded. What a memorable welcome that would be for first-time visitors to Kentucky – for anyone, really.

As word of his red-carpet treatment spread, one small problem arose. When some of these special guests returned home and talked about their red-carpet experience, people did not believe them. Gray quickly remedied that by presenting special guests with official certificates attesting that "Blue Grass Field...has conferred the honor of the Red Carpet..." and personalized it with their names and date of arrival. The scroll was embellished with a seal and a small section of real honest-to-goodness red carpet.

The red-carpet treatment was such a hit that ultimately every flight was met with a red carpet. The certificates were used only for VIPs, but the red carpet was rolled

Presenting flowers to Lydia Hodson, the newly crowned 1972 America's Junior Miss (in center), are Judge Robert Stephens, Mr. and Mrs. Earl Hodson, Bob Babbage, Lt. Gov. Julian Carroll and Mayor Foster Pettit.

out with such regularity that when the new jetways were first introduced, a woman actually refused to get off the plane because she just knew she wasn't in Lexington – there was no red carpet!

The red carpet wasn't the only way Gray could make people feel good about arriving in Lexington. The popularity of the red carpet soon led to the tradition of unrolling a blue-and-white carpet for special occasions to welcome Wildcats, UK dignitaries or Cats fans back to the Bluegrass.

THE POWER AND PERIL OF CELEBRITY

It is safe to say that hundreds of celebrities have come through Blue Grass Airport since it opened in 1946. The degree of celebrity might be debatable – would you consider Miss American Aviation, Queen of Tobaccoland and numerous Mountain Laurel Queens right up there along the likes of Liz Taylor, Charlize Theron and Dakota Fanning? It's all in the eye of the beholder. We certainly know that

Elizabeth Taylor is presented a bouquet by a young admirer when she and Montgomery Clift arrive in 1956 to begin production of *Raintree County*.

Clockwise from top: Vice President Joe Biden and his daughter Ashley arrive for the 2012 Vice Presidential Debate at Centre College; First Lady Barbara Bush in 1992; President George H.W. Bush visits in 1989; Vice President Al Gore in 1996. *Center:* Vice President Dan Quayle in 1992.

A- and B-list Hollywood
stars and directors have come
through the airport every
time a movie went on location in Lexington. Classic
films like *Raintree County*
released in 1957 brought
folks like the aforementioned
Liz Taylor and her co-stars,
Montgomery Clift, Eva Marie
Saint and Lee Marvin, to Lexington.

Kurt Russell

Dakota Fanning

Seabiscuit, starring Tobey Maguire (as jockey Red
Pollard), Jeff Bridges and Chris Cooper, was released
in 2003 to rave reviews. The movie also featured the
talents of two Hall of Fame jockeys – Gary Stevens,
who played handsome rider George Woolf (Red
Pollard's archrival), and Chris McCarron, who cho-
reographed the stunning War Admiral-Seabiscuit
match race sequences filmed at Keeneland.

Speaking of Keeneland
and celebrities, we would
be remiss not to mention
the amazing superstar jockey colony that migrates to
Keeneland every April and
October. The top jocks in
the nation gather there and
often jet off to ride at other
tracks as the race meet pro-
gresses only to fly back the next day to catch a few more
rides at Lexington's historic racetrack. From Kentucky
Derby winners Mike Smith, Jerry Bailey, Edgar Prado
and Lafitt Pincay, to name several, to Triple Crown
winners Ron Turcotte, Steve Cauthen and Jean Cruget,
they have all been frequent flyers at Blue Grass Airport.

What do George W. Bush, Adolph Rupp and the
heavy metal band, Mötley Crüe, have in common?
They are all extraordinarily punctual. When the Bush

Above: In this remarkable image from the filming of the match race in *Seabiscuit*, Gary Stevens (portraying George Woolf)
rides War Admiral while Chris McCarron (stunt double for Tobey Maguire as Red Pollard) tries to catch him on Seabiscuit.

Kurt Russell, Dakota Fanning, Kris Kristofferson
and Elizabeth Shue starred in *Dreamer*, which opened
nationwide in October 2005. A good portion of the
movie was filmed across the road from the airport
at Keeneland, which provided the backdrop for the
Breeders' Cup racing sequence.

entourage says showtime's at 5 p.m., you'd better be
there at 4:30 p.m. because they'd be gone and you'd be
playing catch-up. A similar story about Adolph Rupp
goes that for a 7 p.m. departure, it was Rupp's habit
to board the team bus sometime around 6:30 p.m.
Without looking around to see who might or might

• • • You learned pretty quickly that on time, in Rupp's book, was unpardonably late • • •

airborne in "sixx" minutes or less – a nod to Nikki Sixx, base guitarist and co-founder along with drummer Tommy Lee, of the band.

An area actor and special effects technician remembers realizing with a shock that a dispirited figure in a white suit, pink tie, white shoes, pink socks and his trademark wavy shoulder length hair, wrangling luggage at the airport, was Herbert Khaury, aka Tiny Tim of *Tiptoe Through The Tulips*, fame. And in the "who couldn't help but notice category," the owner of a local research firm reports being greatly distracted by the sight of wrestler-actor André the Giant trying in vain to squeeze his 7-foot-4, 500-pound frame into a rental car outside the terminal.

Rabid fans will do anything to get close to their idols, and a local disc jockey displayed remarkable chutzpah to do so with Bruce Springsteen. Knowing "The Boss" was scheduled to perform in the area, the DJ called Springsteen's publicist, introduced himself as representing a local radio station (failing to mention that its format was Country), and offered to put together a welcoming party at Blue Grass Airport.

Coach Adolph Rupp is greeted by a happy crowd after a win over Tennessee in March 1970.

not be on board, he would settle in his seat and say, "Kick 'er doc." And off they would go. You learned pretty quickly that on time, in Rupp's book, was unpardonably late.

Others recall the pilot of a private plane ferrying Mötley Crüe to and from a gig at Rupp Arena, leaping into bionic action when a phone call signaled the band's imminent approach for departure. Seconds later, a limo screeched to a halt by the plane, the World's Most Notorious Rock Band hopped aboard and was

The publicist gave him the flight information (even legends flew commercial in the 1980s) and at the appointed time, the DJ was there to meet the flight, bearing aloft a limo sign that said SPRINGSTEEN. "The Boss" and the Big Man, Clarence Clemons, had actually settled into the back seat of the jock's car when an irate publicist hurried up to the car and foiled the plan. For years afterwards, the DJ was heard to lament, "I actually had 'The Boss' in my car, man … "

A ROYAL WELCOME IS ALWAYS THE GOAL

Politicians, sports teams, foreign heads of state, musical groups, actors and actresses, all have two things in common: fame and impact. Fame is a given. Be it the Queen of England, Bruce Springsteen, POTUS (that's President of the United States for you non-security types!) or the UK Wildcats, fans want to be able to see their heroes and perhaps collect an autograph or two.

What a lot of people do not realize is that these arrivals have a significant impact on the airport and its operations. Each dignitary visit is beset with its own unique security, transportation, logistical and operational requirements.

Airport staff must work closely with the dignitary's staff to develop plans that facilitate a safe visit that doesn't disrupt normal airport business.

Logistics

All logistics associated with diplomatic arrivals must be coordinated with fixed-base operator TAC Air and airline representatives. This includes determining where the aircraft will be parked; unloading and reloading any cargo or luggage; fueling and servicing; and then providing access for caterers to empty, clean and re-supply the galleys.

Security Plans

Airport staff must coordinate and partner with the U.S. Secret Service, local and state public safety departments, U.S. Customs and Border Patrol (when applicable) and the Transportation Security Administration for a safe and efficient arrival and departure.

Ground Transportation

Ground transportation must be arranged to meet dignitaries planeside and then transport them to their destination along with any cargo or luggage.

Protocols

Protocols for an "expected and proper" greeting must be followed. This includes coordination of a planeside greeting and receiving line, which often involves state and local public officials, special guests and any close acquaintances. During a royal visit, protocol typically includes inviting a child to greet the royal family member.

Airport Executive Director Michael Gobb with daughter Kirsten and wife Kris greet Queen Elizabeth II and Prince Philip in 2007.

If you are envisioning a scene of controlled chaos, don't be fooled. Every facet of the arrival has been planned from the moment the aircraft appears on the radar to the moment it leaves Blue Grass Airport and heads for its next stop. In fact, the arrival, though the culminating act, plays but a small role in the "behind-the-scenes" work and effort that goes into a safe and proper "welcome" for any major dignitary to the city of Lexington and the Commonwealth of Kentucky.

LAS VEGAS CONNECTIONS

Longtime Lexington residents will remember when the answer to "Doing anything this weekend?" was often, "A little gambling in Vegas." These junkets still happen, but not with the frequency that they did in the 1980s and 1990s.

Dan Chandler (middle) and Happy Chandler (left) share a root beer with friend Ken Hart. Lexington had many popular junkets to Las Vegas when Dan Chandler was at Caesars Palace.

Those pre-9/11 weekend junkets to Reno, Vegas or Tunica were all-round easy. On a Thursday afternoon, passengers would pull up and park and walk their suitcase over to a small side gate. They would hand it, and their ticket, over to an airline employee (who probably knew them by name) and stroll right on board. In a few hours they would be placing their first wager in the casino of their choice. By Sunday night, they would be leaving the Blue Grass Airport parking lot for the short drive home, richer or wiser.

Someone who literally embodied the "LexVegas" connection in the Bluegrass was Dan Chandler who grew up in Versailles, Kentucky. As a boy, this youngest son of Kentucky Governor A.B. "Happy" Chandler, rubbed shoulders with the likes of John F. Kennedy and recalled Brooklyn Dodgers owner Branch Rickey flying in to Blue Grass Field from New York on the team's Beechcraft to meet with then-Commissioner of Baseball Chandler at the cabin he used as an office on the family's property in Versailles. The purpose of the trip was to discuss with Commissioner Chandler the plan to integrate Major League Baseball with the then unknown Triple-A player, Jackie Robinson.

As a young man, Dan Chandler mostly "rode the pine" on Adolf Rupp's 1953 and 1954 basketball teams. As an adult, he became the casino host who socialized with the likes of Frank Sinatra at Caesars Palace and is reputed to have raised the expression "My man!" to an art form in Las Vegas gaming circles. An outrageous, outsized personality with a fabulous sense of humor, Chandler would be hired and fired by Caesars Palace more often than Billy Martin by George Steinbrenner. He liked to say he started at the top and spent his life working his way to the middle.

BOND ... JAMES BOND

It is not surprising that two of the most famous no-shows at Blue Grass Airport happen to be associated with the worlds of film and music. One shaken, not stirred. The other, all shook up.

In the 1964 film version of Ian Fleming's *Goldfinger*, CIA Agent Felix Leiter updates James Bond's boss, M, on the suave secret agent's whereabouts.

"It's about 007, sir. We've picked up his homer signal – it's monitored into Friendship Airport Baltimore where he's just landed. He came in on a private jet, ex Geneva. Registered to our old friend, Auric Goldfinger. Their flight plan gives Blue Grass Field as their final destination."

Obviously no one bothered to inform the crew, because when the Bond-bearing Lockheed JetStar touches down, it's not at Blue Grass Field as Leiter reported, but at Northolt, a Royal Air Force station at South Ruislip, six miles north of London Heathrow Airport.

Northolt, we are informed by a documentary on the making of *Goldfinger*, is the longest continually operating Royal Air Force station in Britain and home to Fire Command No. 11 during the Battle of Britain. After the war it became the busiest airport in Europe, until operations were transferred to the new London Airport at Heathrow.

The only "Kentucky" scenes actually shot in Kentucky were the exteriors of Fort Knox and of Goldfinger's caravan approaching the depository. All others were filmed in Miami. Don't be fooled by the shot with a Kentucky Fried Chicken sign conspicuously in the background.

THE KING IS DEAD

You know you are in the South when people remember where they were when they learned that Elvis Presley had died. Perhaps the fact that he was scheduled to perform in less than a week as the first-ever concert in Lexington Center's Rupp Arena made the news of his death poignant enough that it was announced on the public address system at Blue Grass Field. Employees and travelers stopped in their tracks when they heard the shocking news on August 16, 1977. With Elvis' death, Lawrence Welk became the first act to perform in Rupp Arena.

OUR APPROACH IS DIFFERENT

Paul Harvey might have coined the phrase America's "most beautiful air approach" talking about flying into Blue Grass Field, but it seems appropriate that a Lexingtonian, who had been involved with construction projects at the airport, gets to tell "the rest of the story."

Returning from a trip to Dallas one afternoon, one "born and bred" central Kentuckian recollected playing impromptu tour guide for two ladies making their maiden trip to Lexington after the new terminal was built. In Gene Van Meter's own words:

"We were nearing Lexington when I told them to watch to their left, and when the plane dipped its wing for a turn toward the airport, they would see the world-famous Calumet Farm, all trimmed in red with white fences. Then when we leveled off, look to my side for Buckram Farm … Finally I told them they would see Keeneland Race Course on the right, just before

we were to land … As we leveled off after the turn, as always, there seemed to be a few minutes of quietly floating along before the pilots lowered the wheels and flaps. I was hoping someone would come on the intercom of the public address system and say, "Welcome to Kentucky. Welcome to the Bluegrass … the most beautiful place in the world. Welcome to the new Blue Grass Airport!"

It's been many years since the first planeload of people stepped off a Delta Air Lines 21-passenger Douglas DC-3 onto Blue Grass Field in 1946. In that time, the airport has seen the comings and goings of musicians, moguls and magnates, of crowned heads, heads of state, head bangers and head cases, of jocks, jockeys and jet-setters, of actors and athletes, preachers, prisoners and politicians, winners and wannabes, joyful and sorrowful, restrained and unrestrained, solo or with entourage, over the top and under the radar. And it's a fairly safe bet that they never tire of seeing America's "most beautiful air approach" as they float serenely from the sky to land in the heart of the Bluegrass. ✈

PILOTS TRACK THEIR LIVES BY THE NUMBER OF HOURS IN THE AIR, AS IF ANY OTHER KIND OF TIME ISN'T WORTH NOTING.

– MICHAEL PARFIT, *SMITHSONIAN* MAGAZINE, MAY 2000

PRIVATE AVIATION
Dawn of a Modern Airport

BY PATTI NICKELL

When Canadian aviator J.A.D. McCurdy flew his Curtiss biplane into Lexington for the Blue Grass Fair in 1910, he became the first in a long line of non-commercial airline pilots who would make Lexington aviation history.

By the time John Hancock of Wilkes-Barre, Pennsylvania arrived, in his autogyro aircraft in 1931 to attend the Kentucky Derby, private pilots were landing with such frequency at Halley Field that a $5 registration fee would be imposed upon them later that year.

To say that the city's private aviation history has been a rich one is an understatement. Starting with a *Spirit of St. Louis* lookalike piloted by none other than Charles Lindbergh, then fast-forwarding to Air Force One and the Concorde SST – they have all landed here. Queen Elizabeth II has flown in on a Royal Air Force jet several times and the ruler of Dubai, Sheikh Mohammed bin Rashid Al Maktoum, owner of Darley America and Gainsborough Farms (Bluegrass-area Thoroughbred farms), regularly lands his private jumbo jets at Blue Grass Airport.

In the years between McCurdy and the Sheikh, an illustrious group of private aviators and their passengers have flown the friendly skies of the Commonwealth, from American presidents to members of royalty; from stars of the silver screen to superstars of the racetrack. When Triple Crown winner Secretariat arrived at the airport to take up residence at Claiborne Farm, he was welcomed by 150 fans, despite the

best efforts of owner Penny Chenery to keep his arrival time a secret.

It seems that you didn't even have to be real to enjoy a private ride into Lexington. Take James Bond's fictional nemesis Auric Goldfinger in the 1964 film for example – on his way to wreak havoc at Fort Knox, the arch villain's private jet lands at Blue Grass Field (also fictional since the airfield pretending to be in Kentucky is actually in England).

LEXINGTON LEADS THE WAY IN PRIVATE AVIATION

In terms of private aviation, it was the "barnstorming" daredevils of the 1920s and 1930s who first captured the public's imagination as they traveled around the country thrilling spectators with their gravity-defying feats. These rakish aviators were the heroes of the day.

The golden years of private aviation may have begun in the Roaring Twenties, but they reached their zenith in the years following World War II.

The war was the catalyst that led to many of the innovations in flying. In addition, a large group of young men had been trained as pilots during the war, and when it was over they wanted to continue flying and began searching for an outlet.

They found it in private aviation. The two decades between 1950 and 1970 were a boom period for the manufacture of small aircraft. There was an abundance of aluminum, which prior to the war, had not been used significantly in industry, and the military had already completed the necessary research and development. In addition, unused military planes were available for conversion to civilian use.

The private sector took what the military had already developed and then made adaptations as necessary. A Cessna today looks the same as those early planes, with the exception of having a more fuel-efficient engine and more sophisticated avionics.

In its early days, private aviation was considered little more than a "sporting activity for the rich," along the same lines as polo, sailing and horse racing. It was the use of private aircraft for the latter, which made Lexington a litmus test for the rest of the country.

In Lexington, the equine industry was the nexus dominated by affluent people with the money to buy a plane and the time and resources to train as pilots. A private plane made it easier for

Above: The elegant interior of the private plane of Mrs. Warren Wright (Lucille Parker). Mrs. Wright is offered a helping hand as she exits the airplane.
Opposite page: Blue Grass Field was swarming with general aviation aircraft in this photo from 1950. Note the proximity of Versailles Road in the background.

them to travel around looking at horses, and charters were the easiest way to bring their purchases back to the farms.

By the early 1960s, private aviation's impetus had shifted from the thrill of sport to the efficiency it brought to business travel. Fuel was cheap, and Lexington's moderate climate was conducive to year-

round flying. Investing in a company plane proved to be a good business strategy. CEOs who had business operations in three Kentucky cities could make the rounds and still be back home in time for dinner.

By the mid 1960s, private aviation had found its niche. While all forms of aviation have experienced cyclical slumps due to economic factors, private aviation has not seen the extreme ups and downs that deregulation brought to commercial aviation. Personal and business aviation has maintained a solid base of support and today accounts for nearly 65 percent of the operations at Blue Grass Airport.

FIXED-BASE OPERATORS ARRIVE

The term fixed-base operator (FBO) is one that remains largely unfamiliar to most of the nonflying public, but its origins date back to the years immediately following World War I. In 1918, civil aviation in this country was largely un-regulated and transient pilots flying inexpensive military surplus aircraft often found them-selves using farm land as makeshift landing strips, hence, the term "barnstormers."

These pilots, en-dowed with a touch of P.T. Barnum show-manship, were the 20th-century equiv-alent of the Wild West medicine show. They put on flight demonstrations and air shows for the delighted townspeople. In the wake of their success came a cadre of equally nomadic mechanics and flight instructors to support their efforts. Like their circus brethren, they moved from town to town, airstrip to airstrip.

That nomadic existence came to an end with the 1926 passage of the Air Commerce Act resulting in more stringent requirements for the licensing of pilots and aircraft maintenance workers and stricter training regulations for student pilots. What had previously been a business model founded on tran-sience, now evolved into one dependent upon "fixed bases" as aviators settled down in one location with their planes.

Today, these FBOs are essential to the success of any airport. Functioning much as a service station or dealership does for automobiles, FBOs provide a range of aviation services – from providing fuel to emergency maintenance, from aircraft rentals to the sale of vari-ous aircraft parts.

Bohmer Flying Services became the first FBO at Blue Grass Field in 1945, setting up business in the Charles Lindbergh hangar (so named because it had once housed his plane).

Bohmer was joined by Blue Grass Airmotive and Superior Flying Service for a period of time and was followed by Van Dusen Air Incorporated, a worldwide dis-tributor of parts and supplies for the aviation industry. One of Van Dusen's divisions, Air Associates, fig-ured prominently in the movement of horses by air from Lexington to destinations as far away as England, France and Germany.

Various other FBOs and rental/char-ter companies have come and gone at the airport: Lexington Air Taxi, Buckeye Air Service, Sprite Flite Jets, Page-Avjet, which merged with Butler Aviation to

This 1931 photo from Lafayette Studios archives shows a visiting autogyro at what must have been Halley Field. Private aviation was a showcase for great diversity in aircraft.

Blue Grass Airmotive joined Bohmer Flying Services shortly after Blue Grass Field opened. They both served as fixed-base operators.

become Signature Aviation, and Southern Jet, operated by Josephine Abercrombie, owner of Pin Oak Stud Farm.

Warren "Bill" Terry, who developed the Griffin Gate Marriott Resort and owned Coca-Cola bottling plants and Domino Stud Farm, started one of Blue Grass Airport's most colorful FBOs. According to his friend Jack Baugh, Terry hated to fly – he refused to fly – often driving an entire day to avoid having to get on a plane.

Baugh, who owned Almahurst Farm, had gone to Du Quoin, Illinois, to attend the Hambletonian Stakes, harness racing's premier event, and Terry had gone to inspect some bottling plants. Baugh had flown it in about 45 minutes, while it had taken Terry five hours to drive there. The next day, an emergency called Terry back to Lexington early. He reluctantly asked Baugh if he could fly him back to Lexington. Baugh, an accomplished military and private pilot, told him that he would not only fly him to Lexington but would wait and take him back to Du Quoin. After the quick roundtrip Terry said, "You know, I'm going to buy an airplane."

As Baugh said, "Well, Bill Terry was Bill Terry, and not only did he buy an airplane, he bought a Learjet and got a crew and created the charter company called Sprite Flite Jets – as in Coca-Cola's Sprite product. And he brought in a partner, George Evans." Eventually, Baugh bought the charter company from Terry and Evans, and created an FBO at Blue Grass Airport, but kept the name Sprite Flite. The facility he built to house the FBO later became the home of the Aviation Museum of Kentucky.

Following Southern Jet, TAC Air arrived at Blue Grass Airport in 1996. In 2010, TAC Air unveiled a dazzling new 12,000-square-foot terminal and 45,000 square feet of hangar space. This expansion allows them to seamlessly handle up to 250 private aircraft arrivals per day and refuel both commercial and private aircraft with up to 60,000 gallons of fuel on the busiest of days, such as during the 2010 World Equestrian Games.

AT YOUR SERVICE

With the continuing importance of general aviation to the airport's bottom line, a variety of features have been implemented or improved regularly. The most recent upgrade was the relocation and construction of Runway

Jack Baugh was a private aviation enthusiast before he became a fighter pilot for the Air Force. He purchased the FBO Sprite Flite Jets from Warren Terry and partners.

9-27, more commonly known as the crosswind runway.

The 4,000-foot runway, used by private and corporate aircraft, enhances safety conditions when winds are not in the prevailing direction and allows light general aviation traffic to be separated from commercial operations. The relocation of the runway also allowed for increased space for private aircraft parking and hangar development.

During the ribbon-cutting ceremony in 2010, Governor Steve Beshear spoke of how the new runway would not only enhance aircraft safety but would benefit the state's economic development efforts.

"Improvements that enhance the safety and efficiency of air travel for business purposes are an important part of supporting Kentucky's economic development efforts," said Beshear.

The Federal Aviation Administration, Kentucky Department of Aviation and Blue Grass Airport shared

> **66** *General aviation comprises nearly 65 percent of the operations*
> *at Blue Grass Airport and serves as a major economic*
> *engine and vital resource to our community.* **99**
>
> – Airport Board Chairman J. Robert Owens

the $27 million price tag for the runway relocation.

Private aviation also benefits from the ability to clear U.S. Customs in Lexington when flying internationally. The airport has been able to provide this service since 1990. It is a service that private aircraft owners and local corporations appreciate and have come to expect from Blue Grass Airport. It is a tremendous boon to central Kentucky's international business community.

Former Airport Board Member David Trapp chats with Governor Steve Beshear (seated) at the dedication of crosswind Runway 9-27.

COFFEE OR TEA?

Today's commercial flyers, lucky to get a choice of pretzels or peanuts, would be thrilled at the prospect of a meal in the sky on a well-stocked private jet. As with other aspects of private aviation, catering has undergone changes since its inception.

Kate Savage, owner of Bleu Ribbon Hospitality, has been catering private jets for more than 20 years.

During this time she has provided passengers with everything from floral arrangements and assorted cheese trays to dog biscuits and special seat harnesses for pampered pooches.

"In the early days, catering orders were pretty general – at least as far as food was concerned," said Savage. "The crew would place an order, and we would fill it; passengers never specified how many shrimp had to be in a cocktail."

That changed as larger and more sophisticated private airplane operations started coming in to Lexington. It also was a reflection of changing times as owners realized that when it came to catering, the old adage "the sky's the limit," was out the window – just about anything was possible related to food and beverage options when flying.

Not unlike favorite restaurants, caterers develop loyal followings with lots of repeat business.

Below: Visiting 747s from the United Arab Emirates

There are annual cycles in Lexington that make certain private aviation travelers frequent flyers to the Bluegrass. Ballgames, Keeneland racing, Thoroughbred sales and the Kentucky Derby keep general aviation operations hopping, and big business fills in the gaps between those iconic seasons.

With this kind of regularity, caterers get to know their frequent customers' preferences and can often anticipate their menu requests. They are prepared when the calls come in and are quite literally ready to cater to the whims of their clients.

Customers, their representatives or TAC Air typically make catering arrangements. According to Savage, orders can be as diverse as simple snacks to multiple-course gourmet meals and are based on the quantity of food needed or a specific number of people.

She says that if 18 to 20 people are expected to be on board, she and her staff prepare many times that amount of food, which can range from curries and sushi to Spanish omelets and beef stroganoff, all of which is delivered in bulk.

"We cook the food, and then deliver the components required for each menu item in large aluminum foils (disposable pans) for the crew to assemble on board," she said. The service doesn't begin or end there. If it is an international flight, it is the caterer's responsibility to clean out every morsel of food that came in on the airplane and send it to be destroyed. This is a U.S. Customs regulation that must be strictly enforced.

Occasionally, plans change, and the caterer has to have the flexibility to adjust menus, time frames and attitudes. If the flight is delayed an extra day or two – no problem – even if it means that plans and dishes are scrapped so that only the freshest foods are served.

FRACTIONAL OWNERSHIP

Few people have the financial resources to purchase their own jet, and those who do, realize that the purchase of the aircraft is just part of the total investment. Fuel, maintenance, hangar rental, insurance and flight crew are significant operating costs that figure into the equation. A better alternative for those who want the luxury of a private plane but not the total financial commitment is a concept known as fractional ownership.

Launched in 1986, NetJets allows customers to buy a "share" of a plane by pro-rating the price from the market price of a full aircraft. A share entitles an owner guaranteed access – based upon a certain number of hours or days annually. Access is guaranteed to the aircraft type that the owner bought into, or better, if that aircraft type is not available – often with just a day's notice of the owner's intent to fly.

For this flexibility and the prestige that goes with it, owners pay a monthly maintenance fee and an occupied hourly operating rate (generally charged only when an owner or guest is on board).

Other advantages range from five-star service (an onboard concierge and food and beverage choices

Supplies are loaded onto a private aircraft via lift truck for the trip home.

A terrific assortment of private jets in the general aviation area at Blue Grass Airport.

tailored to individual flights) to the boarding process itself. With aircraft located just beyond the TAC Air terminal, boarding is easy with no lines or hassles.

At Blue Grass Airport, whether the client is flying on a personal jet or is participating in fractional ownership, they will be using the world-class services provided by TAC Air. Among the amenities offered by TAC Air is a beautiful terminal including a high-definition movie theater, exercise facilities, sleeping quarters for pilots, conference room and an art gallery featuring works by local artists. Aircraft get coddled, too, with maintenance service, refueling, de-icing, hangar space or whatever else may be necessary to assist the general aviation community.

Aero-Tech's Charles Monette

offer courses accepted as an FAA Industry Training Standard.

"I grew up at the airport where I was the kid in pigtails sweeping hangar floors and washing airplanes," McMahon said in an interview with *Mentor* magazine in 2009, the same year she was chosen by industry and FAA leaders as the FAA National Flight Instructor of the Year.

Monette, who began his aviation career as a radar controller in the U.S. Air Force and opened Aero-Tech in 1971, was his wife's first flight instructor. "I started teaching her when she was 15, and she soloed for the first time on her 16th birthday," Monette recalled.

The couple married in 2006 after a 25-year courtship and continue to operate Aero-Tech together. "I didn't want to rush things," McMahon joked.

TEACHING THE BASICS – AND THEN SOME

From the beginning, the Lexington community embraced aviation, and services supporting private aviation were no exception. Support businesses began popping up with regularity. One of these aviation-related companies at Blue Grass Airport, Aero-Tech, Inc., owned by Charles Monette and his wife Arlynn McMahon, became the first traditional flight school in the nation to

ON THE RECRUITING TRAIL

Lexington proved a fertile field for aviation. In addition to dignitaries and celebrities flying in for visits and the races and Thoroughbreds being shuttled around the world, the University of Kentucky (UK) and its athletic teams have a variety of aviation needs.

NCAA policy prohibits anything other than league-sanctioned charter flights for its student-athletes. When Rick Pitino was basketball coach and the team's official plane was out of service prior to an away game, NCAA policy was tested. There was no lack of private planes ready and willing to transport the team, but before Pitino could accept one of the offers he had to call Sandy Bell, the university's director of compliance, to contact the NCAA and make sure it was within the rules.

While NCAA policy is strictly enforced if student-athletes are traveling, no such rules exist for

Coach John Calipari prepares to board R.J. Corman's private jet as he heads to Kentucky for an interview. He became the head coach for the University of Kentucky men's basketball team in April 2009.

wooing potential coaches. In fact, railroad executive R.J. Corman volunteered the loan of his plane when UK was courting men's basketball Coach John Calipari.

The first time Corman took his plane to Memphis to pick up Calipari for a visit to Lexington, the coach mistook him for the pilot. Corman, known for his sly sense of humor and understated manner, got a chuckle out of it and didn't inform him otherwise. He enjoyed Calipari's friendly and open conversation with the "pilot" sent to pick him up and they became friends. Since then, Corman has been called upon to pick up the latest UK recruit – football Coach Mark Stoops – when he was invited to Lexington to interview and ultimately land the head coaching job.

GROUP CHARTER FLIGHTS

While not a private airplane per se, a commercial charter is the next best thing for a group on the go.

UK Wildcat sports teams may not have been able to revel in private air travel, but "Big Blue" fans certainly could. A chartered commercial L1011, on par with a 747 and capable of holding 500 passengers, was on hand to take "Cat" fans to the Great Alaska Shootout, and similar flights have taken them to Maui, New Orleans, Puerto Rico, San Antonio and New York City to watch the UK men's basketball team play over the years.

Commercial charters at Blue Grass Airport have widely varying clientele, transporting everyone from Commerce Lexington members on their annual Leadership Visit, to prisoners on the routine prison transfers to and from Lexington's federal correctional facility. Regarding the numerous prison transfer flights, which average approximately one per week, airport staff observe, "We were calling it Con Air before the Nicholas Cage movie."

One of the largest differences between commercial charters and private flights, other than the size of the aircraft, is that these flights can arrive and depart at the main terminal rather than the private aviation facilities. Often, commercial airlines also operate group charters.

IT TAKES A VILLAGE

Former First Lady Hillary Clinton may have been referring to raising children when she famously remarked that "it takes a village," but the same phrase could be used to characterize the private aviation community.

Often likened to the "backside" – the part of a track rarely seen by race-goers – private aviation represents its own culture, separate and apart from the world of commercial flyers.

Blue Grass Airport's private aviation community is made up of colorful characters who work, play and, of course, fly together. Many of those colorful characters are women, as private aviation is where most of them got their flying start.

One of the most colorful is Betty Moseley, who, unlike most private pilots, didn't learn to fly until she was 42. Just a few years later, in 1971, she represented Kentucky in the 25th anniversary of the Powder Puff Derby, a transcontinental air race for female pilots.

In her 1969 Piper Cherokee, the *Smitten Kitten*, Moseley competed in North America's largest and longest speed race for women – from Calgary, Canada, to Baton Rouge, Louisiana, and in the process, made history.

"We were on the next to last leg of the race, and I got a May Day call," recalled Moseley. "It was the Louisiana representative, and she was in trouble."

"We were 50 miles out of Little Rock getting ready to do our flyby, and she said she was lost, low on fuel and going to crash," Moseley continued. "So, I told her a little fib – that we had passed the [landmark she refer-

American Bonanza Club fly-in at Blue Grass Airport in September 2008.

> ***I really wanted to bring glamour to flying. I could wear my fur coat and white gloves and check my oil and not get any dirt on me.*** 99

– Betty Moseley, Lexington Pilot

Both Greenwood "Cokie" Cocanougher (above) and Betty Moseley (top) flew in the Powder Puff Derby.

enced] but that I would slow up and help her. We did get her down at an Air Force base. She didn't finish, but she was safe and that was all that mattered to me."

For her valor, Moseley was asked to serve on the women's advisory committee for civil aviation and was enshrined in the Kentucky Aviation Hall of Fame.

Moseley may have 2,300 hours of accident-free piloting under her belt and knows the mechanics of her plane equally as well as any man, but she still refers to herself as a "girly-girl."

"I really wanted to bring glamour to flying. I could wear my fur coat and white gloves and check my oil and not get any dirt on me," the former model said proudly. "My first flight after I got my pilot's

TAC AIR
Taking General Aviation To New Heights

A fixed-base operator (FBO) is a critical component of any airport. TAC Air, a division of Truman Arnold Companies and FBO at Blue Grass Airport since 1996, chose to build its flagship operation in Lexington – from the ground up – using local architects and contractors.

TAC Air's $11.5 million state-of-the-art general aviation terminal and hangar space is the perfect platform for serving the needs of those traveling on private and corporate aircraft from the moment they arrive until they are ready to depart. TAC Air provides fueling and de-icing services for all private and commercial aircraft flying out of Blue Grass Airport.

TAC Air also serves as the gateway to Lexington for the area's major corporations, business executives, dignitaries and those attending special events.

Voted the top FBO chain twice by *Professional Pilot* magazine, Texas-based TAC Air, with 14 locations, is completely attuned to what people are looking for in the 21st century. Their 12,000-square-foot limestone-faced building offers a high-definition theater, fitness facilities, conference rooms, art gallery and gift shop.

Truman Arnold Companies committed to the new facility to better serve its customers and because of the volume of aircraft it handles – over 1,000 per month. Dedicated to serving the region's business aviation needs, TAC Air also demonstrated strong support

Everything is optimized for a world-class customer experience.

for the local aviation community by making a significant contribution to the Aviation Museum of Kentucky.

Serving as FBO for the airport, they have mastered the unique operational challenges associated with the hosting of dignitaries and the cycle of local events, including Keeneland race meets, Thoroughbred auction sales, the Rolex Kentucky Three-Day Event, University of Kentucky sports events and the Kentucky Derby.

Community leaders understand that maintaining an impressive presence on the general aviation side of Blue Grass Airport is the best advertising Lexington can do to support economic development efforts. It's hard to imagine a more welcoming first impression to the Bluegrass.

TAC Air's state-of-the art facilities are impressive inside and out. A behind-the-scenes glimpse of the flight planning room.

license was to Dallas, where a friend and I went shopping at Neiman Marcus. "Would you believe the bill beat us home?"

Moseley reflects on the sense of community that has always been a part of private aviation at the airport.

"I've had so many wonderful parties out here in my hangar," she said. "I even have china that matches the aircraft."

On another occasion, the mood wasn't quite so festive. Recalling Lexington's power outage during an ice storm in 2003, she said, "I came out to the hangar with my cats, and we all cuddled together on one small bed. It was so cold, but we felt safe … just like home."

While Betty Moseley was middle-aged before becoming enamored with flying, Mary Jo Moloney fell in love with aviation as a teenager. The daughter of Dr. George Gumbert, who served on the airport's board

of directors for 22 years and was a co-founder of the Aviation Museum of Kentucky, Moloney had her first flying lesson at age 14 with a family friend. They flew from Louisville to Lexington.

Being a typical teenager, other interests distracted Moloney, and she didn't return to flying until the advanced age of 17.

"I got my license in the early 1980s, right here at Aero-Tech with Arlynn McMahon and Charlie Monette" said Moloney. "They prepared me very well."

A self-described "airport brat," she talked about how some kids grow up at a lake house or on a farm, but she grew up at Blue Grass Airport.

"This was our family's retreat," she said. "We were here in the evenings, in the summertime … basically most of the time."

Moloney reminisced about growing up when

Some general aviation enthusiasts fly aircraft without engines. These are called gliders or sailplanes. In its earliest days, Blue Grass Field was used for training glider pilots. This record-setting Sisu glider was donated to the National Air and Space Museum by Lexington's Jack Baugh.

Above left: A wide variety of private jets on the tarmac. *Above right:* Aircraft maintenance – both for commercial and general aviation aircraft – is a critical service. With more than 140 private aircraft based at Blue Grass Airport and many visiting aircraft, the airport's onsite partner Mustang Aviation provides service 24 hours per day.

Lexington was more of a small town and the airport was something of a novelty.

"We would come out as a family – my brother, my mother, my dad and me – and we would stop at the Starlight Drive-In on Stone Road and get fried chicken boxes and have a picnic at the T-hangars," she said. "We would just watch to see who was landing and who was taking off – this was entertainment to us.

Mary Jo Moloney

Jack Baugh

Moloney recalled "great airport moments" over the years – the 1978 NCAA basketball championship when thousands of fans converged at Blue Grass Airport to welcome home the victorious Wildcats; the visits by Queen Elizabeth and the Concorde.

"So many great memories," she said.

A LOVE OF FLYING

Jack Baugh began his love affair with aviation at an even earlier age than Moloney, building his first model airplane out of balsa wood at the advanced age of five. From there, he never looked back.

A native of Charlotte, North Carolina, Baugh learned to fly when he was 12 years old. He made his first flight to Lexington at age 14, when he accompanied his father, who was in the Standardbred business, to a harness race at the Red Mile trotting track.

Upon graduation from Duke University, Baugh joined the United States Air Force, eventually becoming a jet fighter pilot.

During his time as owner of fixed-base operator Sprite Flite Jets, he said he was privileged to meet a number of people who "helped to make the airport what it is today."

These were people such as Garvice Kincaid, founder of Central Bank and onetime owner of Lexington Airmotive; Wendell Murphy, an Air Force and private pilot, who had a congenital disease which would eventually leave him legally blind; and Bill Terry, from whom Baugh would buy Sprite Flite Jets.

"Wonderful people…all of them," Baugh said.

When asked what these people and all of the others who helped shape private aviation at Blue Grass Airport had in common, Baugh pondered for a moment and then said with a smile, "Love of aviation. Man has always watched the birds and envied their ability to fly."

CHANGE:
The Only Constant in Aviation

BY CELESTE LEWIS

While many industries have experienced peaks and valleys in their life cycles, they seem almost tame when compared to the wild ups and downs (start-ups … acquisitions … mergers … bankruptcies!) found in the commercial airline industry. Blue Grass Airport has not been immune to the upheavals and difficulties in an industry besieged by unpredictable business climates. The one constant in commercial aviation? Change.

The cumulative impact of airline deregulation combined with recessions, terrorism and escalating fuel costs have driven most major commercial carriers to embrace mergers or even seek bankruptcy protection as tactics for survival at some point during the last 30 years. In the wake of major changes, smaller, leaner airlines carved out their territories and regional service became the order of the day.

These national forces played out locally, and Blue Grass Airport would see dozens of route and carrier changes while dealing with its own brand of unprecedented turmoil: the highly charged debate over its own expansion.

Facilities and runway planning and implementation, which routinely take place during a 10-year window, challenge airports to keep pace with developing technology. By the time airport issues are studied, plans developed, recommendations approved and funded, the needs have more than likely changed, sometimes dramatically.

THE EARLY DAYS

Aviation evolved relatively quickly, with technology making giant strides during each of the two World Wars. By the time the first iteration of what would become Blue Grass Airport came to be in the mid 1940s, the strongest of the players in the commercial airline industry were beginning to assert their dominance. Delta, Eastern and Piedmont grew quickly and looked to Lexington, with its universities and established agri-businesses (primarily tobacco, distilled spirits, horse breeding and racing), as an attractive regular stop for their flights between larger destinations.

In the 1960s and 1970s, the airlines were booming. Delta, United, Pan Am, Continental, Trans World Airlines (TWA), American and Piedmont grew into giants that took aviation into the jet age. The city of Lexington and surrounding counties continued to grow. As was happening all across America, people came to depend on the routes and services of a handful of carriers to provide for

Piedmont enjoyed great success in the 1960s and 1970s.

“ IF THERE IS NO STRUGGLE, THERE IS NO PROGRESS. ”

— FREDERICK DOUGLASS

Above left: Airline representatives and experts from the U.S. Bureau of Air Commerce meet in 1937 before the creation of the Civil Aeronautics Authority (CAA). *Above right:* Members of the new CAA take oath of office in 1938.

their travel. Despite ever-expanding needs in the business sector, businesses tended to rely on the same few airlines to transport people and freight as never before.

From its inception, the federal Civil Aeronautics Board (CAB) regulated the airlines. The CAB regulated the cost of fares, routes and market entry of new players in the airline industry. In the early days,

There were concerns and discussion about the need to introduce market forces into the system and phase out government regulation – which became known as "airline deregulation." The Federal Aviation Agency (later renamed the Federal Aviation Administration or FAA) was established and would remain in place to govern safety issues in the industry.

Above left: New Air Safety Board Members Col. Sumpter Smith and Thomas Hardin in 1938. *Above middle:* Edward J. Noble (shown) assumed duties as chairman of the newly created CAA in August 1938. The torch was passed to Robert H. Hinckley in 1939. *Above right:* A member of CAA (seated) is welcomed by Chairman Hinckley in 1939.

the U.S. Postal Service often determined airline routes based on contracts for carrying airmail, not passengers. The industry was considered a public utility and therefore totally under the purview of the federal government.

Over many decades the CAB became cumbersome and slow to respond to the fast-paced airline industry.

From the very beginning, there were advocates and opponents of deregulation. Advocates argued that regulation had outlived its usefulness, that more competition would be beneficial and that smaller markets would be better served by commuter carriers. Opponents maintained that regulation had served the public well, that carriers would undercut each others'

fares and drive the smaller airlines
out of business, that havoc would
be created for airport operators
because of surplus capacity or
diminished demand, that airlines
would place conservative aircraft
orders due to uncertainty and that
smaller markets might lose their
service altogether.

Ultimately, the advocates for deregulation won the battle, although
some would later maintain that in
doing so, they lost the war to improve airline service for the public.

DEREGULATION

The Airline Deregulation Act
of 1978 was a game changer.
Senator Ted Kennedy was the
co-sponsor and champion of the

During WWII, volunteer plotters push pips and standards into place on this early aircraft tracking system while representatives of the CAA, Army and Navy look on.

cause. Although he was later quoted as saying he re-
gretted deregulation, Kennedy was its driver in the
Senate and managed to bring it to the Senate floor as
a bipartisan measure during the Ford administration.
He was then instrumental in getting the measure
passed into law during the Carter administration.

The effect was immediate. Where there had been
only a limited number of trunk airlines, suddenly there
were new players entering the game. The larger airlines
went to a "hub and spoke" model of routes, utilizing
"hub" airports strategically located with connecting
routes being the "spokes," while the new smaller airlines
were utilizing more "point to point" systems. Previously
underserved areas could at last have hope of much-
needed service. Smaller communities like Lexington
worried that they would lose service due to deregulation. The federal government guaranteed smaller communities service for 10 years, but in some cases, routes
to smaller areas would soon be the foundation for new
airlines grabbing their piece of the market and establishing their turf, so to speak, with the new routes.

The number of new start-up airlines serving smaller
markets and reaching further into rural areas mush-
roomed. Start-up airlines with smaller aircraft sprang

up to fill the void of service when a larger airline reduced service to certain areas and even offered new
routes and services not previously introduced. With
deregulation came opportunities for start-up airlines
for the first time since the CAB was established.
Entrepreneurs and investors could once again take a
shot at owning a piece of the sky, letting market forces
be their guide. Southwest Airlines is perhaps the best
example of a deregulation success story. Its transforma-
tion from little "Texas puddle-jumper" to one of the
largest airlines in terms of domestic passengers carried is
proof that deregulation opened up market entry for the
most savvy operators.

THE AFTERMATH

Before deregulation, trunk airlines enjoyed boom
times. Now there was turmoil. A shift of such magni-
tude brought too much change far too quickly, resulting
in instability and the need to restructure. Most difficult
for an industry entrenched in old ways of thinking and
operating was the huge task of changing long-standing
business practices. In addition, competition for routes
and passengers was fierce. With the arrival of many new
smaller, lower cost airlines over the years, a new climate

This 1945 U.S. Army photograph is the first known aerial image of paved runways at Blue Grass Field.

was created and nine of the country's main carriers including Eastern, Pan Am, Continental, TWA and Braniff went bankrupt.

However, there were many positive aspects of deregulation. Established routes to most of the larger cities remained, and fares were more affordable. The average person could see more of the country than ever before with prices low enough to rival the cost of driving. Deregulation made air travel far more affordable for everyone, not just the wealthy or the well-heeled businessman as was once the case. Now people could choose to travel for leisure and fly for fun.

As aircraft became larger and airlines expanded their route networks, it became apparent which routes were profitable; those that weren't were cancelled. The resulting voids in service helped to establish the climate for smaller carriers to succeed. They could offer service to smaller, less populated areas or act as connectors to larger destinations, offering more convenient flights using smaller aircraft.

HEADACHES AND MORE HEADACHES

The extreme growth in aviation created a bottleneck. Air travel statistics for 1974 put the number of passengers at 207.5 million and by 2010 that number had risen to 721.1 million. But who could have predicted that oil, once $20 a barrel, would climb to more than $100 a barrel? The inherent problems of explosive growth and competition with the chilling effect of rising oil costs created havoc for airlines.

If that weren't tough enough, the 1980s, 1990s and 2000s brought even more difficulties for the industry in the way of even higher fuel costs, an economic meltdown and the terrorist attacks on September 11, 2001 (thereafter referred to as 9/11), which ushered in a new era of threats and challenges not previously encountered in aviation.

The horror of 9/11 and the ensuing emotional upheaval in the nation exerted tremendous pressure on the industry to address safety and security issues immediately. The concern over terrorist threats and travel risks

This 1974 photo shows the evolution of Blue Grass Field nearly 30 years later.

HDR, INC.
Where the Past Enlightens the Future

Understanding the technical complexities and functions of an airport is critical when planning for future growth. Long-term engineering partner HDR has the institutional knowledge to ensure that new projects blend seamlessly and easily into existing infrastructure.

HDR stands for the initials of founders H.H. Henningson, Charles Durham and Willard Richardson. Henningson Engineering Company officially became Henningson, Durham & Richardson, Inc. in 1950. The name was later shortened to HDR, Inc.

Iowa native H.H. Henningson wanted to lift small communities from their frontier status through civil engineering. His dream became reality in 1917 when he founded Henningson Engineering Company. The firm grew into one of the largest and most respected architecture-engineering companies in the world. HDR is employee-owned and headquartered in Omaha, Nebraska.

The Lexington office of HDR has a staff of 65 who engineer, design and manage complex construction projects such as those at Blue Grass Airport. HDR's history with Blue Grass Airport began with projects by Witt & Associates in the mid 1980s. Later, Witt & Associates merged with Quest Engineers, which HDR acquired in 2007.

In addition to architecture and engineering, HDR provides consulting, construction and related services through various operating companies. Its professionals are committed to helping clients manage large landmark projects and smaller community projects across the country and around the world. They take great satisfaction in

Bringing strength, beauty and structure to every project

producing work that brings strength, beauty and structure to every project.

At Blue Grass Airport, HDR has expanded air freight facilities, designed the parking garage and rental car ready lot (as a subcontractor to Gresham, Smith and Partners), upgraded security fencing, runway signage, designed and constructed a 35,000-square-yard concrete ramp as part of the terminal expansion project, and managed a wide variety of runway projects.

From an operational standpoint, one of the biggest enhancements at the airport and a critical part of the 2005 Master Plan, was the construction of Runway 9-27. As part of the RW Armstrong team, HDR ensured that the $32 million project, which included construction of a new Taxiway B, expanded aircraft parking and development space for general aviation hangars, was completed in time for the 2010 Alltech FEI World Equestrian Games.

HDR's comprehensive institutional knowledge brings a high degree of value to its work, making the firm one of the most trusted advisors to the airport.

Top: The vault is the electrical nerve center for the airfield and controls more than 800 lights.
Above: An aerial view of Concourse B.

PLANS AND MORE PLANS FOR THE AIRFIELD - A SUMMARY

Blue Grass Airport has continuously sought to improve the airfield and has a significant history of planning efforts over the years. Numerous master plans have been developed and implemented to help guide the airport as it grows. The airport's master planning process includes thoughtful forecasting of future activity and an orderly phased development of the airport over time to accommodate that activity. Based on demographics, airline industry conditions, trends in general aviation, historic growth and economic conditions, the airport and its consulting teams have made plans for future facility improvements to accommodate both the immediate and long-term needs of the commercial airlines and our general aviation community.

1960s

A new terminal and 1,000-foot extension of the runway are proposed for Blue Grass Field in an airport development plan presented in January 1967. The airport board approves the recommendation and the City-County Planning Commission subsequently adopts the plan.

1970s

In 1974, an Airport Master Plan was produced, recommending construction of a 4,000-foot long by 75-foot wide parallel runway 2,800 feet east of the main runway. Since this 1974 Master Plan, some form of parallel runway has been a recommendation in each successive master plan up through and including the 1995 plan.

The 1979 Master Plan Update again recommended a parallel runway; however, the proposed alternative was to be located west of the main runway. Recommendations called for the proposed parallel runway to be 8,000 feet in length and 150 feet in width with 1,150 feet of lateral centerline separation from the existing main runway.

1980s

The 1987 Master Plan Update concurred with the recommendations of the 1979 Master Plan as to the location of the parallel runway west of the main runway; however, it recommended a runway of 6,000 feet in length by 150 feet with only 800 feet of lateral centerline separation from the existing main runway. Additionally, that plan also considered an extension of crosswind Runway 8-26 from 3,500 feet to 4,200 feet.

1990s

In 1990, a Preliminary Environmental Impact Statement reviewed a parallel runway west of the main runway and further modified the previous runway options. The proposed runway was recommended to be 6,000 feet long and 150 feet wide with 1,100 feet of lateral centerline separation to the main runway.

The Master Plan Update conducted in 1995 revised the recommendations of all previous master plans and environmental analyses by suggesting a parallel runway of 9,000 feet in length by 150 feet in width and having 4,300 feet of lateral centerline separation. It was recommended that this new air carrier runway be constructed east of the alignment of existing Runway 4-22.

In November 1999, a Feasibility Study of Alternative Runway Designs analyzed various options for complying with the FAA's Runway Safety Area (RSA) requirements while meeting the necessary runway length criteria on Runway 4-22.

2000s

The recommendation made and selected by the airport board in January 2001 proposed that the 7,000-foot alignment of Runway 4-22 be shifted to the southwest and 600-foot long RSAs be provided at both runway ends. This recommendation, while not meeting the full RSA criteria for Runway 4-22, was deemed to provide acceptable margins of safety and was approved by the FAA in May 2001 and completed in 2006.

This four-phase project included an asphalt overlay of the entire existing length of Runway 4-22 as well as the relocation, upgrading and installation of numerous navigational aids and runway approach lighting. Construction included a one-of-a-kind retaining wall with a mural depicting the area's equine heritage as well as resurfacing the primary parallel taxiway.

The 2005 Master Plan Update identified the need to reconstruct the pavement for the general aviation/secondary runway and recommended relocating it to a 9-27 orientation (east-west), which would allow for more efficient land use and facility development including future corporate and light general aviation facilities.

In 2009, Blue Grass Airport kicked off several airfield projects including the construction of the new Runway 9-27, which was considered critical to maintaining the capability of landing lighter corporate and private aircraft during crosswind conditions. The previous 3,500-foot crosswind Runway 8-26 was removed so construction could begin on the relocated and realigned Runway 9-27. The new runway was constructed at 4,000 feet in length to meet the Kentucky Department of Aviation's planning goals.

2010s

In 2013, a Master Plan Update reflected several objectives for the future including improvements to the existing taxiway system. The Taxiway Safety Enhancement Program represents a multi-year initiative that will reduce runway incursion potential, reduce the potential of aircraft conflicts, enhance separation of aircraft movements and enhance operational flexibility. This will occur through the realignment of the airport's primary taxiway, which will require other initiatives such as the relocation of airport support facilities.

gripped the country and became part of the public psyche, with great adverse impact on the airline industry. A nation that had relied on air travel for business and leisure was suddenly reluctant to fly – dealing a severe blow to the commercial airlines with already compromised bottom lines.

After 9/11, as the nation returned to some degree of normalcy, passengers experienced new security regulations. These changes introduced more hassle to the traveling public, further dampening their desire to travel by air. For many, especially frequent business and leisure travelers, flying just wasn't fun anymore. Nor was it efficient in terms of time spent or cost.

With the layering of deregulation, intense competition, escalating oil prices, economic turmoil and the threat of terrorism at a previously unprecedented level, the airline industry was reeling. Instability, in the form of bankruptcies, layoffs and mergers became commonplace in the years following deregulation and only now, some 30 years later, are we seeing stability return in the overall financial health of the airlines.

RUNWAY CONTROVERSY

At Blue Grass Airport, talk turned to expansion for many reasons even before deregulation. Lexington was growing, businesses wanted to set up for future growth and local access to comprehensive air service was seen as a "must" for continued growth and prosperity.

To meet the needs for growth and safety, a new and longer runway was viewed as necessary for three reasons: a capacity concern based on projected passenger enplanements; a need for a redundant air carrier runway; and a runway that would fully comply with FAA design requirements, particularly those associated with Runway Safety Areas (RSA) off each runway end. RSAs are designed to reduce the risk of damage to airplanes in the event of an airplane undershooting, overshooting or veering off the runway.

While the debate had been going on for 20 years, in 1998 the issue of airport expansion reached a boiling point in the form of a proposed 9,000-foot second runway parallel to the existing 7,000-foot runway. Many in the aviation industry were adamant that this was necessary to keep pace regionally and nationally and to

accommodate larger, heavier passenger jets requiring longer runways for takeoffs and landings and the potential for expanded cargo flight needs of a growing city.

The executive director of Blue Grass Airport at that time, Michael Flack, expressed his concern over public expectations that the airport "remain the same" and warned that an airport without the expansion would be "a drag on the community and local economy."

Along with the jet age came a heightened awareness of the environment. People were sensitive to the impact of development on water, land and noise levels. Central Kentuckians have a passionate relationship with the land and a long-standing history of protecting the natural beauty of the area.

The airport's location among the surrounding historic Thoroughbred farms belied an uncomfortable relationship from the start. The first land dispute had been in 1941 when local landowners petitioned to stop the development of the airport when first proposed at its current location. There had been an acceptance over the years but that was about to change. There were limits to what the community would tolerate.

HOW RUNWAYS ARE NUMBERED

Runways are numbered between 01 and 36. The number indicates the runway's heading according to the points on a compass with north at 360 degrees, east at 90 degrees, south at 180 degrees and west at 270 degrees. There is no runway zero. The two-digit number is essentially 1/10th of the magnetic heading of the runway plus or minus 5 degrees (i.e. one digit per ten degrees). A runway pointing to the north with a heading of 355 degrees will be generally given the number 36 (1/10th of 360° plus or minus 5 degrees).

Since the same runway pavement can be normally used in either direction, it will have a second number, which will always differ by 18 (180° or halfway across the compass). For better clarity in radio communications, each digit of a runway number is pronounced individually, i.e., runway three six, runway two seven, runway one five, etc.

Our Beautiful Approach

Flying into Lexington is often described as a "unique and charming" experience rivaled by none. To glance out the airplane window and take in the approach is a sight to behold and entirely different from many airports set in rural areas or on the outskirts of cities that offer an industrial and highly paved area as a first glimpse of the community. Blue Grass Airport is nestled in the middle of a lovely green space of farmland offering vistas of bucolic beauty as you land. Business people and community leaders often tell stories of flying in potential employees for interviews or hosting corporate executives for site selection visits who report falling in love with Lexington at first sight on the approach to the airport – deciding then and there that they want to live here.

APPROACH TO RUNWAY 22

KEENELAND RACE COURSE
KEENELAND TRAINING TRACK IN FOREGROUND

DARLEY STUD

SHADWELL FARM

BATTLE LINES ARE DRAWN

What made Blue Grass Airport unique – its prized location in the heart of horse country – also made it

Mike Flack, executive director of Blue Grass Airport, supported expansion to keep pace with growth.

a lightning rod for future development. Area residents quickly took sides; the battle lines were drawn. The opposition to the proposed new runway lined up in the form of groups calling themselves Airport Watch, representing the surrounding neighborhoods and SOIL (Save Our Irreplaceable Land), representing the interests of nearby horse farms such as Shadwell, Calumet and Jonabell (now Darley) and Keeneland.

Airport Watch vehemently opposed eating up the valuable land with the new runway. They were concerned the noise and added stress the expansion might create. Fliers and bumper stickers were distributed; commercial airtime was purchased; consultants were hired; and twice the runway opponents convinced the Urban County Council to pass resolutions opposing the runway plan.

Even beyond the Bluegrass region the fight was being watched. A *Chicago Tribune* article in 1997 noted that, "Airport expansion is controversial in almost any community, but in Lexington, the thought of evicting Thoroughbreds to lay tarmac has incited landowners ranging from Arab sheiks to Kentucky colonels."

Lexington's mayor at the time, Pam Miller, insisted on cooler heads and was wary of the proposed expansion plan. At one of the many meetings on the airport proposal she said, "I see all the emphasis given to one plan – the parallel runway – and I want to make sure the FAA hears the message loud and clear: This community wants all alternatives studied and wants all [options] given significant attention."

In the end, the alliance of the two opposing groups proved too formidable for the airport, and the plan was scrapped.

Above: Airport Watch member and Firebrook subdivision resident Karen Shrader opposed the concept of a second runway maintaining that the Versailles Road corridor needed to stay the same. *Left:* Scenic Calumet Farm

with noise pollution and safety hazards they were sure would affect their homes and neighborhood. One member of Airport Watch pointedly remarked, "That's one corridor of Lexington that really needs to stay the same." SOIL fought to save the land so critical to the horse industry and fought to spare their horses and businesses

The perceived need was legitimate at the time the runway expansion was first proposed in 1978, but new studies confirmed the weakness of the argument calling for the longer runway. There had been technological developments in the industry and a paradigm shift coinciding with the many years the controversy

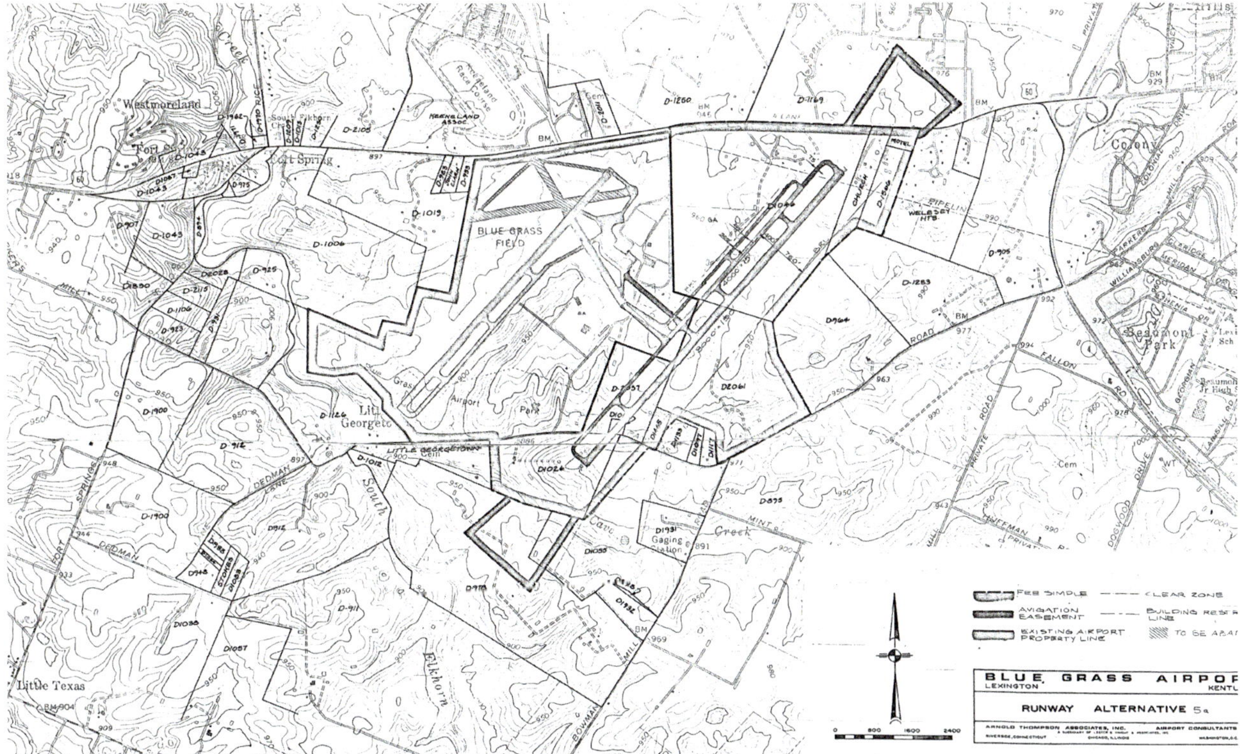

A site plan showing a parallel runway concept

raged. As energy costs soared, planes were designed to be lighter and smaller, and therefore, used less fuel and required less runway. Smaller midsize airplanes requiring shorter runways took the place of the behemoth runway-gobbling aircraft that had been proliferating a decade earlier.

In April 1998, Executive Director Michael Flack left Lexington to lead the airport in Columbia, South Carolina. When Michael Gobb became the new executive director of Blue Grass Airport in August 1998, his arrival marked the beginning of a more conciliatory stance on the expansion issue and the controversy subsided.

Expansion would ultimately need to be revisited, and in 2000 the runway controversy returned. The airport board once again looked at a proposed runway that would run parallel to Versailles Road. The discussion centered on safety compliance issues underscoring the argument for the existing runway to be longer and the need for "redundancy" or a second runway to use in the event of a runway closure.

The old rancor returned as the community and airport factions squared off. This time cost became the deciding factor as the proposed new runway carried a price tag of

Gas is $1.06 per gallon.

The biggest airport in the world opens in Hong Kong.

Cirrus Aircraft successfully flight-tests the CAPS ballistic emergency aircraft parachute.

MetroJet operated by US Airways begins operations.

BMW buys Rolls-Royce motor cars for $570 million.

Although it wins no Academy Awards, the wildly successful movie *Armageddon* grosses more than $550,000,000 worldwide.

Europeans agree on a single currency – the Euro.

A first-class postage stamp is 32 cents.

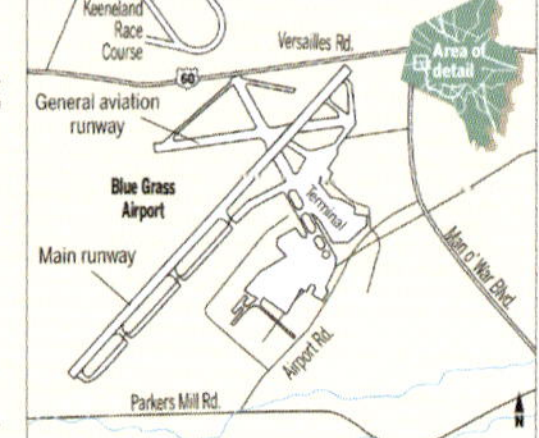

This *Lexington Herald-Leader* headline from 2003 said it all.

$50 million dollars and an alternative choice – lengthening the existing runway – was budgeted at $28 million. An addition that provided for 600-foot RSAs at each end of the current runway was also finally accepted.

The debate forced Lexington to examine its identity, and the resulting outcome suggested that Lexington was happy to remain a regional airport for the time being, especially if this would preserve the Bluegrass farmland setting it prized above all.

At one point in the lengthy expansion dialogue, the idea was put forth to move the airport altogether, perhaps to a neighboring county, eliminating the constraints of the current location. Beyond the astronomical costs of building a new commercial airport would be the sad reality that flying into the Bluegrass might then look like the descent into just about anywhere. The unique arrival that travelers to Lexington experience would cease to be.

THE COMPETITION

Though land issues have defined the footprint of Blue Grass Airport, for the foreseeable future it continues to be a competitive airport, one very attuned to bringing the best in air travel to central Kentucky.

Lexington's airport competes for routes and passengers with Cincinnati/Northern Kentucky International Airport and Louisville International Airport, both within a short driving distance of Lexington. A newer, smaller airport in nearby Georgetown handles additional private and small cargo planes – convenient for a huge corporation like Toyota Motor Manufacturing Kentucky located in Scott County.

For a community to strike the right balance between cost and convenience, some juggling skills are required. The ease of flying, as long as it is convenient and relatively cost-effective, keeps people on planes instead of opting to drive or use other transportation. Every community strives for the winning formula with the right combination: ticket price, routes, frequency and aircraft size.

Dr. Ray Garman, a licensed pilot and former airport board member, believes that Blue Grass Airport's management team understands that Lexington is competing with other airports and they counter by offering conve-

Allegiant focuses on offering attractive vacation packages to Lexington customers.

nience and friendly service. He said, "From my perspective, the people who work here appreciate and respond to the Bluegrass community and recognize the attractiveness of the venue compared to nearby airports."

Blue Grass Airport comes up a winner for most locals who have the option of booking flights elsewhere. Lexington's airport is a quick commute, has closer parking and a less-crowded, much more compact terminal allowing for faster check-ins, shorter security lines and far less walking – an important factor when traveling with luggage and children.

The fact that Blue Grass Airport has access to many hubs and is one stop to most anywhere in the world prompts airport Executive Director Eric Frankl to say, "This community, for the population size, is very blessed to have a convenient local airport with the amenities, service and number of non-stop destinations that are offered."

REGIONAL JET SERVICE AND LEISURE TRAVEL

In many ways the smaller airlines face the same pressures as the big ones. Today's markets require shuffling of routes and providers with cost and efficiency guiding their decisions.

Even in times of belt-tightening and economic caution, rather than discontinue routes altogether, the regional airlines may choose to reduce the number of flights offered to a destination during a day or week: perhaps only one flight in the morning and one flight in the afternoon or three flights per week rather than daily service. This flexibility is more compatible with flights taken predominantly by leisure travelers since the scheduling requirements of business travelers can strongly influence arrival dates and times.

Fewer, fuller flights are a common practice today as opposed to more frequent flights with empty seats. What might be lost from offering the convenience of several flights per day to a given destination is offset by efficiency and lower costs.

With many of the same stresses and vulnerabilities that affect large airlines, some smaller airlines primarily serving leisure travel began specializing in vacation destinations. It has been important for them to be creative, to design customized incentives and to build partnerships to sell specific destinations. Strategic alliances with hotels and resorts to offer appealing packages at attractive prices for the consumer has enabled the smaller airlines to remain viable players in the game.

A clear example of the industry's volatility is the AirTran Airways story. In 2009, AirTran and Blue Grass Airport officials announced that the low-cost airline would be coming to Lexington in early 2010 offering flights to the popular destinations of Fort Lauderdale and Orlando, Florida.

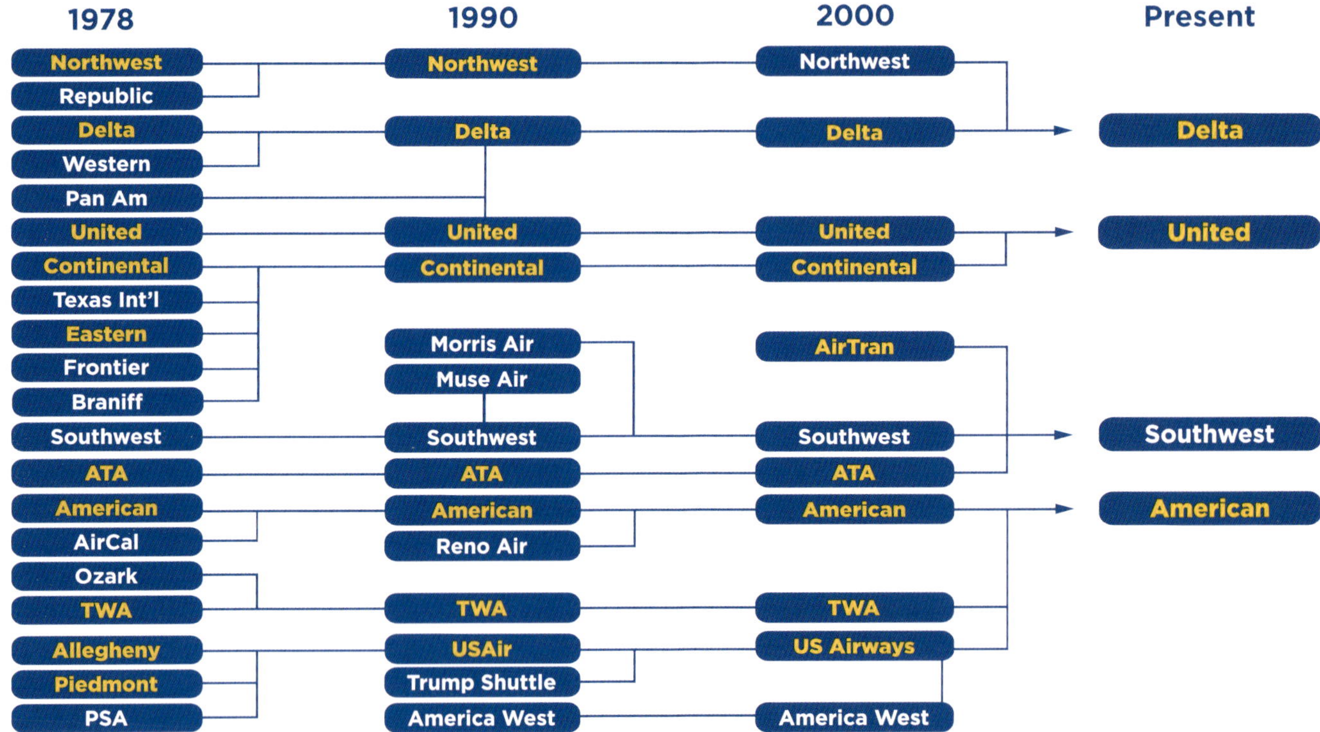

Since the Airline Deregulation Act of 1978, airline mergers and acquisitions have led to a consolidated industry. Airlines that have served Lexington are highlighted in gold.

After operating a short time in Lexington, AirTran was purchased by Southwest Airlines and discontinued operations in Lexington. Fortunately for Blue Grass Airport, Allegiant (another low-cost airline) stepped up and added non-stop flights on its 150-seat jets to Orlando and Tampa Bay and ultimately Fort Lauderdale and Punta Gorda, Florida. It was a great trade-off since Allegiant is a leader in offering travel packages that include lodging, car rental and tickets to Florida amusement parks and attractions.

Many airlines carve out niches in the markets. By 2011, Blue Grass Airport saw record growth in the area of leisure travel. Eric Frankl, Blue Grass Airport's executive director explained, "It really has had its ups and downs. For example, Delta used to have non-stop service from Lexington to Orlando but discontinued the route. Then AirTran provided service to Orlando. Now Allegiant has a route to Orlando. The fact that it's a different product and a different aircraft doesn't matter – the fact that Blue Grass Airport can continue to offer service to that market does matter to our customers. Leisure and travel vacation packages are vibrant and growing."

MERGERS – A CIRCULAR JOURNEY

As mergers swallow up many of the smaller carriers and make giants of the combined larger airlines, the old days of the large legacy airlines seem to be coming back. United's merger with Continental, Delta's acquisition of Northwest and now American's merger with US Airways are just part of a larger trend that continues to create ripples of change for airports and travelers.

The economic realities of running an airline are more daunting than ever with security concerns and the soaring costs of fuel being the two largest issues. In this era of higher costs, it seems that many of the smaller airlines created after deregulation have found it hard to hold on in today's economic climate, and certainly there are advantages to combining forces.

Some of the mergers have grabbed headlines as when Delta's merger with Northwest made Delta the largest airline in the world. Mergers have enabled several of the airlines to survive a turbulent era and begin to grow again with new routes and services. The airline industry seems to be emerging stronger than ever but not without changes and adjustments to the communities they serve and the overall flight experience.

ATS CONSTRUCTION
Completing Monumental Projects Without Incident

ATS Construction (ATS) is a third-generation family-owned construction company serving central Kentucky since the 1950s. This full-service highway and runway contractor, which employs a dedicated professional staff, has been doing construction at Blue Grass Airport for more than 10 years.

They build necessary roads, runways and ramps and maintain a large portion of Blue Grass Airport's paved surfaces, which total more than 7.59 million square feet. Because installing and maintaining paved surfaces is the airport's largest capital expense, having an experienced local partner like ATS is critical to ensuring safe and efficient operations.

Over the past decade, they have been involved in numerous projects including runways, taxiways and ramps. They have moved in excess of 2 million cubic yards of rock and dirt, constructed over 30,000 square feet of retaining walls, placed in excess of 35,000 cubic yards of concrete and laid over 20,000 linear feet of storm lines during this time.

During the resurfacing of the main runway in 2006, ATS laid approximately 61,150 tons of bituminous asphalt and 20,575 tons of stone in a single weekend. This process took place with great care to safely coordinate the project between the airport, two asphalt plants and 150 dump trucks transporting asphalt to the site – a monumental undertaking by a valued partner.

> *More than 150 dump trucks were used to resurface the main runway.*

ATS employees and subcontractors worked around the clock to resurface Runway 4-22 in 2006. Airlines were notified one year in advance that the main runway would be closed for 48 hours.

PREPARING FOR CRISIS
and the Unthinkable Happens

BY MICHELLE RAUCH

It takes an inherent amount of trust to travel by air. Whether you're a passenger on a commercial flight or behind the controls of a private plane, you must have trust. If you are a passenger, your safety is in the hands of your pilot. If you are a pilot, you must trust your training, your instincts and the mechanical abilities of your aircraft. You must also trust those on the ground who serve to assist you in an emergency.

It is the responsibility of the airlines and the airport to ensure the safety of the traveling public. As safety and security demands have changed, so has the airport as it adapts to those changes. At Blue Grass Airport, this evolution has occurred carefully over the years in an effort to maintain the balance between safety and customer service while preserving its unique Bluegrass ambiance.

As a teenager of the 1940s, Gene Van Meter and his friends loaded up into a 1939 Chevrolet and cruised out to the airport and onto the runway. It was a treat to take the Chevy for a spin on the ultra smooth surface and they topped out at 95 miles per hour. It was their open road and they relished the freedom. The airport was in its infancy and so were security and emergency preparedness.

The U.S. Army built the first fire and rescue building at Blue Grass Field in the summer of 1945. It was equipped with a fire truck, an ambulance and radio equipment. Its intended purpose was to transport military patients to and from the Veterans Administration (VA) Hospital in Lexington and the Darnall General Hospital in Danville. The airport was not equipped for full-scale responses to aircraft emergencies. That responsibility fell on the shoulders of the city and county departments with the closest fire station nearly seven miles away.

Progress was made in the 1950s. The airport invested in a pickup truck equipped with a carbon dioxide fire extinguisher system. Fortunately, this modest equipment sufficed for the time and carried the airport safely into the 1960s. In 1965, the Southeastern Airport Managers Association recognized airport manager Logan Gray with its annual safety award. Times were changing, and so would public opinion regarding the airport's emergency preparedness.

By 1966, there were 156,000 take-offs and landings at the airport. Newly introduced jet service posed a challenge. The airport was only equipped with the pickup truck purchased in the 1950s and still relied on nearby fire departments for emergencies. Manpower was limited to two daytime emergency personnel and a uniformed night watchman. Federal Aviation Administration (FAA) guidelines suggested that an airport the size of Lexington's should have a combination truck that

The airport purchased its first emergency response vehicle in 1954.

Public safety team during a May 2011 training exercise.

> **"BE PREPARED... THE MEANING OF THE MOTTO IS THAT A SCOUT MUST PREPARE HIMSELF BY PREVIOUS THINKING OUT AND PRACTICING HOW TO ACT ON ANY ACCIDENT OR EMERGENCY SO THAT HE IS NEVER TAKEN BY SURPRISE."**
>
> – ROBERT BADEN-POWELL

A small twin-engine airplane crash took nine lives in April 1967. Fayette County and Keeneland fire rigs are at the scene.

carried a dry chemical extinguishing system, firefighting foam and water plus additional rescue equipment. The guidelines also cited the need to have five trained firefighters on site. Logan Gray agreed and was outspoken about the airport's needs, but the costs were prohibitive. As airport administrators admitted that the emergency support was inadequate, they faced public scrutiny. An April 1966 headline in the *Lexington Leader* read: "There may not always be time to get fire rigs to the airport." It was clear that emergency preparedness at Blue Grass Field needed to take a big step forward.

Two accidents made emergency preparedness front and center and gave context to the FAA guidelines. On October 29, 1966, a helicopter snagged power lines at the end of the runway killing local civic leader Julia Allen Short. Short was one of a handful of female helicopter pilots in the world. Five months later, on April 3, 1967, another high profile crash made headlines.

Logan Gray (left) meets with officials into the night at the crash site.

Safety involves more than crash-rescue operations and emergency medical services. Snow removal is critical to the safe and efficient operation of the airport. In the early days, snow removal was accomplished with little more than a pick-up truck with a snow plow attached. In modern times, sophisticated snow removal equipment is essential to airport operations.

Nine people affiliated with the University of Kentucky were killed when their small twin-engine plane crashed at Keeneland just after takeoff. At the time, it was the worst air disaster in central Kentucky history. It prompted debate on the airport's ability to respond to a disaster. In 1969, a little more than two years after these accidents, the Air Line Pilots Association labeled Blue Grass Field "dangerous" citing the lack of fire and rescue equipment as the reason behind that rating.

Logan Gray reacted and two months later appointed Edward Hammel as the airport's first chief of rescue operations. The appointment was followed by the airport board's approval of a $70,000 investment in emergency and fire rescue equipment and facilities. A fire and rescue truck was included in the purchases. Planning began in earnest for a full-time airport fire department.

In March 1970, Blue Grass Field's fire and rescue team was in place. The team conducted its first firefighting drill using the new crash and rescue truck. The exercise was a success and illustrated how firefighting chemicals paired with water could knock down a fire long enough for firefighters to pull passengers from a burning plane.

The value of the fire-and-rescue team that was established in 1970 was fully appreciated in 1987. A twin-engine private jet traveling from Dallas to New York radioed for help after one of its engines caught fire. Controllers guided the plane into Blue Grass Airport, but the pilot lost all power prior to landing. He crashed just short of the runway on Versailles Road. The plane burst into flames on impact. Airport rescue personnel responded in seconds. Two people died that day, but two others were saved because of the immediate response from the rescue team.

With the airport poised to respond to fire and rescue emergencies, attention turned to security. The beginning of what would be decades worth of changes started with federally mandated measures. In December 1972, two months before the federal law required it but following a hijacking incident with local connections, commercial passengers at Blue Grass Field had to walk through metal detectors and have carry-on luggage searched. Airport screening was implemented as awareness of airline hijacking incidents increased globally. In spite of changes at commercial airports across the country, those on the general aviation side of the airport still enjoyed a lot of freedom.

GROWING PAINS

In the early 1970s, Blue Grass Field was an airport with virtually no boundaries. Former Airport Board Member David Trapp remembers it well. "In the old days you could drive out to the airport and walk up to the airplane, crank it up and go fly. I had a bike out here and rode the bike all around." Trapp, who grew up in a family that owned a hangar and airplanes, loves aviation and considers himself fortunate to have spent nearly every day at the airport since the early 1960s. By the late 1970s, a six-foot security fence had been installed around the perimeter of the airport. Trapp remembers the days when change was in the air. He watched as increased security spread from the commercial airlines to the private aviation side of the airport.

Large photo: Emergency response vehicles and crash crew in 1960. The crash crew consisted of one fireman, four volunteers from men on duty in the hangars and two men from each of the three airlines at the field. The fire truck is 20 years old at the time. *Above clockwise starting at top left:* Testing firefighting equipment in 1970; Logan Gray with firefighting truck in 1966; Firefighting training exercise in 1974; Safety measures include new beacon; Increased security measures in the early 1970s.

STITES & HARBISON, PLLC
Trusted Advisors to Blue Grass Airport

For more than a half-century, the professionals of Stites & Harbison have served Kentucky airports. These airports regularly face complicated business, regulatory and legal opportunities and challenges. Stites & Harbison provides essential counsel to help Blue Grass Airport navigate myriad opportunities and challenges, including assistance with complex legal contracts, delicate land acquisition negotiations, relocation issues, employment matters, project financing and accident litigation.

Tom Halbleib

Stites & Harbison, one of the largest law firms in the region, is the successor to one of the oldest law practices in the nation, tracing its origins back to 1832.

The firm handles sophisticated transactions, difficult litigation and complex regulatory matters for Blue Grass Airport and has served as a trusted advisor since 1999.

As the airport's legal advisor, Stites & Harbison attorneys provide guidance at board meetings and during many contract negotiations, assist with the development of policy recommendations and generally advise the airport year-round. Their legal team advises Blue Grass Airport regarding dispute avoidance whenever possible, and when disputes arise, they help the airport address and resolve them efficiently and effectively.

Although many Stites & Harbison attorneys have served the airport with distinction, two leaders merit particular mention – Governor Steve Beshear and the late Kennedy Helm III, former chairman of Stites & Harbison. For several years prior to his election, Governor Beshear provided exemplary leadership for the Stites & Harbison team that served Blue Grass Airport.

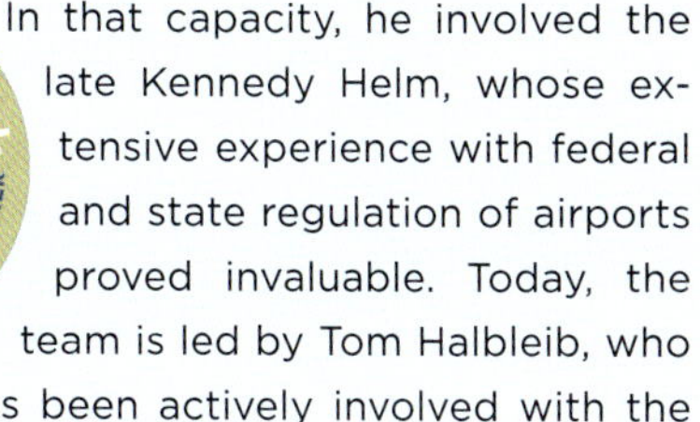

In that capacity, he involved the late Kennedy Helm, whose extensive experience with federal and state regulation of airports proved invaluable. Today, the team is led by Tom Halbleib, who has been actively involved with the airport since 1999.

One of the Top Places to Work in Kentucky every year since 2005

U.S. News & World Report and *The Best Lawyers in America* have ranked Stites & Harbison as a National Tier 1 firm in three practice areas and as a Metropolitan Tier 1 firm in 61 practice areas for the 2014 "Best Law Firms" in America. In addition to working to provide the quality client service to merit such ratings, Stites & Harbison also strives to provide an outstanding work environment for its staff and professionals. Since the Kentucky Chamber of Commerce launched its "Best Places to Work in Kentucky" award during 2005, it has recognized Stites & Harbison as one of the Top Places to Work in Kentucky every year.

Stites & Harbison's willingness to invest in developing the necessary technical knowledge, and its commitment to quality service delivery, provide a good example of how a trusted advisor can help Blue Grass Airport pursue opportunities, resolve challenges professionally and maintain focus on its vision for the future.

SOUTHERN AIRWAYS FLIGHT 49
A Notorious 1972 Hijacking Finds Its Way To Lexington

On November 10, 1972, Melvin Cale, Louis Moore and Henry D. Jackson, Jr., each facing criminal charges for other offenses, decided that their future prospects might be sunnier in Cuba than in the United States. Armed with pistols and hand grenades, the three boarded Southern Airways Flight 49 in Birmingham, Alabama – to add hijacking to their already alarming rap sheets. As the blue and yellow Southern Airways Douglas DC-9, decorated with the cheerful inscription, "HAVE A NICE DAY," approached cruising altitude, the door to the cockpit burst open and a man, holding a gun to the head of the flight attendant declared, "We're taking over the airplane." The trio demanded $10 million in cash, a demand Southern Airways scrambled to try to meet.

As the November 27, 1972 issue of *Time* magazine reported, "Southern Airways of Atlanta prides itself on its antebellum hospitality. Its airplanes even have smile faces painted on the nose ... But no one was smiling after one of the most theatrical and spectacularly prolonged episodes in the chronicles of skyjacking."

For Captain William R. "Billy Bob" Haas, co-pilot Harold Johnson and 31 passengers, there began a 29-hour, 13-stop, 4,000-mile odyssey involving tense negotiations with the FBI, threats to crash the plane into the nuclear reactor at Oak Ridge, Tennessee, and multiple stops to refuel. One of those stops was Blue Grass Field. The hijackers, believing that humiliation was a means of crowd control, had already forced all the male passengers to strip to their underwear. When ground crewman Darrell Melton approached to refuel the plane, he was ordered to do the same.

Sam Wheat, who worked at the airport's Avis Rent-A-Car operation at that time, recalled the brisk November day and the nervous young man refueling the airplane with engines running so that the hijackers could make a fast getaway. Some 40 years later, Darrell Melton recalls that he was told to look nonchalant while refueling the airplane dressed only in his underwear and a borrowed Piedmont T-shirt on that 32-degree day. He was at least given a blanket (again, Piedmont) to wrap up in as he drove to the airplane alone.

While he was refueling, he could see one of the hijackers pointing a gun at him with another holding a gun to a woman's head. As soon as he disconnected the fuel hose, but before he could finish rolling it up, the pilot flashed the landing lights at him as a warning and gave the engine full throttle. The 22-year-old Melton remembers news media, FBI officials and airport police descending on him when he returned from refueling and remarking that he looked calm. His response? "It hadn't sunk in yet!"

Ironically, it was not during the stop in Lexington, but the one in Tennessee, that buckets of Kentucky Fried Chicken were loaded onto the plane to sustain passengers, crew and hijackers. Along with the fried chicken, bulletproof vests, pep pills and alcohol demanded by the hijackers, there was a reported $2 million in ransom money hurriedly raised by Southern Airways in a desperate attempt to placate them.

A DC-9 flown by Southern Airways Vice President Jim Godwin, with 38 FBI sharpshooters aboard and a Navy plane with more armed FBI officials, tailed the hijacked

> *While he was refueling, he could see one of the hijackers pointing a gun at him with another holding a gun to a woman's head.*

A Southern Airways DC-9 similar to the airplane involved in the 1972 hijacking

Left: A map tracing the route of the hijacked airplane. *Right:* Co-pilot Harold "Billy" Johnson and a passenger were taken by ambulance to a Miami hospital following the 29-hour ordeal.

plane with lights out looking for an opportunity to disable the airplane – a chance they got in Orlando, where they tried to shoot out the tires of the hijacked plane while it stopped to refuel.

The co-pilot, who said that the hijackers were shocked and enraged by the FBI's actions in Orlando, was shot in the arm as he dived behind a seat for safety. Hijacker Moore maintained years later that they never meant to hurt anyone and that shooting the co-pilot was an accident.

The saga ended when Haas landed the plane, its tires shredded by FBI gunfire during the Orlando landing, on a runway at José Martí International Airport, just southwest of Havana, Cuba. Far from being welcomed as heroes, Cale, Moore and Jackson were captured. Cuban officials confiscated the money and swiftly marched the three off

> *A DC-9 with 38 FBI sharpshooters and a Navy plane with more armed FBI officials tailed the hijacked plane.*

to a Cuban jail to serve eight years before being deported to serve even more time in a U.S. prison. At the urging of a Georgia congressman, the Cuban government eventually returned the ransom money to Southern Airways. How had they managed to smuggle their guns aboard? By wrapping them in a raincoat, which they passed from one to the other as they boarded.

The aftermath of this notorious hijacking? In January 1973, the FAA implemented a landmark anti-hijacking rule stating that all airline passengers must pass through metal detectors and that all carry-on baggage be inspected. Airports were also required to have a law enforcement officer in the boarding area during the screening and boarding process. Previously, the FAA had only required air carriers to conduct a weapons scan of those passengers who fit the profile of a hijacker.

Top: Area firefighters in a 2011 training exercise. *Above:* Training in the classroom is an important part of preparation for an emergency response team.

There were some growing pains. New requirements mandated that the general aviation community be photographed and fingerprinted before a badge was issued that allowed access inside the airport's perimeter fence. That badge then had to be swiped at the general aviation access gates tracking people as they came and went – a far cry from the freedom and openness of earlier years. Eventually, the general aviation community adapted and tougher security measures became part of a normal routine. Trapp acknowledges the challenge of operating under new parameters while allowing necessary access for people who work in general aviation and those who use the airport for business and pleasure.

TRAINING AND MORE TRAINING

For airport public safety staff (formerly called fire and rescue), the operational model begins with a unique certification. All of the personnel in the department are "tri-certified." They are certified police officers, firefighters and emergency medical service (EMS) personnel. That certification requires hundreds of hours of training. In the 1980s, officers needed 400 hours of training at the police academy. By 2013, 750 hours were required with an additional 700 hours for basic fire training and 400 hours for EMS.

Every year public safety officers are required to complete 100 additional hours of professional development training, 40 hours of police training and 12 hours of EMS training. That's every officer, every year. If employees do not have those certifications, they cannot be employed as public safety personnel at the airport. It is serious business. The training enables them not only to meet, but to exceed, FAA guidelines. Also, in compliance with FAA training requirements, a full-scale emergency exercise is staged every three years. During the interim years, "tabletop" exercises (reviews held in a meeting room, not in the field) are performed to ensure airport and community preparedness.

FIRE TRAINING CENTER

Blue Grass Airport was one of only a handful of airports in the country to be chosen by the FAA as a preferred site to build an aircraft firefighting and rescue-training center in 1996. Two years later, the $5 million facility opened, and subsequently as many as 500 firefighters attend training at the facility annually. Managed by a department with extensive experience, the training center has attracted firefighting professionals from across the region.

The regional center has the latest technology and includes two aircraft simulators that allow safe, live fire training scenarios. The simulators replicate several types of emergency situations. Computer-controlled and propane-fired, they simulate fires involving large-scale flammable liquid, engines, wheels and brakes, as well as fires inside the cabin. Trainees also learn how to stop a disaster in its tracks and perform rescues. They are trained for small and large-scale emergencies.

In 2009, the center received a $1 million refurbishment. That investment brings the total to more than $6 million in infrastructure solely for training personnel. While Blue Grass Airport is regarded as one of the region's leading training centers for airport emergency responders, local firefighters from across Kentucky and the region are also trained here.

9/11 CHANGES EVERYTHING

Prior to September 11, 2001 (9/11), Blue Grass Airport was growing, not only with construction, but also with the addition of more non-stop flights. The ease of parking, getting to the ticket counter and arriving at the airline gate all within the distance of a few hundred feet was always a great selling point for flying in and out of Lexington. It was hassle-free travel at its best. "You didn't have to be here an hour ahead of time. You could be here ten minutes ahead of time and get on your plane. The terrorist attacks

One year after 9/11, a memorial service was held at the airport to honor those whose lives were lost in the tragedy.

on 9/11, of course, changed all of that," said former Airport Board Chairman Bernie Lovely. The impact upon business was negative and immediate.

When flights resumed, customers spoiled by the ease of flying in and out of Blue Grass Airport faced unprecedented change. "It created a lot of consternation in them and therefore, it was even more important that we worked very hard on customer service and community relations," Lovely said.

Congress passed legislation establishing the Transportation Security Administration (TSA) two months after the terrorist attacks. The TSA was given the responsibility of screening all passengers and baggage for explosives. By December 2002, every airport in the country was required to have an explosive detection system installed. Since federal law mandated the security changes, Blue Grass Airport's management team saw an opportunity to be a test site for the new screening technology and seized it. It was a chance to embrace change for the betterment of the community. The installation of this new baggage screening system placed Lexington in a leadership role among the airports in the field of aviation security.

There were two options for the new baggage screening equipment: placement in the lobby or behind the scenes. At the time, Lexington was one of only five airports in the country that opted for the behind-the-scenes scanners. It was also the smallest airport in the U.S. to have the advanced screening system. The choice was in keeping with what customers were accustomed to — hassle-free travel. Changes during the post-9/11 era brought new procedures and frustrating delays, but passengers in Lexington hardly knew it. Seven months after the deadline for advanced baggage screening implementation, the airport had a resurgence of air travel and was

THE IMPACT OF SEPTEMBER 11, 2001, ON BLUE GRASS AIRPORT

September 11, 2001 – At 9:45 a.m. EST, due to terrorist attacks on the World Trade Center in New York and the Pentagon in Washington, D.C., the Federal Aviation Administration (FAA) orders all aircraft to land at the nearest airport as soon as practical. At this time, there are more than 4,500 aircraft in the air on Instrument Flight Rules (IFR) flight plans. It is the first unplanned shutdown of U.S. airspace. It is estimated that by 12:15 p.m., the airspace over the 48 contiguous states was clear of all commercial and private flights. Blue Grass Airport, Louisville International Airport and Cincinnati/Northern Kentucky International Airport are evacuated for security sweeps.

September 13, 2001 – Airplanes remain grounded as Blue Grass Airport works on completing an FAA checklist imposing tougher security requirements. Blue Grass Airport receives clearance for arrivals and departures shortly after noon, and the first flight leaves Lexington for Atlanta at 12:50 p.m.

September 18, 2001 – During the previous year, Blue Grass Airport announced numerous additions to its non-stop destination lineup. However, following 9/11, airport officials say nothing is certain. About 20 percent of flights to and from Lexington have been canceled since the terrorist attacks last week and airlines are announcing massive cutbacks to stem their losses.

September 29, 2001 – Continental announces that it has dropped plans for non-stop service from Blue Grass Airport to LaGuardia Airport in New York City. The company had announced twice-daily flights on September 5, less than a week before the terrorist strikes on the World Trade Center and the Pentagon. The ban on air travel, and low traffic after it was lifted, forced the already ailing industry to cut flights and lay off employees.

October 6, 2001 – Thirty-five National Guardsmen are stationed at five Kentucky airports, including three guardsmen at Blue Grass Airport. The guard is called out after President Bush asks governors to assist in enhancing airport security at more than 400 locations in the wake of the September 11 attacks. Guards are stationed at the airport's security checkpoint and will be on duty any time there is a departing flight.

October 14, 2001 – Under federal security rules issued the previous week, airline passengers are limited to bringing a single piece of carry-on luggage, rather than two, in addition to another small bag, such as a purse or briefcase.

November 17, 2001 – The airport parking garage regains use of approximately 500 parking spaces, but all cars parking in the previously restricted area have to be inspected. Following the September 11 attacks, the FAA eliminated all parking within 300 feet of terminals across the country as a safeguard against car bombings. The ruling eliminated 30 percent of Blue Grass Airport's parking.

regarded as a model for airport screening. Growth continued. Three years after 9/11, service to five more cities was added in addition to one more airline.

The progress made in Lexington encouraged the U.S. Department of Homeland Security to choose Blue Grass Airport as one of only 12 airports in the country to serve as a security hub for general aviation aircraft needing to fly into Reagan National Airport in Washington, D.C. That airport was closed to general aviation traffic for four years after the 9/11 attacks. "This is a ringing endorsement for Lexington Blue Grass Airport," said U.S. Representative Hal Rogers, chairman of the House Homeland Security Appropriations Subcommittee. The Lexington airport was in the company of much larger airports on that approved "gateway" list including Seattle-Tacoma, Boston Logan, Houston Hobby, New York LaGuardia and Chicago Midway.

In the years following 9/11, the airport's public safety department continued to grow and bring in other local agencies for training. The FAA requires a full-scale mock disaster once every three years. On August 10, 2005, an exercise was held at the airport. Three hundred participants from 20 agencies reacted and trained to a simulated aircraft accident with "victims." Sadly, their training would be tested one year and seven days later.

TRAINING, TESTING AND THE UNTHINKABLE

Less than an hour before sunrise on August 27, 2006, emergency responders from Blue Grass Airport, Lexington Division of Police and Fire, Fayette County Sheriff's department and neighboring county EMS units received a call they will never forget. It was a call that put all their training on the line. Delta Comair Flight 5191 from Lexington to Atlanta had crashed at 6:07 a.m. on a farm directly adjacent to the airport after taking off on the wrong runway.

Flight 5191, a 50-seat Bombardier Canadair Regional Jet, had been cleared to take off on Runway 22, which was 7,000 feet long and used for commercial airline traffic. Instead it taxied to a closed Runway 26, a 3,500-foot runway used for small private aircraft, as it prepared to take off. Without adequate runway length,

the midsize airplane failed to lift off, hitting an earthen berm, fence and trees before bursting into flames. It was the worst domestic U.S. crash in nearly six years.

Airport public safety staff Jon Sallee, Pete Maupin, Richard Graham, Pat Alford and Carl

FEDERAL AVIATION ADMINISTRATION (FAA)

FACT SHEET: Chronology of Events on September 11, 2001

Notes: All times are EST. Flight departures are actual takeoff times.

0800. American Airlines Flight 11, a Boeing 767 with 92 people on board, takes off from Boston Logan airport for Los Angeles.

0814. United Airlines Flight 175, a Boeing 767 with 65 people on board, takes off from Boston Logan airport for Los Angeles.

0821. American Airlines Flight 77, a Boeing 757 with 64 people on board, takes off from Washington Dulles airport for Los Angeles.

0840. FAA notifies the North American Aerospace Defense Command's (NORAD) Northeast Air Defense Sector about the suspected hijacking of American Flight 11.

0841. United Airlines Flight 93, a Boeing 757 with 44 people on board, takes off from Newark airport for San Francisco.

0843. FAA notifies NORAD's Northeast Air Defense Sector about the suspected hijacking of United Flight 175.

0846. (approx.). American Flight 11 crashes into the north tower of the World Trade Center.

0902. (approx.). United Flight 175 crashes into the south tower of the World Trade Center.

0904. (approx.). The FAA's Boston Air Route Traffic Control Center stops all departures from airports in its jurisdiction (New England and eastern New York State).

0906. The FAA bans takeoffs of all flights bound to or through the airspace of New York Center from airports in that Center and the three adjacent Centers – Boston, Cleveland and Washington. This is referred to as a First Tier groundstop and covers the Northeast from North Carolina north and as far west as eastern Michigan.

0908. The FAA bans all takeoffs nationwide for flights going to or through New York Center airspace.

0920. The FAA establishes an open phone line with other government agencies and the military to share information about missing or suspicious aircraft.

0926. The FAA bans takeoffs of all civilian aircraft regardless of destination – a national groundstop.

0940. (approx.). American Flight 77 crashes into the Pentagon.

0945. In the first unplanned shutdown of U.S. airspace, the FAA orders all aircraft to land at the nearest airport as soon as practical. At this time, there were more than 4,500 aircraft in the air on Instrument Flight Rules (IFR) flight plans.

1007. (approx.) United Flight 93 crashes in Stony Creek Township, PA.

1039. Reaffirming the earlier order, the FAA issues a Notice to Airmen (NOTAM) that halts takeoffs and landings at all airports.

1215. (approx.). The airspace over the 48 contiguous states is clear of all commercial and private flights.

> **I remember when everything just stopped, and that's when we, as a group of first responders, had a prayer session.**

– Sgt. Scott May, Lexington Division of Police

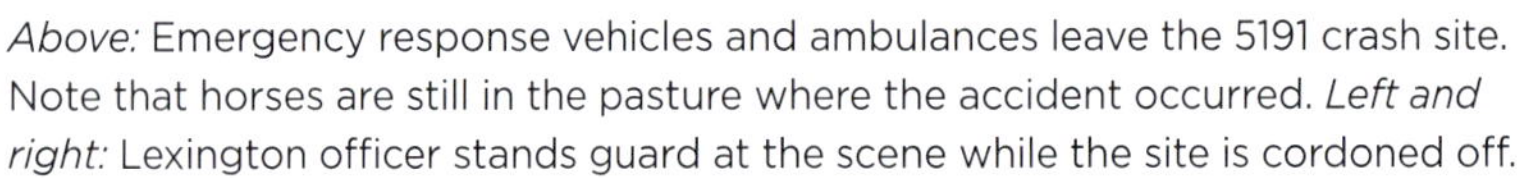

Above: Emergency response vehicles and ambulances leave the 5191 crash site. Note that horses are still in the pasture where the accident occurred. *Left and right:* Lexington officer stands guard at the scene while the site is cordoned off.

Faulconer, along with Lexington Police Officer Bryan Jared, were the first responding officers. Sallee, Maupin and Jared pulled first officer James Polehinke from the burning plane. As they were rushing Polehinke to the nearest hospital, a flood of police cruisers, fire engines and ambulances converged on the scene. Lexington Police Sergeant Scott May was also among the first to arrive. "There was a big rush to get there and do as much as we could, hoping for survivors and looking for them," Sergeant May said. The response was instant and in-stinctual. However, May added, it did not take long to realize there would be no additional survivors and

it became apparent as empty ambulances formed a caravan leaving the crash site.

Forty-seven passengers, a flight attendant and the captain had all died in the fiery crash. "We had never trained to respond to an aircraft accident where everyone died," recalled the airport's Director of Public Safety and Operations Scott Lanter. "We've always trained to go in and save everybody. We were able to make only one rescue and that was tough for a lot of the people at this airport," Lanter said.

The 5191 crash was a sobering lesson. "I remember when everything just stopped, and that's when we, as a group of first responders, had a prayer session,"

Sergeant May recalled. Then it was back to work with many, including May, working more than 20 hours at the crash site that first, very long, day.

When Lanter arrived he assumed command of the scene. Lanter was faced with the challenge of working with other local, state and federal agencies, including the FAA and National Transportation Safety Board (NTSB). He says everyone was equipped to work well together because of a strongly rooted history of collaborating in the past. The addition of federal authorities didn't change that relationship. NTSB Board Member (and later Chairman) Deborah Hersman, who led the investigation of the crash, called the people and support network at the airport and in Lexington unparalleled. "I have to say, it was a very difficult experience, but if any-

the design, layout and lighting of the runway. Power plant specialists studied the engines looking for signs of equipment failure. Aircraft performance specialists made sure the jet was performing as it should. The post-crash environment was scrutinized, too. This included the emergency response from the airport to the city's fire and rescue. No stone was left unturned.

THE AFTERMATH

Nearly a year later, in July 2007, the NTSB released its findings during a nine-hour hearing in Washington, D.C. Family members of the victims were present, including 5191 Captain Jeff Clay's widow. The crowd listened as the probable cause was issued: pilot error. Specifically, the NTSB determined the captain and first

The community shows its support for the victims' families and loved ones.

thing could be made easier, it was because of the people here in Lexington," Hersman said.

In the days, weeks and year that followed, the teamwork continued between local and federal authorities. Hersman noted that it is not unusual to encounter infighting during a crisis, but that didn't happen in Lexington. "That was one of the things that within the first 24 hours was very clear to me … that everyone was going to pull together. This was not a community that was going to pull apart when the tragedy happened."

With the arrival of the NTSB, attention switched to the investigation. Nearly 20 people with specialized areas of expertise looked into every angle of the accident. A former air traffic controller looked at operations at the tower that morning. Another expert looked into

officer failed to use the available cues that would have alerted them they were on the wrong runway during taxi. The board also concluded the pilots failed to perform a routine crosscheck to verify the airplane was on the correct runway prior to takeoff. The NTSB recommended that the FAA should prohibit the issuance of a takeoff clearance during an airplane's taxi to its departure runway until after the airplane has crossed all intersecting runways.

Though the NTSB report was very sobering, there were also two positive findings. The first was that "the first officer's survival was directly attributed to the prompt arrival of the first responders and their ability to extricate him." Second, "the emergency response was timely and well coordinated." These two findings

> **" *Sometimes people are placed in a position to respond and you just know what you have to do. You go on automatic.* "**
>
> – Gerry van der Meer, Flight 5191 Memorial Commission Co-chair

validated the airport's focus on safety and the dedication of the airport's public safety team. They also served to help reassure a community rocked by the tragedy.

Dr. Ray Garman, former chair of the airport board and co-chair of the Flight 5191 Memorial Commission, had this observation about the crash and its impact on the community: "I think everyone who lived in the Bluegrass – perhaps even as wide as Kentucky – knew at least one person who was on that plane because they came from the philanthropic community, the business community and social community of Lexington. We all had a sense of loss, and you could feel it."

A makeshift memorial at the airport

The profound loss prompted an intense reaction among people in the community. They wanted to help and comfort, and there were countless unsung heroes. From the companies bringing in food for the responders; to people who stopped what they were doing to stand on the side of the road with posters bearing written words of support for the families of the victims; to school children who created a banner for the victim's families staying at the Crowne Plaza Campbell House hotel – the community responded in countless ways.

Gerry van der Meer was the general manager of the Crowne Plaza Campbell House at that time and later served as co-chair of the Flight 5191 Memorial Commission. He and his staff opened their doors to the families who poured into Lexington and needed a central gathering place during the crisis. "Sometimes people are placed in a position to respond and you just know what you have to do. You go on automatic," van der Meer recalled. Local businesses, churches and individuals contributed food, water and comfort. The depth and breadth of response has been described as immeasurable. "People, when they see hurt or pain, are naturally drawn to help in whatever way they can," van der Meer said.

No one asked for help during the crisis. Yet help was available at every turn. "We are humbled by the support we have been shown," Michael Gobb, Blue Grass Airport executive director at the time of the accident, said of the community response.

Because of the accident, the community learned a profound lesson about loss and the resilience of the human spirit. NTSB Chairman Hersman noted, "You remember the grace that you saw people display in the darkest days of their lives and the people around them, how they just really open their arms to take care of them. I think that what we saw there – and all over Lexington – was that in the end, we are our brother's keeper. They took care of each other during a difficult time."

POST-5191 SAFETY CHANGES

While the NTSB ultimately determined the cause of the Comair 5191 crash was pilot error, its investigation uncovered deficiencies that demanded immediate attention. "We learned a lot from this accident, and I feel aviation is safer because of what happened here in Lexington. We learned, we made changes and now things are different," NTSB Chairman Hersman said. After the investigation the NTSB released 10 recommendations to the FAA and one to the National Air Traffic Controllers Association.

The new recommendations to the FAA included the following:

- *Requiring all crewmembers on the flight deck to confirm and cross-check the airplane's location to ensure they are at the assigned departure runway prior to takeoff*
- *Installing an automatic system that will alert pilots when a takeoff is attempted on an unintended taxiway or runway*
- *Requiring enhanced taxiway centerline markings and surface painted holding position signs at all runway entrances*
- *Prohibiting clearance for takeoff from the control tower during the taxi; clearance may only be given after the plane has crossed intersecting runways and has arrived at the departure runway*
- *Air traffic controllers should refrain from performing administrative tasks while moving aircraft are in their sight*

Other recommendations that surfaced in the report had been addressed before; however, the 5191 investigation prompted the board to re-issue them. At the top of the list: runway safety. The 5191 crash reinforced why runway safety is on the NTSB's Most Wanted List of transportation safety improvements. Pilot and air traffic controller professionalism also made that list which had been a problem during the events leading up to the accident. The report emphasized the need for the FAA to work with the National Air Traffic Controllers Association to reduce controller fatigue. Scheduling and shift modifications were among the areas needing to be addressed to ensure that the cognitive performance of air traffic controllers is always at its best. Additional training for controllers and managers in charge of scheduling was also proposed to address the causes and symptoms of fatigue. Procedures should be implemented to promote retention of well-trained controllers.

Five years after the crash, NTSB Chairman Hersman spoke to the families of the crash victims noting that the FAA has moved forward on five of the recommendations coming out of the NTSB Comair 5191 report.

5191 MEMORIAL

The 5191 Memorial Commission was formed shortly after the crash to create a lasting tribute to the lives lost. Dr. Ray Garman, chairman of the Aviation Museum of Kentucky at the time of the accident, and Gerry van der Meer, general manager of the Crowne Plaza Campbell House, served as co-chairs. The commission included victim's family members, community nonprofit leaders, representatives of entities dealing with the aftermath of the tragedy and airport staff. They started by taking time to build a sense of trust and consensus among the group.

A fund was established through the Blue Grass Community Foundation for the creation of the memorial and later an endowment, as well, to cover expenses and upkeep. Finding the perfect location for the memorial was not an easy task and ultimately a partnership was formed with Hospice of the Bluegrass to place the memorial in its Garden of Remembrance at the Arboretum, State Botanical Garden of Kentucky, adjacent to the University of Kentucky campus.

"There was a lot of crying in the beginning and later on there were a lot of smiles," van der Meer recalled of

Gas is $2.80 per gallon.

Virgin America begins operations.

Apple CEO Steve Jobs announces the iPhone.

Airbus A380 makes its first flight to the United States.

NASA launches the Phoenix spaceship.

Bob Barker airs his last episode of *The Price is Right*.

Queen Elizabeth II becomes the oldest monarch in the history of the United Kingdom.

A first-class postage stamp is 41 cents.

JEFF WILLIAMS
PAIGE MICHELLE WINTERS
BRIAN WOODARD
JOANN WRIGHT
BETTY BUTLER YOUNG
FLIGHT 5191
AUGUST 27, 2006
REBECCA ADAMS
LYLE ORVILLE ANDERSON

the delicate and often difficult process of developing a suitable memorial for a tragedy of that scale.

Creating a memorial that recognizes the ultimate human tragedy of lost lives while at the same time providing a place to grieve, reflect and find peace is a monumental undertaking. That balance was struck with the creation of the 5191 memorial. The responsibility was placed in the hands of sculptor, Douwe Blumberg.

The Los Angeles native, who now calls Northern Kentucky his home, was chosen from 49 applicants to create the memorial. Although the award-winning sculptor had the vision to complete more than 200 private and public commissions, the 5191 memorial was a unique undertaking. This was Blumberg's first memorial for an accident of this scale. His approach to his art is summarized on his website. "When I do a piece, my goal is to capture something special in it. I'm not interested in 'pretty,' I want a spark of life: movement, drama, that something that will make you look twice ... that power."

What Blumberg created is part art and part act of sheer engineering: "49 Birds in Flight - A flock of kindred souls pointed towards the heavens." The sculpture, standing at 18 feet, is as wide as it is tall and is made of cast aluminum and magnesium alloy. The names of the victims are etched on the granite base and the body of each bird holds a stainless steel canister containing mementos of the victims.

Blumberg talked about his vision during an interview with Kentucky Educational Television. "Birds in flight have always had a close association with a soul," he reflected and these are no exception. The birds, and the personal mementos tucked inside them from friends and relatives of the victims, represent the ineffable spirit of each lost life.

Finding the right location for the memorial required just as much time and thought, and another perfect balance was struck five years after the crash when the 5191 memorial was dedicated at the Arboretum. It's a location that is not too public, nor too secluded. The surroundings compliment the sculpture and invite reflection. More than 600 people attended the dedication at the Arboretum including NTSB Chairman Hersman. "See how they shine. Indeed all forty-nine. All special. All loved. Always remembered," Hersman said.

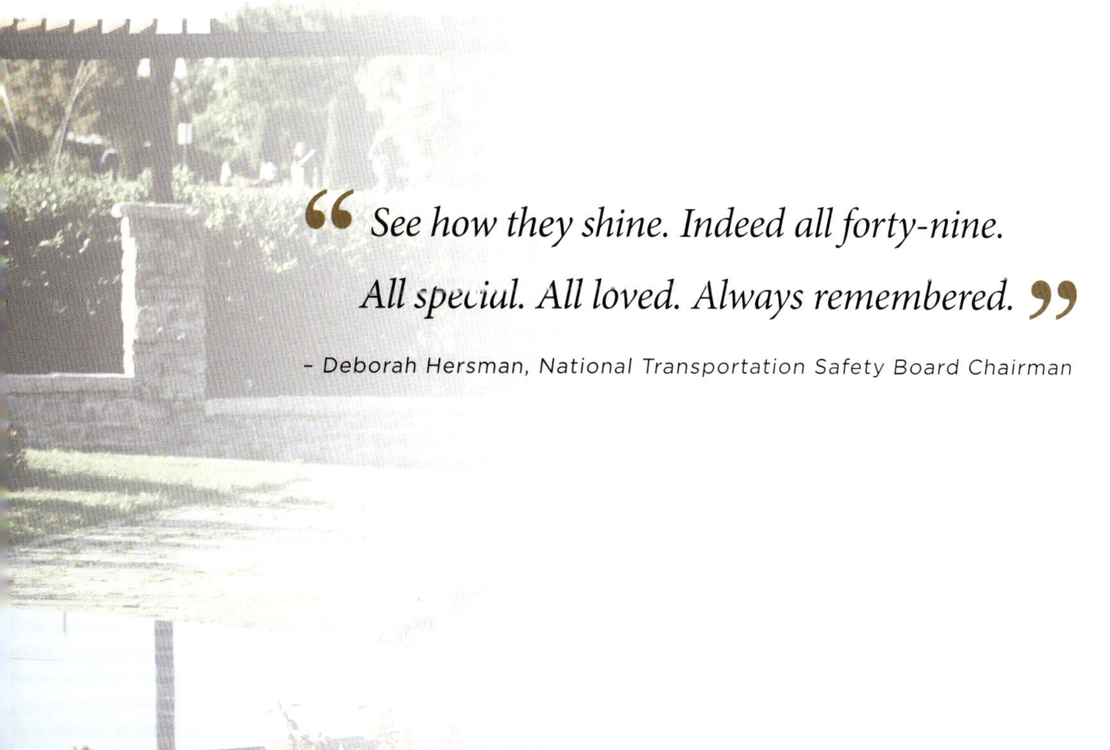

> **See how they shine. Indeed all forty-nine. All special. All loved. Always remembered.**
>
> – Deborah Hersman, National Transportation Safety Board Chairman

COMMUNITY
Connects Us All

BY KATHIE STAMPS

Communities are often forged and forever branded as a result of critical decisions made by their early leaders. Lexington is no exception. The epicenter of Kentucky's Bluegrass did not have the typical attributes that enable a community to grow and thrive when it was founded unceremoniously at a small camp in 1775 at McConnell Springs, a watering hole at the edge of the wilderness. It didn't have the commercial potential provided by a riverside or seaside port. Even by the standards of the day, it was pretty much in the middle of nowhere.

Its primary resource was clear natural spring water and a rolling landscape where, quite literally, the buffalo roamed. This land was left beautifully intact by the nomadic lifestyle of the Native Americans hunting the region during the millennia before the settlers arrived.

The early settlers found that it was a perfect place to breed and nurture livestock, and agriculture set the tone for this young community. It is interesting to note that horses and cattle in Kentucky are raised on "farms," as if they literally grow the animals out of the soil and mineral-rich water that feeds the lush Bluegrass pastures, whereas out West they tend to livestock on "ranches." Those minerals, especially the calcium from the limestone, have been credited with the superiority of the stock.

Although the Kentucky, Ohio and Mississippi rivers (the 18th- and 19th-century version of our interstate transport) were not convenient to Lexington, it did not seem to impede its growing economy. Higher education helped fill the void created by the lack of major industry, and Transylvania University, established in 1780, helped Lexington become known as the "Athens of the West." Ultimately, Lexington would grow to become one of the nation's largest cities not located on a navigable body of water.

Rail lines proliferated in the late 1800s and through the turn of the century. For many enterprises, rail provided viable transportation solutions, and railroads became the economic drivers for inland cities and regions. For passengers, train travel was in vogue, and it didn't matter what your social and economic status might be, you could get where you wanted to go by rail.

In the first quarter of the 20th century, automobiles took hold of the public's imagination – and their pocketbooks. Roads and highway systems were developed across the nation as the popularity of traveling by automobile increased.

The aeronautical advances made during World War I were incorporated into new airplanes that were more practical for both private enthusiasts and commercial enterprise. America embraced the modern age and never looked back.

As the use of automobiles and airplanes grew, infrastructure for both was developed to accommodate the new transportation patterns. Local leaders and government agencies with foresight built interstate highways and airports. In locales where these entities partnered to build for the future, the economic playing field was effectively leveled, and some businesses and industry sectors had the good fortune to gain a strategic advantage as a result.

The one-of-a-kind mural painted on a large retaining wall at one end of the airport's main runway combines scenes from several area farms to portray the iconic Kentucky horse farm.

The commitment to nurturing aviation was critical and the involvement and support of the community produced added benefits – a stronger, more vibrant, more diverse economy and a local culture with access to national and international influences.

FAST FORWARD TO TODAY

Today, Blue Grass Airport serves more than one million passengers annually, through five major airlines and non-stop service to 13 hub cities, including Atlanta, Charlotte, Chicago, Detroit and Minneapolis, plus connecting service to hundreds of worldwide destinations. This success is largely due to the airport's geographic location related to hub cities. The hub city proximity gives Blue Grass Airport access that other airports of similar size may not have.

WHO OWNS AND OPERATES THE AIRPORT?

Like many commercial service airports in the U.S., Blue Grass Airport is owned by an independent unit of local government. In this case, it is the Lexington-Fayette Urban County Airport Board, operating with powers granted by statutes of the Commonwealth of Kentucky. This type of entity is commonly referred to as an "airport authority." Blue Grass Airport is operated by a governing board, which sets policy and represents the interest of the community. The board, in turn, hires an executive director, who employs the appropriate staff to carry out the day-to-day functions of the airport.

The city of Lexington passed an ordinance on December 27, 1945, creating an airport board to manage the operation of Blue Grass Field. This ordinance stated that the board, to be known as the "City of Lexington-Fayette County Airport Board," would consist of six members, three of whom would be appointed by the city of Lexington

and three by the county of Fayette. The members of the board were to be appointed by the city manager and the first members appointed would serve for terms of one, two and three years, respectively. Upon the expiration of the first terms, successors would be appointed for three-year terms. The ordinance also stated that members of the airport board would serve without compensation except for the position of secretary-treasurer, who may or may not be a member of the board, who can receive a salary of $500 per year.

When city and county government merged in June 1972, the new charter changed the name to the "Lexington-Fayette Urban County Airport Board," and all six members were appointed by the mayor and confirmed by members of the Urban County Council with up to two four-year terms.

Fifty-three years after it was first established, the board was expanded

from six to 10 members as a direct result of controversy surrounding airport expansion.

In 1998, the state enacted legislation that expanded the Lexington-Fayette Urban County Airport Board to 10 members. One member of the airport board was to be a representative of Lexington-Fayette Urban County Government designated by the mayor. The nine other members, two of whom must live within a three-mile radius of the airport, were to be appointed by the mayor and approved by the Lexington-Fayette Urban County Council.

The airport is not funded by local tax dollars but instead is self-supportive by collecting revenue generated by the varied activities of airlines, tenants, service providers and passenger use. Major construction projects have typically been funded through bond issues and federal grants, although in the early days, bank loans were used for funding improvements and infrastructure.

Opposite page: Blue Grass Airport often hosts Commerce Lexington networking events in the terminal. *Above:* During the 2010 Alltech FEI World Equestrian Games, Blue Grass Airport experienced one of the busiest times in the airport's history with a passenger boarding increase of 39 percent from the year prior.

With an annual economic impact of $370 million and 3,478 jobs for Lexington, the airport is an important component of Lexington's economy, contributing to both the Lexington area and other parts of Kentucky. For starters, Blue Grass Airport is the primary scheduled airline service provider for not only central Kentucky, but also for much of eastern and southern Kentucky, serving a 54-county area.

Because of the airport, residents of Lexington and the region can more conveniently access the national air transportation system, allowing them to conduct business in all parts of the U.S. and internationally, to visit family and friends and to enjoy vacation destinations. The airport also makes it easy for hundreds of thousands of visitors to come to Lexington for business and for amenities that the region offers. The Lexington Convention and Visitors Bureau works with the airport to bring conventions to the region. When they arrive, convention visitors are greeted by in-airport signage, an airport welcome center and use of the executive lounge.

The airport occupies 1,076 acres directly across from a national historic landmark racetrack and the leading Thoroughbred auction sales company in the

2012

The average price of a gallon of gas is $3.61.

Continental Airlines, in operation since 1934, fully merges into United Airlines.

Felix Baumgartner becomes the first person to break the sound barrier without any machine assistance during a record space dive.

Eighty-four percent of U.S. domestic flights arrive within 15 minutes of their scheduled arrival time – a record since the government began tracking them in 1988.

The summer Olympic Games are held in London, England.

NASA's most advanced Mars rover, Curiosity, lands on the red planet.

Neil Armstrong, the first man to walk on the moon, dies at 82.

The United States Hunter Jumper Association's International Hunter Derby Championship is one of many equine competitions that the Kentucky Horse Park plays host to annually.

world – Keeneland. It is in the heart of Lexington's "green belt," a zoning mechanism ensuring that the beautiful Thoroughbred horse farms surrounding it for miles are preserved rather than developed.

Known as the "Horse Capital of the World," Lexington has an extensive equine industry supported by the airport. Besides iconic Keeneland, the Kentucky Horse Park figures prominently with many national equine-related associations onsite and a full calendar of regional, national and even international events taking place on the grounds.

With more than 350 horse farms located in the Bluegrass, it is no surprise that two of the largest equine veterinary practices in the world are nearby. Hagyard Equine Medical Institute, with more than 50 vets plus support staff, was founded in 1876, and moved to Lexington in 1891. Rood & Riddle Equine Hospital opened in

Lexington in 1986 and quickly grew to a staff of more than 50 vets and 200 support personnel.

Two Thoroughbred auction companies are based in Lexington and are considered economic drivers for the

Lexington has earned the name "Horse Capital of the World."

airport, the hospitality industry and a myriad of supporting businesses. Keeneland, with four auctions each year and race meetings in April and October, is across Versailles Road from the airport. Fasig-Tipton Company is the oldest Thoroughbred auction firm in North America and is located on Newtown Pike, where Glengarry Field/Cool Meadow, the airport that preceded Blue Grass Field, was located.

The airport is such an integral part of the regional equine industry that it has an air cargo operation – H.E. "Tex" Sutton Forwarding Company, LLC – dedicated to transporting horses to and from Blue Grass Airport.

RECOGNIZED FOR EQUALITY AND EXCELLENCE

Federal regulations require airports to set disadvantaged business enterprise goals and Lexington's airport has consistently surpassed those goals for the past 10 years, winning a national award from the Federal Aviation Administration for excellence in the process.

Blue Grass Airport is considered one of the top employers of minority business in Fayette County and has hosted multiple minority conferences and educational seminars with local partners including Small Business Opportunities Seminars, where small businesses learn to collaborate with others on Request for Proposal submittals.

Porter G. Peeples, president and CEO of the Urban League of Lexington and former airport board member, has high praise for the airport's efforts on behalf of minorities and disadvantaged businesses. "Blue Grass Airport goes beyond what is expected or required to meet minimum standards related to disadvantaged busi-

In 2009, Airport Board Member P.G. Peeples *(left)* and Engineering Director Mark Day *(right)* accepted the national Disadvantaged Business Enterprise Advocate Partner Award from FAA representative Fanny Rivera.

ness enterprise. They do what is right to help give people the opportunities they need to succeed."

MAKING AN IMPRESSION

Inside and out, Blue Grass Airport makes a beautiful first impression for travelers who fly to Lexington. Perhaps being located across from a national historic landmark (Keeneland) and one of the most picture-perfect horse farms (Calumet Farm) sets the tone for Lexington's airport. From the start, zoning in the area surrounding the airport was an important issue for city leaders and neighboring farms. Their efforts paid off and the emphasis on beauty and tranquility are still in the forefront today.

On approach, it is the gently rolling Kentucky countryside and Calumet Farm that captivate travelers' visual sense. Inside the terminal, Blue Grass Airport has invested heavily in improvements to ensure an accessible facility for the traveling public.

As it finished projects on its master plan and readied itself for the 2010 Alltech FEI World Equestrian Games – the international equivalent of the Olympic Games for equine sport – the airport had one of its busiest construction seasons in history.

Shops operated by retailer, The Paradies Shops, provide passengers with an assortment of local merchandise.

Left: Bronze equine sculptures created by world-renowned artist Gwen Reardon are located in a "paddock" area neighboring the rental car facility. *Above:* Passengers receive assistance at the Information Center with mascot Big Lex in the background. *Below:* The airport's trompe l'oeil mural and the equine-themed landscape won the prestigious Jay Hollingsworth Speas Award.

Airport officials and local dignitaries unveil the terrazzo floor in the terminal lobby that reflects the historical lineage of the world's top Thoroughbreds. From left to right, Les Kimbrough, Porter G. Peeples, Roszalyn Akins, Bernard Lovely, John Davis, Mayor Jim Newberry, Councilmember Linda Gorton, Commissioner Winn Turney, J. Robert Owens and Eric Frankl.

A $2.6 million renovation to the terminal's lobby level included new airline ticket counters, replacement of the ceiling system with energy-efficient products including an iconic, locally produced, Big Ass Fan,™ updated way-finding signage and relocation of the Information Center. Encouraging passengers to come back and explore the rich equine heritage, a beautiful concentric design on the terrazzo floor was installed charting the sire lineage of 800 Thoroughbreds through more than 300 years of Thoroughbred genealogy.

Shortly after the 2010 Alltech FEI World Equestrian Games, the lobby in the airport terminal became the permanent home to a piece of stained glass artwork depicting a blue horse named Big Lex, the mascot of the Lexington Convention and Visitors Bureau. Adapted from a painting by Edward Troye in the 1800s, John F. "Zig" Zeigler of Zeigler Stained Glass in Lexington created the piece and with the assistance of LexArts, donated it to the airport.

Building on the equestrian theme, the exterior of the airport has its own "paddock" between the terminal and rental car facility that closely resembles the actual paddock across the road at Keeneland. Artist Gwen Reardon created life-size bronze horse and handler sculptures set on three walking rings representing the three Triple Crown races. Keeneland donated recycled-rubber "brick" pavers and other landscaping elements for the project, developed and sponsored by the Triangle Foundation, a local charitable foundation dedicated to creating and improving public spaces in Lexington.

When a $35 million runway safety project necessitated the construction of a large embankment and

A $16 million concourse expansion in 2007 provided additional passenger gates and seating areas.

a 30-foot-by-800-foot retaining wall facing historic Keeneland, rather than leaving the wall blank and marring the view, the airport commissioned a trompe l'oeil mural by internationally recognized artist Eric Henn. Depicting a stone bridge, a federal-style house and images from Kentucky horse farms, the mural was so successful that it was awarded the Jay Hollingsworth Speas Airport Award in 2006. The award is highly coveted within the aviation industry and recognizes projects that achieve compatible relationships between airports and the landscapes that surround them.

The staff at the Lexington Convention and Visitors Bureau (Lexington CVB) understands the importance of air travel to a destination and, if you ask them, they will tell you how much they love their airport and why.

Their charge is to market Lexington to meeting planners and business and leisure travelers in order to "put heads in beds." They watch area hotel occupancy rates like brokers track the stock market. Their goal: keeping Lexington's hospitality industry hopping and Bluegrass attractions vibrant.

When a meeting planner considers bringing a convention to Lexington they always ask about the airport, with one of the first questions being "How convenient is the lift?" This is tourism industry-speak for the total number of non-stop flights, connecting flights and overall ease of arriving and departing by air.

With Blue Grass Airport's non-stop flights to major cities and the ability to fly to many destinations in the world with one stop, the answer is simple. They can assure potential meeting and convention clients that getting to and through Lexington's airport is easy.

Not only is getting through security screening as efficient as possible, but deplaning is also quick. From landing and taxiing to picking up luggage at baggage claim, because of the facilities, amenities and scale, the whole process is without hassle. Travelers to Lexington can get a rental car or a cab and be at their hotel faster than they can get to baggage claim from a gate in some of the big airports. Another perk – at least 15 hotels in Lexington offer shuttle service from the airport, most of them free of charge for hotel guests.

The airport's friendly staff is another selling point for the Lexington CVB. A typical convention in Lexington will bring in 1,200 to 1,400 people, but the airport has accommodated attendees of conferences for many times that number. Take locally based corporation Alltech for example. In addition to hosting frequent international colleagues and customers, the Alltech International Symposium draws approximately 3,000 people from more than 70 countries every year – with the majority of them traveling through Blue Grass Airport.

One of Lexington CVB's largest market segments is equine, a truly international industry with racing, breeding, eventing and pleasure riding on continents around the globe.

Nearly one million people visit the Kentucky Horse Park every year. They explore the park, conduct business with on-site equine associations, attend horse shows, watch the annual Rolex Kentucky Three-Day Event and participate in numerous other activities.

Keeneland attracts a half-million visitors annually as racing draws fans from around the country and sales bring buyers from around the world. In addition to Keeneland, the city of Lexington gets quite a bit of spillover from another race taking place at Churchill Downs in Louisville on the first Saturday in May.

Many Kentucky Derby guests, including tour and incentive groups, prefer to stay in Lexington instead of Louisville during Derby weekend. As central Kentuckians know, Churchill may have the race, but Lexington has the reason with world-famous hospitality and an incredible horse farm ambience that entices many visitors to start or end their Derby festivities in the Bluegrass.

While a lot of central Kentucky's international leisure travelers are attracted to Lexington for the many

Keeneland Race Course, located across Versailles Road from the airport, is famed for its Thoroughbred race meets and horse sales.

Bourbon aging in barrels at Buffalo Trace Distillery in Frankfort.

equine-related activities that take place in the Bluegrass region, bourbon is also a big draw. Most people visiting for distillery tours or bourbon tastings will stay overnight in Lexington instead of other towns, according to the Kentucky Distillers' Association.

Two years prior to the Alltech FEI World Equestrian Games, the Lexington CVB instituted a training program for tourism ambassadors. This ambassador program requires a half-day class to learn about area tourism and for ambassadors to maintain a certain level of involvement throughout the year. All frontline employees of the airport have been certified through the program.

HEALTH AND SAFETY MATTER

The airport has historically had close ties to both law enforcement agencies and military units. The Lexington Division of Police bases its helicopter at Blue Grass Air-

port. Its flights support efforts to lower crime and to keep the community safe. The airport is also used for prisoner transport flights since the Federal Medical Center prison (formerly known as the Federal Correctional Institute) is located in Lexington.

Blue Grass Airport is also the headquarters of the 138th Field Artillery of the Kentucky National Guard. It has operated its armory and operational maintenance shop on the southeast part of the airport since 1972. The Guard unit employs 97 full-time Guardsmen and 488 part-timers. Its annual economic output exceeds $31.8 million.

The design and layout of the airport, its parking structures and its location on Versailles Road at Man o' War Boulevard – a straight shot from downtown Lexington – make air travel super convenient for Lexingtonians. Going a step beyond convenience, the airport serves as a critical component in medical emergencies.

Kentucky Organ Donor Affiliates (KODA), formed in 1987, is a nonprofit organ and tissue procurement agency serving 112 hospitals and three transplant centers. KODA has utilized the facilities of Blue Grass Airport and its charter plane services on numerous occasions. In 2012, there were 103 occasions for "fly-outs" so that transplant surgeons and KODA team members could recover organs at a hospital outside of Lexington or out of state.

"These life-saving flights make it possible to recover organs and transport them for transplantation in a timely manner," said Jenny Miller Jones, KODA's director of education. "Using the charter service out of Blue Grass Airport makes saving lives possible."

Founded in 1968 as the Central Kentucky Blood Center and renamed in 2007, the Kentucky Blood Center is the largest FDA-licensed blood bank headquartered in the state. Located in Lexington, the Kentucky Blood Center's service area includes nearly 70 hospitals and clinics in more than 60 Kentucky counties, with distributions of more than 100,000 blood components annually.

When the blood centers receive blood components from other areas of the country or need to share blood with other centers, these life-saving products are usually transported through Blue Grass Airport. As a collection site for the National Marrow Donor Program (NMDP), the blood center collects stem cells that are then couriered by air for patients awaiting transplant. Kentucky Blood Center is also a Dendreon collection facility, a treatment option for prostate cancer patients. The patient's own cells are collected in Lexington and immediately shipped through Blue Grass Airport to a facility in Atlanta or Southern California, where the cells are treated and returned to the patient as a transfusable drug.

"Without access to a top-notch airport, we would not be a Dendreon or NMDP facility. And these are important services we provide to the community," said William Reed, president and CEO of Kentucky Blood Center. "The airport is also a vital component in our disaster preparedness plan because we need to be able to import or export blood components very quickly whenever necessary."

> **"** *Using the charter service out of Blue Grass Airport makes saving lives possible.* **"**
>
> – Jenny Miller Jones, Kentucky Organ Donor Affiliates

Medical transport helicopter

Dr. David Stevens, one of the founding members of the blood center, has served on Blue Grass Airport's board of directors. Likewise, Eric Frankl, Blue Grass Airport's executive director, now serves on the Kentucky Blood Center board.

Making the airport a trusted and valuable member of the community is Frankl's goal. "Most people think of the airport in terms of commercial aviation, of taking a flight, for business or pleasure," he said. "They may not have any idea that a rare blood type or organ transplant can be flown directly in to our airport and may save their life."

2ND SUNDAY AND MORE

Air circuses and aerial shows drew people from the community to early local airstrips in days gone by. Putting on air shows at busy commercial airports in the 21st century is not always a viable way to engage the public. Taking their place are family-friendly events that promote health and physical activity. Once a year, the airport

actually closes its 4,000-foot runway to air traffic and opens it for people to run, walk, bike and generally experience the mind-boggling vastness of a runway.

The first such event, called 2nd Sunday (named for the second Sunday in a given month), began when then-council member Jay McChord had a meeting with Frankl in early 2010. McChord recalls seeing a rendering of a runway under construction at that time.

"I asked, could you ride a bike on it or run on it? And he said, 'Probably,'" McChord said. McChord's brain started spinning. He wanted to incorporate the airport into Lexington's monthly 2nd Sunday bike ride, with people riding their bicycles from downtown to the airport, taking a lap on a runway that was under construction and

Left: The airport opens its crosswind runway annually to host a 5K run in partnership with United Way of the Bluegrass. *Opposite page inset:* 2nd Sunday participants enjoy yoga on the runway. *Above:* Cyclists and walkers exercise while exploring vintage aircraft.

then riding back. Before long, the runway became the venue itself instead of just a midway point.

"The airport was visionary enough and gracious enough to say okay," McChord said. In June 2010, 2nd Sunday took place at the airport with thousands of people on the runway.

"It was just crazy," McChord said. He was delighted, of course, that Blue Grass Airport management saw it as a community day, even setting out vintage planes and helicopters. Airport and city fire trucks

were also on display, as were police helicopters and motorcycles. While thousands of people were running and playing on Runway 9-27, they also had the opportunity to watch planes land and take off on the nearby commercial runway.

2nd Sunday was inspired by a community event in Bogota, Colombia, where a city street was closed so people could run and have fun. It was successfully adapted for Lexington in 2008 by McChord and Diana Doggett, an agent with the Family and Consumer Sciences Extension at the University of Kentucky. Each of the 120 counties in Kentucky is encouraged to cordon off an existing piece of infrastructure and use it for walking, biking and other forms of physical activity for the entire community.

The 2nd Sunday event even earned a first-place award for Blue Grass Airport in the "best special event" category by Airports Council International-North America.

2nd Sunday is not the only community-oriented activity that takes place on a closed runway. When United Way of the Bluegrass wanted to do a fundraiser in the form of a 5K race, they contacted McChord, who suggested Blue Grass Airport. The first United Way "5K on the Runway" took place in June 2012 and again in June 2013.

MESSER CONSTRUCTION CO.
Actively Engaged in the Community Where They Work

Over the years, Blue Grass Airport has had the benefit of working with a variety of companies that have been great long-term partners, like Messer Construction Co. Their business track record brings stability and institutional knowledge, which provide immediate benefits to every construction project.

Founded in 1932, Messer has built a solid reputation for providing outstanding value and delivering fast track, design-build projects with companies like Eli Lilly, Honda of America Co., Yamaha Motor Corporation and Valvoline.

At Blue Grass Airport, they have handled construction projects such as the 1990 terminal expansion, the parking garage and the Concourse B addition. Beyond new construction, Messer has also played a significant role in multiple complex renovation projects within the terminal and concourse areas of the airport.

When major construction projects happen at a busy airport, the highest priority is safety. Messer's commitment to keeping staff and visitors safe during the building process has earned them national recognition. Working in and around occupied spaces is an art that Messer has mastered.

Messer Construction Co. has contributed more than $500,000 and countless volunteer hours to the Lexington community since 2006 – one of the nine communities where they have established regional offices. Their philosophy of "working where we live" develops deep, trusting relationships with clients, stakeholders, subcontractors and suppliers as evidenced by the relationship they have developed with Blue Grass Airport.

Messer has handled new construction such as the concourse and parking garage, as well as renovation projects at Blue Grass Airport.

AND LET'S NOT FORGET TRAVEL AMENITIES

From the earliest days, keeping the traveling public comfortable on their air travel adventures was important. As aviation progressed, handing out goggles and heavy blankets gave way to more refined comforts. Once the novelty of flying wore off, and as more travelers saw how other cities accommodated their flying public – it was "game on" for airports to treat their customers well.

While Lexington did not have a "real" airport with restrooms, electricity, telephone service, paved roads and runways for decades, once Blue Grass Field opened, the public and those providing service to them expected more.

When commercial flights began servicing Blue Grass Field, restaurants came and went every few years. The volume just wasn't there in the early days for proprietors to make a profit – but the traveling public expected it and the potential lured operator after operator to make a go of it. Sundry shops, pinball machines and observation decks were added for the convenience and entertainment of the public.

Today, business travelers find everything they need at Blue Grass Airport, including free wireless internet access throughout the terminal – light years from the bare basics of Halley Field and Cool Meadow and certainly unimaginable technology and convenience when compared to the earliest days of Blue Grass Field.

In 2006, the airport unveiled a new executive lounge, The Club at Blue Grass, featuring complimentary snacks and beverages, flat-screen televisions, meeting facilities, copying and faxing services, all with a high level of personalized service. Private meeting facilities located near gates and the concourses make it easy to conduct business or interview prospective employees at the airport anytime – the ultimate convenience for businesses dealing with sensitive issues, located out of town or that have limited facilities. Blue Grass Airport is one of only a few small-hub airports nationwide to offer an airport-operated executive lounge.

In late 2012, mobile boarding pass check-in was introduced at the airport, allowing passengers to have their boarding pass sent directly to their smartphone or tablet, which is then scanned at the security checkpoint and the airline gate, allowing passengers to bypass the ticket counter.

Travelers at Blue Grass Airport have a number of shopping and dining options. In Concourse B, the nation's first-ever *New York Times* Bookstore opened in 2005. It is operated by The Paradies Shops, an airport retailer with more than 550 stores in 75 markets. It also operates the Blue Grass MarketPlace in the airport's lobby. In June 2012, the Kentucky Ale Taproom began offering travelers a taste of the Bluegrass, including Alltech's Kentucky Bourbon Barrel Ale and Town Branch Bourbon. A MarketFresh restaurant, located prior to security checkpoint, also opened in 2012. Dunkin' Donuts and Pepper's Mexican Grill opened on the second level in 2013 and 2014, respectively.

AVIATION MUSEUM OF KENTUCKY

The Aviation Museum of Kentucky, conveniently located on Blue Grass Airport property, was dedicated on August 6, 1993, in what was originally the Diamond Shamrock hangar at the airport. In 2010, the museum moved to its current location, the 20,000-square foot building formerly occupied by fixed-base operator TAC Air. Leasing the facility from Blue Grass Airport, the president and chief operating officer and the 18-member board of directors of the museum work to accomplish their mission: preserving the history of aircraft for the public and educating area youth on careers in aviation.

For aviation enthusiasts, school groups and Scout troops, the Aviation Museum of Kentucky is quite a treat. About 10,000 people visit the museum every year, from all 50 states and 80 countries, to see in one location all manner of aircraft, including biplanes and vintage World War II fighter planes. In addition to permanent displays, the museum receives three or four new pieces of memorabilia every year.

Every summer, 300 to 400 young people, aged 10 to 15, attend one of the aviation camps at the museum. About 30 percent are girls. More than 5,000 young people have been introduced to aviation since the summer camps began in 1995. For some it's just summer fun; for others it has led to careers in the military or in aviation as a pilot, mechanic, engineer, air traffic

GRESHAM, SMITH AND PARTNERS
Enhancing Customer Experience Through Design

Gresham, Smith and Partners (GS&P) has served as a trusted and valued advisor to Blue Grass Airport for more than two decades. This longstanding relationship is possible because of a staff that includes experts in many different facets of aviation design, from roadways to curbsides, terminals to gates, and everything in between.

GS&P designed the airport's parking structure and a phased multiyear terminal renovation that reflects the culture of the Bluegrass region and provides a beautiful customer experience for those flying in and out of Blue Grass Airport.

Their vast array of in-house expertise, including architecture, engineering, interior design, wayfinding, environmental consulting and comprehensive planning services, gives them the best team possible to meet the airport's needs.

GS&P's award-winning aviation group has an impressive resume that includes small regional airports as well as the busiest airports in the world. They have worked with more than 35 of the nation's top 100 airports.

They are also heavily involved in aviation industry organizations, which helps them stay abreast of international standards and best practices. This ongoing dedication to "honing their craft" gives them additional opportunities to provide value to their clients while responding to their needs.

Their philosophy? Airports are as unique as the communities they represent, and they work to reflect that individuality through a wide range of design and planning expertise. GS&P certainly accomplished that in Lexington!

Concourses A and B are great examples of Gresham, Smith and Partners' work at Blue Grass Airport.

Inset: Best-selling author Rita Mae Brown autographs books at Blue Grass Airport on opening day of the nation's first *New York Times* Bookstore. *Above:* Passengers enjoy the upscale amenities and business services of The Club at Blue Grass. This airport-operated lounge opened in 2005 and provides a comfortable respite from traveling.

controller, flight attendant, meteorologist, clerk, freight handler, travel agent or any number of other positions related to aviation.

From an economic perspective, the aviation industry contributes more than $10 billion in revenue and supports 130,000 jobs in Kentucky. In addition, Kentuckians have contributed to aviation's rich history, and many of their accomplishments are showcased at the museum.

Solomon Van Meter, born at Shenandoah Hall in Lexington, invented the modern "backpack" parachute and filed for a patent in 1911. In 1937, Willa Brown Chappell, of Glasgow, Kentucky, became the first African-American female to become a licensed pilot in the United States. Albert Ueltschi, founder of FlightSafety International in 1951, was from Franklin County. Prior to his career in academia, Earlington, Kentucky, native Dr. Lee Todd, former president of the University of Kentucky, was an electrical engineer and his company, Projectron Inc., developed the cathode ray tube used by Rediffusion Simulation's flight simulators.

The history of the museum itself dates back to 1978, when former Air Force mechanic Wendell Murphy, founder of the local Avis franchise, and George Gumbert, M.D., an orthopedic surgeon and member of the Lexington-Fayette Urban County Airport Board, cofounded a small group they called the Kentucky Aviation History

Solomon Van Meter

Above: A wonderful assortment of aircraft on display at the Aviation Museum of Kentucky. *Below:* Wendell Murphy and Dr. George Gumbert were instrumental in launching the museum.

Roundtable. It was an opportunity for people to get together and talk about their airplanes and flying. The group put up their first exhibit in the lobby of Blue Grass Airport, which included a swatch of fabric from the Wright brothers' Kitty Hawk aircraft in a sterling silver replica of the plane. For years the members of the roundtable talked about a permanent home for the memorabilia they had collected, and in 1993 the museum became a reality.

The Aviation Museum of Kentucky is considered a boutique museum when compared with larger, more nationally recognized institutions such as the National Museum of the Air Force, located at the Wright-Patterson Air Force Base in Ohio, or the Smithsonian National Air and Space Museum in Washington, D.C. The Aviation Museum of Kentucky is a nonprofit organization, funded by entrance fees, memberships and donations.

The museum also houses the Kentucky Aviation Hall of Fame, designated as the Commonwealth of Kentucky's official aviation hall of fame by the Kentucky General Assembly, which has inducted four to five people every year since 1996, from brigadier generals and Tuskegee Airmen to astronaut Story Musgrave, who earned his pilot's license at Blue Grass Field while attending graduate school at the University of Kentucky in the mid 1960s.

With a museum reflecting Kentucky's rich aviation heritage and an airport proudly showcasing the equine legacy of the Bluegrass region, travelers can get a "sense of place" just passing through Lexington's jewel of an airport.

That character, when combined with gracious southern hospitality and an ongoing commitment to provide customers with the highest levels of safety, service and technology, makes Blue Grass Airport a Kentucky tradition to be savored.

ACKNOWLEDGEMENTS

By Fran Taylor

What a privilege it has been to work on this project. Everyone we approached was excited about being involved, extraordinarily kind and open to sharing his or her resources. Airport board members (past and present), aviation enthusiasts and airport employees shared memories, mementos and offers to help. The aviation partners we contacted offered information and photos. Plus, the subject matter was fascinating and full of surprises at every turn.

I can't begin to thank chapter writer Scott May enough for his contributions and encouragement. He has been researching early aviation in central Kentucky for the past six years and was a wealth of information. Scott wrote the first chapter in the book and shared his research and photographs. He was also endlessly patient with my many queries.

This book would not have been possible without the rich repository of photos and news stories from the archives of the *Lexington Herald-Leader* housed at the Lexington Public Library. The *Kentuckiana Digital Archives* at the University of Kentucky are also a treasure trove of images enriching this and every regional research project. Sharon Ruble, former *Lexington Herald-Leader* photo imaging director, went above and beyond to find wonderful images to bring the stories in this book to life and prepare them for publication.

Suzanne Dorman, the talented designer for this project, worked early mornings, nights, weekends and every spare moment to put this book together – beautifully.

Amy Caudill, the director of marketing and community relations for the airport, was absolutely indispensable throughout this very long and complex project. This book would never have happened without her, and it is all the better for her dedication and painstaking attention to detail.

Grady Walter at Stablemate Creative did a tremendous job editing the book. He and Rob Kandt were proofing gurus and helped rectify grammatical and typographical errors.

The chapter writers, all of whom gave great local and sometimes personal perspective to their subject matter, were game to tackle work not in their immediate area of expertise – which meant more research time and a tougher challenge. It was a pleasure getting to know them better through this process.

After living in central Kentucky for nearly 40 years, I thought I knew a lot about the Bluegrass. I knew that people were in love with UK basketball and Keeneland and that most adults can name their favorite horses, jockeys and bourbons. I've learned that you can poll people about whether they prefer white fences or black fences, and it will pretty much be a toss-up between the two. But, I had no idea how many people loved aviation. What a revelation.

Were it not for Eric Frankl and Amy Caudill deciding that this story should be told and making it happen, and the airport board supporting this decision, I would never have learned firsthand about the American heroes who helped shape our early aviation history. I wouldn't have understood the sagas of visionary community leaders, who against all odds built the early airfields and Blue Grass Field. And, I would never have realized the role that aviation played in helping our community grow while keeping the rich heritage of the Bluegrass intact. A heartfelt thank-you to all who supported this project.

CONTRIBUTORS

Rena Baer *(The Birth of Blue Grass Field)* is a Lexington freelance editor, writer and former journalist with the *Charlotte Observer* and the *New York Times* Regional News Group. She still considers it her civic duty to read the newspaper every day.

Robert Bolson *(It's Official: We are a Commercial Airport!)* is a freelance writer, award-winning corporate marketing and advertising professional, gregarious gourmand, recreational photographer and life-long resident of Lexington. He has written about various topics, from travel and lifestyle trends, to haute couture and Thoroughbred racing.

Dan Dickson *(The Jet Age: Dawn of a Modern Airport)* writes for several regional and national publications covering business, travel and state government. He is a former news reporter and anchor at television stations in Lexington and Louisville.

Ave Lawyer *(The Famous and Infamous)* divides her time between freelance writing and marketing projects and conceiving and directing site-specific productions for On The Verge theater company, of which she is a founding member.

Celeste Lewis *(Change: The Only Constant in Aviation)* is a visual artist and freelance writer, living in her hometown, Lexington. A happily repatriated Kentuckian, she has also lived and worked in the Rocky Mountains where she wrote for several publications in Utah and Wyoming.

Scott May *(Lexington Catches Flying Fever)* is a native of Danville, Kentucky, who now lives in Lexington. He has been involved in aviation since the late 1980s. He is a pilot of both airplanes and helicopters, which he flies for the Lexington Division of Police.

Patti Nickell *(Private Aviation: Dawn of a Modern Airport)* is a Lexington-based freelance writer whose travel features appear in the *Herald-Leader*. In addition, her articles have appeared in the *Los Angeles Times, Chicago Tribune, Miami Herald, Seattle Times, Vancouver Sun, Toronto Star*, and *Charlotte Observer*, among other papers.

Michelle Rauch *(Preparing for Crisis and the Unthinkable Happens)* is an award-winning journalist. After nearly 20 years in television news, she turned her focus from broadcasting to teaching high school students multimedia production and freelance writing.

Kathie Stamps *(Community Connects Us All)* is a writer and voice-over artist based in Lexington. She writes business profiles and feature stories for regional and national publications.

Maryjean Wall, Ph.D. *(Equine Transport: When Horses Fly)* is a part-time instructor in history at the University of Kentucky. She is author of *How Kentucky Became Southern: A Tale of Outlaws, Horse Thieves, Gamblers, and Breeders,* and she had a long career as an Eclipse award-winning and Pulitzer Prize-nominated journalist.

PHOTO CREDITS

Every effort was made to correctly identify sources and to credit photographers and collections for this project. If any errors have been made we are truly sorry and will correct those credits in future editions.

Three photo sources were absolutely indispensible in telling the story of aviation in central Kentucky. The first two were the collections of the *Lexington Herald-Leader* and the University of Kentucky Archives. These incredibly rich sources of information and photographs documenting the history of the Bluegrass are readily available to researchers and accessible through the Lexington Public Library and the Kentuckiana Digital Library managed by the University of Kentucky. The photos that have been preserved in these collections are priceless and are one of Kentucky's greatest treasure troves for anyone interested in history. A special thanks to Jason Flahardy at the University of Kentucky for pulling images from the many collections held there and to Ron Garrison at the *Lexington Herald-Leader* for his many helpful suggestions and efforts with the John C. Wyatt Collection of photographic images.

Our third invaluable source was local photographer Bill Straus. With nearly 90 photos in the book, Straus made the contemporary history of the airport come alive. You may have seen Straus at work over the last 30-plus years documenting aviation in central Kentucky, racing and sales at Keeneland, University of Kentucky sports, business and civic events and on Commerce Lexington Leadership Visits – just some of his many assignments over the years. We are deeply grateful for his talent, enthusiasm and partnership in helping to make this project possible.

ABBREVIATIONS

BSP – Bill Straus Photography (Bill Straus); BGA – Blue Grass Airport; HESFC – H.E. Sutton Forwarding Company (Tex Sutton); JH – Joseph Hayden Collection; KA – Keeneland Association; KL Keeneland Library; KHS – Kentucky Historical Society, C. Frank Dunn Collection; LHL – *Lexington Herald-Leader*, John C. Wyatt Collection; LOC – Library of Congress, Washington, D.C.; NASA – National Aeronautics and Space Administration; NASM – National Air and Space Museum, Smithsonian Institution; NPM – National Postal Museum, Smithsonian Institution; PFA – Photos From Above (Faron Collins); UKA – University of Kentucky Archives and Special Collections.

PHOTO POSITION KEY:

(top to bottom of page) t = top, m = middle, b = bottom, (left to right of page) l = left, c = center, r = right.

7 BSP. **8/9** NASA. **10** LOC. **11** NPM t; LOC b. **12** Bain Collection, LOC t; UKA b. **13** KL t; National Photo Company Collection, LOC b. **14** Public Domain t and b. **15** Samuel Halley Family Collection. **16** KHS. **17** KHS l; LOC r. **18** LHL. **19** Scott May Collection t; KHS b. **20** Davis-Monthan Aviation Field Register t; KHS b. **21** Samuel Halley Family Collection l; Glenn Greathouse m; unattributed r. **22/23** UKA. **24** UKA t; Lafayette Studios, UKA b. **25** UKA. **26/27** Lafayette Studios, UKA. **28/29** UKA. **30** *Modern Mechanic*s t; Dr. George Gumbert b. **31** LHL. **32** U.S. Army Air Corps. **33** Works Progress Administration, UKA. **34** Herb Block Foundation. **35** Public Domain. **36** Lafayette Studios, UKA t; KHS b. **37** Originally published by Lexington Board of Commerce. **38** KL. **39** Lexington-Fayette Urban County Government t; LHL b. **40/41** UKA. **42/43** UKA. **44** LHL. **45** Lafayette Studios, UKA. **46** U.S. Air Force t; LHL b. **47** LHL. **48** LOC l and m; NASM t; U.S. Army Air Corps r and b. **49** NASM t; LOC m. **50** U.S. Army t; Lafayette Studios, UKA b. **51** Lafayette Studios,

UKA. **52** Lafayette Studios, UKA t; LHL b. **53** LHL. **54** LHL. **55** Asiir Collection, Creative Commons. **56** LHL. **57** LHL. **58** BGA. **59** LHL. **60/61** LHL. **62/63** LHL. **64** LHL. **65** Milward Family Collection. **66** BGA t; JH b. **67** LOC t; LHL b. **68** LOC t; UKA b. **69** Delta Air Lines t; Flying Hostesses of Eastern Air b. **70** Chris Ware illustration. **71** BGA t; Avis Rent-A-Car m; Hertz Rental Car b. **72** BSP. **73** BGA. **74** BSP. **75** Public Domain. **76** BSP t; HESFC b. **77** LHL. **78** Seaboard Archives. **79** LOC tl and tr; KL b. **80** KL. **81** LHL. **82** KA t; Public Domain bl; LHL br. **83** BSP. **84** LHL. **85** BSP l and r; KA m. **86** BSP. **87** HESFC. **88** BSP. **89** Delta Air Lines. **90** JH. **91** UKA. **92** LHL. **93** Eastern Air Lines t; LHL bl; JH br. **94** LHL. **95** BSP tl and b; stock photo tr. **96** BGA t; LHL b. **97** LHL. **98** LHL. **99** LHL. **100** LHL t; Lyle Wolf, GRW b. **101** Lyle Wolf, GRW t; LHL m and b. **102** BSP t; BGA b. **103** Lyle Wolf, GRW t; Betty Moseley bl; Jim Combs Family Collection br. **104** LOC t; U.S. Army Air Corps b; NPM r. **105** Samuel Halley Family Collection t; NPM m; Lafayette Studios, UKA b. **106** Lafayette Studios, UKA t; LHL m; LOC b. **107** Richard Forston Collection t; LOC b. **108** KL t; NPM m; LHL b. **109** LHL t and b. **110** Scott May Collection tl; LHL tr; LHL m; Peggy Papania Collection b. **111** LHL l and t; NPM mr; JH b. **112** NPM t; LHL b. **113** JH t; NPM m; KA bl; LHL br. **114** LHL t, m and br; NPM bl. **115** LHL t and m; NPM br. **116** JH tl; BSP tr; LHL ml; LHL br. **117** LHL tl; NPM m; LHL br. **118** LHL tl; BSP m; Lyle Wolf, GRW bl; NPM br. **119** BGA t and b; LHL m. **120** BGA l; LHL r. **121** LHL t; NPM ml; BSP mr; LHL bl. **122** NPM t; LHL b. **123** NPM tr; BGA ml; BGA b. **124** BSP tl; BGA m; LHL b. **125** NPM t and b; BSP m. **126** BSP. **127** BGA. **128** NPM t and m; BSP b. **129** BSP t, ml and bl; NPM br. **130/131** BSP. **132** BSP l; Stablemate Creative r. **133** BSP t and ml; Alltech bl; Ron Spriggs br. **134** University of Kentucky Athletics t;

UKA b. **135** LHL t; Jonathan Palmer b. **136** LHL. **137** BSP. **138** LHL l; BSP r. **139** BSP. **140** LHL. **141** BSP t and m; LHL b. **142** LHL tr, tl, ml and b; JH mr. **143** LHL. **144/145** LHL. **146** Paul Atkinson t; BSP ml, m, bl and br. **147** BSP tl and tr; John Stephen Hockensmith b. **148** LHL. **149** British Postal Museum t; BSP b. **150** Chandler Family Collection. **151** Corbis. **152** BSP; **153** Peggy Papania Collection, BSP. **154** LHL. **155** BGA. **156** UKA t; JH b. **157** Jack Baugh Collection. **158** BSP t; Stablemate Creative m. **159** BSP. **160** Kate Savage. **161** BSP. **162** LHL, Charles Bertram. **163** BSP. **164** BSP t; Roberts Family Collection ml and mr. **165** TAC Air t and br; BSP bl. **166** NASM. **167** BSP. **168** NPM t; LHL b. **169** BGA. **170/171** LOC. **172** Scott May Collection, U.S. Army Air Force t; BGA b. **173** BSP t; Keith Philpott b. **175** BGA. **176/177** PFA. **178/179** PFA. **180/181** PFA. **182/183** PFA. **184/185** PFA. **186** LHL tl and br; PFA bl. **187** BGA. **188** LHL. **189** Maurice B. Quirin. **191** BSP. **192** BGA t; LHL b. **193** BSP. **194** LHL. **195** JH. **196** LHL. **197** Bob Hower, Quadrant Photography tl; BSP ml and bl; Kentucky Chamber of Commerce tr; *U.S. News & World Report* and *The Best Lawyers in America* mr. **198** Delta Air Lines. **199** Chris Ware illustration l; Associated Press r. **200** BSP. **201** BGA. **204/205** LHL. **206** LHL. **208** BSP. **210** Lexington Convention and Visitors Bureau. **211** BSP. **212/213** BSP. **214** Suzanne Dorman t; James Archambeault b. **215** BGA t; BSP b. **216/217** BSP. **218** BSP. **219** KA. **220** Buffalo Trace Distillery. **221** BSP. **222/223** BSP. **224** BSP l; BGA r. **225** BSP. **226** BSP tl; BGA tr; Kentucky Educational Television b. **227** BSP t; BGA b. **228/229** BSP.

INDEX